Ernest L. Clarke

$3 00

Bromsgrove

Janr. 02

The English Theological Library

General Editor

Frederic Relton, A.K.C.

Vicar of St. Andrew's, Stoke Newington

With General Introduction by

The Lord Bishop of London

THE WORKS

OF

BISHOP BUTLER

A NEW EDITION WITH PREFACE AND NOTES BY

J. H. BERNARD, D.D.

FELLOW OF TRINITY COLLEGE AND ARCHBISHOP KING'S LECTURER
IN DIVINITY IN THE UNIVERSITY OF DUBLIN

VOL. II.

London
MACMILLAN AND CO., LIMITED
NEW YORK: THE MACMILLAN COMPANY
1900

GLASGOW: PRINTED AT THE UNIVERSITY PRESS
BY ROBERT MACLEHOSE AND CO.

THE ANALOGY OF RELIGION NATURAL & REVEALED

TO THE

CONSTITUTION AND COURSE OF NATURE

TO WHICH ARE ADDED

TWO BRIEF DISSERTATIONS

I. OF PERSONAL IDENTITY
II. OF THE NATURE OF VIRTUE

By JOSEPH BUTLER, D.C.L.

LATE LORD BISHOP OF DURHAM

Ejus [Analogiæ] hæc vis est, ut id quod dubium est ad aliquid simile, de quo non quæritur, referat; ut incerta certis probet.—QUINTIL. i. 6.

London

MACMILLAN AND CO., LIMITED

NEW YORK: THE MACMILLAN COMPANY

1900

GENERAL INTRODUCTION

THEOLOGY is concerned with setting forth the truth of God as He has revealed it in His Word to His Church. This truth needs new application to the conditions and circumstances—intellectual and social—of each generation. As various problems arise in the world of man, various aspects of God's truth receive additional emphasis and explanation. Theology grows according to the growth of human knowledge. It brings out of the treasure-house of Scripture "things new and old."

A student of theology who wishes to gain accurate knowledge on any particular point, must refer to the time when that point was forced into prominence by some movement or tendency of thought. At such times men's minds, with the full force of their intelligence and their learning, were directed to the full investigation of a question which pressed for immediate solution. At such periods a subject was fully studied and thought out. It is only when we are in contact with minds to which these subjects were of vital importance that we feel their full significance.

and its literary merits are of a very high order. It may be read by readers of every class. Doubtless the forms of appeal to the popular consciousness vary in every age, and methods which once were powerful soon grow antiquated. But pulpit oratory, after all, lasts longer than other forms of oratory, and the roll of English preachers has produced finer examples of eloquence than exist elsewhere.

The strenuous pursuit of truth, sobriety, high thoughts, commanding power of expression—these are great qualities. They are all to be found in the books which are to be issued in this series. Introductions and notes will serve to bridge over the gulf which must always to some degree separate the thought of the past from the thought of the present. It is better to read one great book than a series of little books. It is better to seek for the truth where its issues were most seriously felt, than to rest content with tabulated arguments in its favour. Theological students will profit by contact with great minds. It is for their guidance especially that this series is designed. They would gain in power to face the problems of our own time if they were better acquainted with the great heritage of the past, and were animated by the same spirit as their predecessors, whose lot was cast in no less difficult days.

M. LONDON.

PREFACE TO BUTLER'S ANALOGY

In this edition of the *Analogy* a marginal analysis of Butler's argument has been provided, which it is hoped may be an aid to readers. Butler's style is so concise, and each word is so carefully chosen, that it is not possible to reproduce in a phrase or two all that he means to teach in a paragraph; but the experience of many years' lecturing on the *Analogy* has convinced me that even an imperfect conspectus of the argument is better than none. Students are only too easily diverted from Butler's main theses by the nicety with which he formulates small points of detail; and yet it is the former, not the latter, which it is important to keep in view. I have numbered the paragraphs for convenience of reference, but have not broken them up into shorter sections, as has been done, *e.g.*, by Mr. Gladstone in his handsome edition. I am persuaded that Butler's reasoning is more easily followed if the text is printed as he left it, and that any alteration of his arrangement in paragraphs is likely to breed misunderstanding.

I have supplied some notes, mainly with the purpose of elucidating Butler's meaning and of directing attention to the controversies with which he was concerned, and the authors who may be supposed to have influenced him. The references to eighteenth century writers have, in most cases, been derived from my own reading; but they might be multiplied indefinitely by any one who would be at the pains of examining the tedious volumes which record the progress of the Deistic controversy. Mr. Leslie Stephen's *English Thought in the Eighteenth Century* furnishes in an attractive form a convenient introduction to the study of the conditions under which the *Analogy* was produced; and it is indispensable to students of the period. I have thought it right to indicate a few points, where it seems to me that the Bishop's arguments are no longer convincing. But it would be impossible adequately to treat the numerous problems which he touches, especially in the Second Part, without writing a treatise on systematic theology. And so I have left untouched a great deal upon which it would be tempting to enlarge, being convinced that the duty of an editor is to interpret rather than to criticise his author.

The text is reprinted from the Oxford edition of 1844, corrected by the aid of the careful edition of Bishop Fitz-Gerald (London, 1860). The Index is, in the main, that prepared by Bentham (afterwards Regius Professor of Divinity at Oxford from 1763 to 1776) and revised by Butler himself. A few additions have been made to it, but I have judged it better not to disturb the general arrangement, and have retained Butler's original comments. A sketch of Butler's life, and a brief appreciation of the value of his contributions to theology and to ethics, will be found in the Editor's Preface to Vol. I. of this edition of his works.

J. H. BERNARD.

THE ANALOGY OF RELIGION

NATURAL & REVEALED

TO THE

CONSTITUTION AND COURSE OF NATURE

TO THE

RIGHT HONOURABLE

CHARLES, LORD TALBOT

BARON OF HENSOL

LORD HIGH CHANCELLOR OF GREAT BRITAIN

THE FOLLOWING TREATISE IS, WITH ALL RESPECT, INSCRIBED

IN ACKNOWLEDGMENT OF THE HIGHEST OBLIGATIONS

TO THE LATE LORD BISHOP OF DURHAM

AND TO HIMSELF, BY HIS LORDSHIP'S

MOST DUTIFUL, MOST DEVOTED

AND MOST HUMBLE

SERVANT

JOSEPH BUTLER

ADVERTISEMENT

PREFIXED TO THE FIRST EDITION.

If the reader should meet here with anything which he had not before attended to, it will not be in the observations upon the constitution and course of Nature, these being all obvious; but in the application of them: in which, though there is nothing but what appears to me of some real weight, and therefore of great importance; yet he will observe several things, which will appear to him of very little, if we can think things to be of little importance, which are of any real weight at all, upon such a subject as religion. However, the proper force of the following treatise lies in the whole general analogy considered together.

It is come, I know not how, to be taken for granted, by many persons, that Christianity is not so much as a subject of inquiry; but that it is, now at length, discovered to be fictitious.[1] And accordingly they treat it, as if, in the present age, this were an agreed point among all people of discern-

[[1] Butler draws a like mournful picture in his *Charge to the Clergy of Durham* (1751), which begins with the words: "It is impossible for me, my brethren, upon our first meeting of this kind, to forbear lamenting with you the general decay of religion in this nation; which is now observed by every one, and has been for some time the complaint of all serious persons." His testimony is confirmed by Burnet in the Preface to the third edition of his *Pastoral Care* (1713); and in the ninth chapter of Southey's *Life of Wesley* similar evidence will be found. Cp. also Collins' *Butler*, pp. 93-95. But see, for the other side of the picture, Dr. Overton's Preface to Law's *Serious Call*, p. xi.]

ment; and nothing remained, but to set it up as a principal subject of mirth and ridicule,[2] as it were by way of reprisals, for its having so long interrupted the pleasures of the world. On the contrary, thus much, at least, will be here found, not taken for granted, but proved, that any reasonable man, who will thoroughly consider the matter, may be as much assured, as he is of his own being, that it is not, however, so clear a case, that there is nothing in it. There is, I think, strong evidence of its truth; but it is certain no one can, upon principles of reason, be satisfied of the contrary. And the practical consequence to be drawn from this is not attended to by every one who is concerned in it.

May, 1736.

[2] [So too Berkeley in 1721: "In these wiser times, a cold indifference for the national religion, and indeed for all matters of faith and Divine worship, is thought good sense. It is even become fashionable to decry religion, and that little talent of ridicule as applied to such wrong purposes that a good Christian can hardly keep himself in countenance." *Works* (Fraser's ed.), iii. 195.]

CONTENTS

PART I.

OF NATURAL RELIGION.

CHAPTER I.

CHAPTER II.

CHAPTER III.

INTRODUCTION.

[1.] PROBABLE evidence is essentially distinguished from demonstrative by this, that it admits of degrees; and of all variety of them, from the highest moral certainty, to the very lowest presumption.[1] We cannot indeed say a thing is probably true upon one very slight presumption for it; because, as there may be probabilities on both sides of a question, there may be some against it: and though there be not, yet a slight presumption does not beget that degree of conviction, which is implied in saying a thing is probably true. But that the slightest possible presumption is of the nature of a probability, appears from hence; that such low presumption, often repeated, will amount even to moral certainty. Thus a man's having observed the ebb and flow of the tide to-day, affords some sort of presumption, though the lowest imaginable, that it may happen again to-morrow: but the observation of this event for so many days, and months, and ages together, as it has been observed by mankind, gives us a full assurance that it will.

Probable evidence admits of degrees.

[2.] That which chiefly constitutes Probability is expressed in the word Likely, *i.e.* like some truth,[2] or true event; like it, in itself, in its evidence, in some more or fewer of its circumstances. For when we determine a thing to be probably true, suppose that an event has or will come to pass, it is from the mind's remarking in it a likeness to some other event, which we have observed has come to pass. And this observation forms, in numberless daily instances, a presumption, opinion, or full conviction, that such event has or will come to pass; according as the observation is, that

In what it consists;

[1] [Cp. Part II. vi. 11 below.]

[2] Verisimile. [That is, the maxim at the basis of reasoning of this kind is that "the like is also the likely."]

the like event has sometimes, most commonly, or always so far as our observation reaches, come to pass at like distances of time, or place, or upon like occasions. Hence arises the belief, that a child, if it lives twenty years, will grow up to the stature and strength of a man; that food will contribute to the preservation of its life, and the want of it for such a number of days, be its certain destruction. So likewise the rule and measure of our hopes and fears concerning the success of our pursuits; our expectations that others will act so and so in such circumstances; and our judgment that such actions proceed from such principles; all these rely upon our having observed the like to what we hope, fear, expect, judge: I say upon our having observed the like, either with respect to others or ourselves. And thus, whereas the prince[3] who had always lived in a warm climate, naturally concluded in the way of analogy, that there was no such thing as water's becoming hard, because he had always observed it to be fluid and yielding: we, on the contrary, from analogy conclude, that there is no presumption at all against this: that it is supposable there may be frost in England any given day in January next; probable that there will on some day of the month; and that there is a moral certainty, *i.e.* ground for an expectation, without any doubt of it, in some part or other of the winter.

frequently resorted to.

Moral certainty.

Probable evidence is (1) imperfect,

[3.] Probable evidence, in its very nature, affords but an imperfect kind of information; and is to be considered as relative only to beings of limited capacities. For nothing which is the possible object of knowledge, whether past, present, or future, can be probable to an infinite Intelligence; since it cannot but be discerned absolutely as it is in itself, certainly true, or certainly false. But to Us, probability is the very guide of life.[4]

(2) appropriate to our condition,

(3) applicable in questions which are

(*a*) difficult,

[4.] From these things it follows, that in questions of difficulty, or such as are thought so, where more satisfactory evidence cannot be had, or is not seen; if the result of examination be, that there appears upon the whole, any the lowest presumption on one side, and none on the other, or

[3] The story is told by Mr. Locke in the chapter of Probability. [*Essay on the Human Understanding*, iv. 15. 5.]

[4] [See Note A on Butler's Doctrine of Probability, at the end of this Introduction.]

a greater presumption on one side, though in the lowest degree greater; this determines the question, even in matters of speculation; and in matters of practice, will lay us under an absolute and formal obligation, in point of prudence and of interest, to act upon that presumption or low probability, though it be so low as to leave the mind in very great doubt which is the truth. For surely a man is as really bound in prudence to do what upon the whole appears, according to the best of his judgment, to be for his happiness, as what he certainly knows to be so. Nay further, in questions of great consequence, a reasonable man will think it concerns him to remark lower probabilities and presumptions than these; such as amount to no more than shewing one side of a question to be as supposable and credible as the other: nay, such as but amount to much less even than this. For numberless instances might be mentioned respecting the common pursuits of life, where a man would be thought, in a literal sense, distracted, who would not act, and with great application too, not only upon an even chance, but upon much less, and where the probability or chance was greatly against his succeeding.[5]

(*b*) practical,

(*c*) important.

[5.] It is not my design to inquire further into the nature, the foundation, and measure of probability; or whence it proceeds that *likeness* should beget that presumption, opinion, and full conviction, which the human mind is formed to receive from it, and which it does necessarily produce in every one; or to guard against the errors, to which reasoning from analogy is liable. This belongs to the subject of Logic; and is a part of that subject which has not yet been thoroughly considered. Indeed I shall not take upon me to say, how far the extent, compass, and force, of analogical reasoning, can be reduced to general heads and rules; and the whole be formed into a system. But though so little in this way has been attempted by those who have treated of our intellectual powers, and the exercise of them; this does not hinder but that we may be, as we unquestionably are, assured,

Questions of (*a*) psychology and

(*b*) logic excluded.

[5] See Part II. vi. 3. [Butler returns to the same subject, Part I. vii. 11 and Part II. vii. 43. Compare also the *Charge to the Clergy of Durham*, § 4: "Would it not be madness for a man to forsake a safe road and prefer to it one in which he acknowledges there is an even chance he should lose his life, though there were an even chance likewise of his getting safe through it?"]

As a fact, argument from analogy carries weight.

that analogy is of weight, in various degrees, towards determining our judgment and our practice. Nor does it in any wise cease to be of weight in those cases, because persons, either given to dispute, or who require things to be stated with greater exactness than our faculties appear to admit of in practical matters, may find other cases in which it is not easy to say, whether it be, or be not, of any weight; or instances of seeming analogies, which are really of none. It is enough to the present purpose to observe, that this general way of arguing is evidently natural, just, and conclusive. For there is no man can make a question, but that the sun will rise to-morrow, and be seen, where it is seen at all, in the figure of a circle, and not in that of a square.

Origen on the difficulties of Scripture.

[6.] Hence, namely from analogical reasoning, Origen[6] has with singular sagacity observed, that "he who believes the Scripture to have proceeded from Him Who is the Author of Nature, may well expect to find the same sort of difficulties in it, as are found in the constitution of Nature."

Extension of his remark (*a*) negatively,

And in a like way of reflection it may be added, that he who denies the Scripture to have been from God upon account of these difficulties, may, for the very same reason, deny the world to have been formed by Him.

(*b*) positively;

On the other hand, if there be an analogy or likeness between that system of things and dispensation of Providence, which Revelation informs us of, and that system of things and dispensation of Providence, which experience together with reason informs us of, *i.e.* the known course of Nature; this is a presumption, that

with a qualification.

they have both the same author and cause; at least so far as to answer objections against the former's being from God, drawn from any thing which is analogical or similar to what is in the latter, which is acknowledged to be from Him; for an Author of Nature is here supposed.[7]

[6] Χρὴ *μέν τοί γε τὸν ἅπαξ παραδεξάμενον τοῦ κτίσαντος τὸν κόσμον εἶναι ταύτας τὰς γραφὰς πεπεῖσθαι, ὅτι ὅσα περὶ τῆς κτίσεως ἀπαντᾷ τοῖς ζητοῦσι τὸν περὶ αὐτῆς λόγον, ταῦτα καὶ περὶ τῶν γραφῶν*. *Philocal.* p. 23. ed. Cant. [chap. ii. § 5. It is an interesting question whence Butler derived this quotation, of which he gives a free translation in the text. The *Philocalia* of Origen is not a work which (as Bishop Westcott has reminded the editor) Butler is likely to have read in the original; and it is highly probable that he found this observation of Origen, so apposite to his own train of reasoning, in some theological treatise of the day. Nevertheless it is remarkable that the word *ἀναλογία* occurs in the preceding paragraph (§ 4) of the *Philocalia.*]

[7] [The idea is admirably expressed by Berkeley in *Alciphron*, vi. 31

[7.] Forming our notions of the constitution and govern- Unfounded hypotheses.
ment of the world upon reasoning, without foundation for
the principles which we assume, whether from the attributes a
of God, or any thing else, is building a world upon hypothesis,
like Des Cartes. Forming our notions upon reasoning from b
principles which are certain, but applied to cases to which
we have no ground to apply them, (like those who explain
the structure of the human body, and the nature of diseases
and medicines from mere mathematics without sufficient data,)
is an error much akin to the former: since what is assumed
in order to make the reasoning applicable, is Hypothesis.
But it must be allowed just, to join abstract reasonings with Legitimate to argue:
the observation of facts, and argue from such facts as are (1) from like to like;
known, to others that are like them; from that part of the (2) from a part to the whole;
Divine government over intelligent creatures which comes
under our view, to that larger and more general government
over them which is beyond it; and from what is present, (3) from the present to the future.
to collect what is likely, credible, or not incredible, will be
hereafter.[8]

[8.] This method then of concluding and determining This applicable to religion.
being practical, and what, if we will act at all, we cannot § 4
but act upon in the common pursuits of life; being evidently § 5
conclusive, in various degrees, proportionable to the degree
and exactness of the whole analogy or likeness; and having § 6
so great authority[9] for its introduction into the subject of
religion, even revealed religion; my design is to apply it
to that subject in general, both natural and revealed: taking Butler's postulate
for proved, that there is an intelligent Author of Nature, may be justified.
and natural Governor of the world. For as there is no
presumption against this prior to the proof of it: so it has 1
been often proved with accumulated evidence; from this 2 a
argument of analogy and final causes; from abstract reason- b
ings;[10] from the most ancient tradition and testimony; and c

(published in 1732, four years before the *Analogy*): "It will be sufficient if such analogy appears between the dispensations of grace and nature as may make it probable (although much should be unaccountable in both) to suppose them derived from the same Author, and the workmanship of one and the same Hand." See Part II. ii. 4 below and the editor's note thereon.]

[8] [Cp. Part II. ii. 4.]

[9] [I suppose that Butler means the authority of Origen, whose maxim has just been cited. Mr. Gladstone refers to *St. John* iii. 12.]

[10] [Butler gives an outline of such an argument based on "abstract reasonings,"—in modern parlance, an *a priori* proof,—in ch. vi. § 3; the *a posteriori* or 'design' argument, from final causes, as it was

d from the general consent of mankind. Nor does it appear,
so far as I can find, to be denied by the generality of those
3 who profess themselves dissatisfied with the evidence of
religion.

A priori speculations as to the best of worlds are idle.

[9.] As there are some, who, instead of thus attending to
what is in fact the constitution of Nature, form their notions
of God's government upon hypothesis: so there are others
who indulge themselves in vain and idle speculations, how
the world might possibly have been framed otherwise than
it is; and upon supposition that things might, in imagining
that they should, have been disposed and carried on after
a better model, than what appears in the present disposition
and conduct of them. Suppose now a person of such a turn
of mind, to go on with his reveries, till he had at length
fixed upon some particular plan of Nature, as appearing to
him the best. One shall scarce be thought guilty of detraction
against human understanding, if one should say, even before-
hand, that the plan which this speculative person would fix
upon, though he were the wisest of the sons of men, probably
would not be the very best, even according to his own notions
of *best;* whether he thought that to be so, which afforded
occasions and motives for the exercise of the greatest virtue,
or which was productive of the greatest happiness, or that
these two were necessarily connected, and run up into one
and the same plan. However, it may not be amiss once
for all to see, what would be the amount of these emendations
and imaginary improvements upon the system of Nature, or

Their logical consequences.

how far they would mislead us. And it seems there could
be no stopping, till we came to some such conclusions as these:
(1) that all creatures should at first be made as perfect and as
happy as they were capable of ever being: that nothing, to
(2) be sure, of hazard or danger should be put upon them to do;[11]
(3) some indolent persons would perhaps think nothing at all:
(4) or certainly, that effectual care should be taken, that they
should, whether necessarily or not, yet eventually and in fact,
always do what was right and most conducive to happiness,
which would be thought easy for infinite power to effect;
a either by not giving them any principles which would endanger
b their going wrong; or by laying the right motive of action

developed, *e.g.* by Paley in his *Natural Theology*, has always been more popular and attractive.]

[11] [Cp. Part I. iv. 9.]

in every instance before their minds continually in so strong a manner, as would never fail of inducing them to act conformably to it: and that the whole method of government by punishments should be rejected as absurd; as an awkward round-about method of carrying things on; nay, as contrary to a principal purpose, for which it would be supposed creatures were made, namely, happiness.

[10.] Now, without considering what is to be said in particular to the several parts of this train of folly and extravagance; what has been above intimated, is a full direct general answer to it, namely, that we may see beforehand that we have not faculties for this kind of speculation. For though it be admitted, that, from the first principles of our nature, we unavoidably judge or determine some ends to be absolutely in themselves preferable to others, and that the ends now mentioned, or if they run up into one, that this one is absolutely the best; and consequently that we must conclude the ultimate end designed, in the constitution of Nature and conduct of Providence, is the most virtue and happiness possible: yet we are far from being able to judge what particular disposition of things would be most friendly and assistant to virtue; or what means might be absolutely necessary to produce the most happiness in a system of such extent as our own world may be, taking in all that is past and to come, though we should suppose it detached from the whole of things. Indeed we are so far from being able to judge of this, that we are not judges what may be the necessary means of raising and conducting one person to the highest perfection and happiness of his nature. Nay, even in the little affairs of the present life, we find men of different educations and ranks are not competent judges of the conduct of each other. Our whole nature leads us to ascribe all moral perfection to God, and to deny all imperfection of Him. And this will for ever be a practical proof[12] of His moral character, to such as will consider what a practical proof is; because it is the voice of God speaking in us.[13] And from hence we con-

A full answer: our faculties are incompetent to such speculations, for, (1) (2) (3) (4) the moral perfection of God

[12] [Cp. Part. I. iii. 24, 28 *sub fin.*, where he explains what is meant by a 'practical proof,' *i.e.* a 'proof from fact,' and therefore a proof which ought to influence practice; cp. Part I. vi. 15.]

[13] [This may be assumed, inasmuch as we postulate an *Intelligent* Author of Nature. Cp. Serm. vi. § 7, and Part I. iii. 15 below.]

guarantees the happiness of virtue.

clude, that virtue must be the happiness, and vice the misery, of every creature; and that regularity and order and right cannot but prevail finally in a universe under His government.[14] But we are in no sort judges, what are the necessary means of accomplishing this end.

How accomplished we know not.

The observed order of Nature

[11.] Let us then, instead of that idle and not very innocent employment of forming imaginary models of a world, and schemes of governing it, turn our thoughts to what we experience to be the conduct of Nature with respect to intelligent creatures; which may be resolved into general laws or rules of administration, in the same way as many of the laws of Nature respecting inanimate matter may be collected from experiments. And let us compare the known constitution and course of things with what is said to be the moral system of Nature; the acknowledged dispensations of Providence, or that government which we find ourselves under, with what religion teaches us to believe and expect; and see whether they are not analogous and of a piece. And upon such a comparison it will, I think, be found, that they are very much so: that both may be traced up to the same general laws, and resolved into the same principles of divine conduct.

compared with the moral order.

Such analogy

[12.] The analogy here proposed to be considered is of pretty large extent, and consists of several parts, in some, more, in others, less, exact. In some few instances perhaps it may amount to a real practical proof; in others not so. Yet in these it is a confirmation of what is proved other ways. It will undeniably shew, what too many want to have shewn them, that the system of Religion, both natural and revealed, considered only as a system, and prior to the proof of it, is not a subject of ridicule, unless that of Nature be so too. And it will afford an answer to almost all objections against the system both of natural and revealed Religion; though not perhaps an answer in so great a degree, yet in a very considerable degree an answer to the objections against the evidence of it: for objections against a proof, and objections against what is

proves that Religion is not a subject of ridicule,

and answers objections against (1) the *System* and (in part) against (2) the *Evidence* of Religion.

[14] [Kant turns the argument the other way. Happiness in proportion to merit is, he urges, a demand of the moral law; and as such equal distribution is not observed here on earth, we are morally obliged to conclude that there will be hereafter not only a further state of existence where present inequalities will be redressed, but also an All Righteous and All Powerful Judge Who will have both the will and the power to reward the righteous and punish the wicked. Cp. Part II. viii. 11.]

said to be proved, the reader will observe are different things.[15]

[13.] Now the divine government of the world, implied in the notion of religion in general and of Christianity,. contains in it; that mankind is appointed to live in a future state;[16] that there every one shall be rewarded or punished;[17] rewarded or punished respectively for all that behaviour here, which we comprehend under the words, virtuous or vicious, morally good or evil:[18] that our present life is a probation, a state of trial,[19] and of discipline,[20] for that future one; notwithstanding the objections, which men may fancy they have, from notions of Necessity, against there being any such moral plan as this at all;[21] and whatever objections may appear to lie against the wisdom and goodness of it, as it stands so imperfectly made known to us at present:[22] that this world being in a state of apostasy and wickedness, and consequently of ruin, and the sense both of their condition and duty being greatly corrupted amongst men, this gave occasion for an additional dispensation of Providence; of the utmost importance;[23] proved by miracles;[24] but containing in it many things appearing to us strange, and not to have been expected;[25] a dispensation of Providence, which is a scheme or system of things;[26] carried on by the mediation of a divine person, the Messiah, in order to the recovery of the world;[27] yet not revealed to all men, nor proved with the strongest possible evidence to all those to whom it is revealed; but only to such a part of mankind, and with such particular evidence, as the wisdom of God thought fit.[28] The design then of the following treatise will be to shew, that the several parts principally objected against in this moral and Christian dispensation, including its scheme, its publication, and the proof which God has afforded us of its truth; that the particular parts principally objected against in this whole dispensation, are analogous to what is experienced in the constitution and course of Nature, or Providence; that the chief objections themselves which are alleged

The principles of religion: (*a*) natural,

and (*b*) revealed.

The points objected to analogous to the constitution and course of Nature, similar objections lying

[15] [Cp. Part I. vii. 12.]
[16] Ch. i.
[17] Ch. ii.
[18] Ch. iii.
[19] Ch. iv.
[20] Ch. v.
[21] Ch. vi.
[22] Ch. vii.
[23] Part II. ch. i.
[24] Ch. ii.
[25] Ch. iii.
[26] Ch. iv.
[27] Ch. v.
[28] Chs. vi. vii.

shews like traces of Wilkins' influence, and indeed reproduces his illustration.[1]

[1] The argument has, of course, been urged by many other writers. For example, Clarke in his *Evidences* (Prop. xv.) declares that "though their faith extended no further, than only to a belief of the possibility of the truth of the Christian Revelation; yet even this alone ought to have weight enough to determine reasonable creatures, to live soberly, righteously, and godly." And Clarke proceeds to quote a passage from Arnobius (*adv. Gentes*, Bk. II.), which puts the prudential argument concisely and well. Cp. Part II. viii. 9 below.

Dr. Samuel Clarke (1671-1729), who was Rector of St. James', Westminster, was counted one of the most eminent English philosophers of the day. His influence, direct and indirect, upon Butler was considerable. Butler when a young man had a spirited correspondence with him on the subject of Clarke's arguments for the Being of God (see, further, note to Part I. vi. 3); and Clarke's ethical doctrine, which treated the distinction between right and wrong as lying deep in the "eternal fitness" of things, is recognised by Butler as containing an indispensable element of truth (see Note E appended to Part I. Ch. vi.).

THE ANALOGY OF RELIGION

TO THE

CONSTITUTION AND COURSE OF NATURE.

PART I.

OF NATURAL RELIGION.

CHAPTER I.

Of a Future Life.

[1.] STRANGE difficulties have been raised by some concerning personal identity, or the sameness of living agents, implied in the notion of our existing now and hereafter, or in any two successive moments; which whoever thinks it worth while, may see considered in the first Dissertation at the end of this treatise.[1] But without regard to any of them here, let us consider what the analogy of nature, and the several changes which we have undergone, and those which we know we may undergo without being destroyed, suggest, as to the effect which death may, or may not, have upon us; and whether it be not from thence probable, that we may survive this change and exist in a future state of life and perception.

Personal identity: how affected by death.

[2.] I. From our being born into the present world in the helpless imperfect state of infancy, and having arrived from thence to mature age, we find it to be a general law of nature in our own species, that the same creatures, the same individuals, should exist in degrees of life and perception,

I. The Law of Growth

[1] [See *Dissertation* I. Note the definition of personal identity given here, viz. "the sameness of living agents."]

these effects do in no wise appear to imply the destruction of a living agent. And besides, as we are greatly in the dark, upon what the exercise of our living powers depends, so we are wholly ignorant what the powers themselves depend upon; the powers themselves as distinguished, not only from their actual exercise, but also from the present capacity of exercising them; and as opposed to their destruction: for sleep, or however a swoon, shews us, not only that these powers exist when they are not exercised, as the passive power of motion does in inanimate matter; but shews also that they exist, when there is no present capacity of exercising them: or that the capacities of exercising them for the present, as well as the actual exercise of them, may be suspended, and yet the powers themselves remain undestroyed. Since then we know not at all upon what the existence of our living powers depends, this shews further, there can no probability be collected from the reason of the thing, that death will be their destruction: because their existence may depend, upon somewhat in no degree affected by death; upon somewhat quite out of the reach of this king of terrors. So that there is nothing more certain, than that *the reason of the thing* shews us no connexion between death, and the destruction of living agents. Nor can we find any thing throughout the whole *analogy of nature*, to afford us even the slightest presumption, that animals ever lose their living powers; much less, if it were possible, that they lose them by death: for we have no faculties wherewith to trace any beyond or through it, so as to see what becomes of them. This event removes them from our view. It destroys the *sensible* proof, which we had before their death, of their being possessed of living powers, but does not appear to afford the least reason to believe that they are, then, or by that event, deprived of them.

or (ii) from the analogy of nature.

Argument from the Law of Continuance confirmed by the facts of growth.

[6.] And our knowing, that they were possessed of these powers, up to the very period to which we have faculties capable of tracing them, is itself a probability of their retaining them, beyond it. And this is confirmed, and a sensible credibility is given to it, by observing the very great and astonishing changes which we have experienced; so great, that our existence in another state of life, of perception and of action, will be but according to a method of providential conduct, the like to which has been already exercised even with regard to ourselves; according to a course of nature, the like to which we have already gone through.

Imagination the parent of false presumptions;

[7.] However, as one cannot but be greatly sensible, how difficult it is to silence imagination enough to make the voice of reason even distinctly heard in this case; as we are accustomed, from our youth up, to indulge that forward delusive faculty, ever obtruding beyond its sphere;[6] of some assistance indeed to apprehension, but the author of all error: as we plainly lose ourselves in gross and crude conceptions of things, taking for granted that we are acquainted with, what indeed we are wholly ignorant of: it may be proper to consider the imaginary presumptions, that death will be our destruction, arising from these kinds of early and lasting prejudices: and to shew how little they can really amount to, even though we cannot wholly divest ourselves of them. And,

e.g. that the soul is composite and therefore discerptible.

[8.] I. All presumption of death's being the destruction of living beings, must go upon supposition that they are compounded; and so, discerptible. But since consciousness is a single and indivisible power, it should seem that the subject in which it resides must be so too. For were the motion of any particle of matter absolutely one and indivisible, so as that it should imply a contradiction to suppose part of this motion to exist, and part not to exist, *i.e.* part of this matter to move, and part to be at rest; then its power of motion would be indivisible; and so also would the subject in which the power inheres, namely, the particle of matter: for if this could be divided into two, one part might be moved and the other at rest, which is contrary to the supposition. In like manner it has been argued,[7] and, for any thing appearing to the contrary, justly, that since the perception or consciousness, which we have of our own existence, is indivisible, so as that it is a contradiction to suppose one part of it should be here and the

But the simplicity of consciousness may indicate the simplicity of the soul.

[6] [Cp. what he says of Imagination as a "source of discontent" (Part I. v. 20 below), and his remarks in *Public Sermons*, I. § 15.]

[7] See Dr. Clarke's *Letter* to Mr. Dodwell, and the defences of it. [The passage will be found at p. 101: "As evidently as the known properties of matter prove it to be certainly a discerpible substance, whatever other unknown properties it may be endued with; so evidently the known and confessed properties of immaterial beings prove them to be indiscerpible, whatever other unknown properties they likewise may be endued with." Cp. further Clarke's *Evidences of Natural and Revealed Religion*, p. 266 (ed. 1738), and see Note B at end of this chapter.]

other there; the perceptive power, or the power of consciousness, is indivisible too: and consequently the subject in which it resides; *i.e.* the conscious being. Now upon supposition that living agent each man calls himself, is thus a single being, which there is at least no more difficulty in conceiving than in conceiving it to be a compound, and of which there is the proof now mentioned; it follows, that our organized bodies are no more ourselves or part of ourselves, than any other matter around us. And it is as easy to conceive, how matter, which is no part of ourselves, may be appropriated to us in the manner which our present bodies are; as how we can receive impressions from, and have power over any matter. It is as easy to conceive, that we may exist out of bodies, as in them; that we might have animated bodies of any other organs and senses wholly different from these now given us, and that we may hereafter animate these same or new bodies variously modified and organized; as to conceive how we can animate such bodies as our present.[8] And lastly, the dissolution of all these several organized bodies, supposing ourselves to have successively animated them, would have no more conceivable tendency to destroy the living beings ourselves, or deprive us of living faculties, the faculties of perception and of action, than the dissolution of any foreign matter, which we are capable of receiving impressions from, and making use of for the common occasions of life.

No necessary connexion between thought and the bodily organism.

[9.] II. The simplicity and absolute oneness of a living agent cannot indeed, from the nature of the thing, be properly proved by experimental observations. But as these *fall in* with the supposition of its unity, so they plainly lead us to *conclude* certainly, that our gross organized bodies, with which we perceive the objects of sense, and with which we act, are no part of ourselves; and therefore shew us, that we have no reason to believe their destruction to be ours: even without determining whether our living substances be material or immaterial. For we see by experience, that men may lose
(*a*) their limbs, their organs of sense, and even the greatest part of
(*b*) these bodies, and yet remain the same living agents. And

Daily observation confirms this.

For example:

[8] [Butler here follows the line suggested by Cicero: "Mihi quidem, naturam animi intuenti, multo difficilior occurrit cogitatio multoque obscurior, qualis animus in corpore sit, tamquam alienae domui, quam qualis, cum exierit et in liberum caelum quasi domum suam, uenerit." (*Tusc. Quaest.* I. xxii. 51.)]

conveying them to, the perceiving power, in a manner similar or like to the manner in which our organs of sense prepare and convey them. Both are in a like way instruments of our receiving such ideas from external objects, as the Author of Nature appointed those external objects to be the occasions of exciting in us. However, glasses are evidently instances of this; namely of matter which is no part of our body, preparing objects for and conveying them towards the perceiving power, in like manner as our bodily organs do. And if we see with our eyes only in the same manner as we do with glasses, the like may justly be concluded, from analogy, of all our other senses. It is not intended, by any thing here said, to affirm, that the whole apparatus of vision, or of perception by any other of our senses, can be traced through all its steps, quite up to the living power of seeing, or perceiving: but that so far as it can be traced by experimental observations, so far it appears, that our organs of sense prepare and convey on objects, in order to their being perceived, in like manner as foreign matter does, without affording any shadow of appearance, that they themselves perceive. And that we have no reason to think our organs of sense percipients,[10] is confirmed by instances of persons losing some of them, the living beings themselves, their former occupiers, remaining unimpaired. It is confirmed also by the experience of dreams; by which we find we are at present possessed of a latent, and, what would otherwise be, an unimagined unknown power of perceiving sensible objects, in as strong and lively a manner without our external organs of sense as with them.

confirmed by experience, (*a*)

(*β*)

[13.] So also with regard to our power of moving, or directing motion by will and choice: upon the destruction of a limb, this active power remains, as it evidently seems, unlessened; so as that the living being, who has suffered this loss, would be capable of moving as before, if it had another limb to move with. It can walk by the help of an artificial leg; just as it can make use of a pole or a lever, to reach towards itself and to move things, beyond the

(*b*) The limbs are not self-directive.

[10] [Butler again follows Cicero's line of reasoning: "Nos enim ne nunc quidem oculis cernimus ea, quae videmus . . . ut facile intelligi possit animum et videre et audire, non eas partes, quae quasi fenestrae sint animi, quibus tamen sentire nihil queat mens, nisi id agat et adsit" (*Tusc. Quaest.* I. xx. 46).]

length and the power of its natural arm: and this last it does in the same manner as it reaches and moves, with its natural arm, things nearer and of less weight. Nor is there so much as any appearance of our limbs being endued with a power of moving or directing themselves; though they are adapted, like the several parts of a machine, to be the instruments of motion to each other; and some parts of the same limb, to be instruments of motion to other parts of it.

[14.] Thus a man determines, that he will look at such an object through a microscope; or being lame suppose, that he will walk to such a place with a staff a week hence. His eyes and his feet no more determine in these cases, than the microscope and the staff. Nor is there any ground to think they any more put the determination in practice; or that his eyes are the seers or his feet the movers, in any other sense than as the microscope and the staff are. Upon the whole then, our organs of sense and our limbs are certainly instruments, which the living persons ourselves make use of to perceive and move with: there is not any probability, that they are any more; nor consequently, that we have any other kind of relation to them, than what we may have to any other foreign matter formed into instruments of perception and motion, suppose into a microscope or a staff; (I say any other kind of relation, for I am not speaking of the degree of it); nor consequently is there any probability, that the alienation or dissolution of these instruments is the destruction of the perceiving and moving agent.

The bodily members are but the soul's instruments.

[15.] And thus our finding, that the dissolution of matter, in which living beings were most nearly interested, is not their dissolution; and that the destruction of several of the organs and instruments of perception and of motion belonging to them, is not their destruction; shews demonstratively, that there is no ground to think that the dissolution of any other matter, or destruction of any other organs and instruments, will be the dissolution or destruction of living agents, from the like kind of relation. And we have no reason to think we stand in any other kind of relation to any thing which we find dissolved by death.

Hence bodily dissolution in no way necessitates the death of the living agent.

[16.] But it is said these observations are equally applicable to brutes: and it is thought an insuperable difficulty, that

Does not such reasoning apply to brutes?

they should be immortal, and by consequence capable of everlasting happiness.[11] Now this manner of expression is both invidious and weak: but the thing intended by it, is really no difficulty at all, either in the way of natural or moral consideration. For first, suppose the invidious thing, designed in such a manner of expression, were really implied, as it is not in the least, in the natural immortality of brutes; namely, that they must arrive at great attainments, and become rational and moral agents; even this would be no difficulty: since we know not what latent powers and capacities they may be endued with. There was once, prior to experience, as great presumption against human creatures, as there is against the brute creatures, arriving at that degree of understanding, which we have in mature age. For we can trace up our own existence to the same original with theirs. And we find it to be a general law of nature, that creatures endued with capacities of virtue and religion should be placed in a condition of being, in which they are altogether without the use of them, for a considerable length of their duration; as in infancy and childhood. And great part of the human species go out of the present world, before they come to the exercise of these capacities in any degree at all. But then, secondly, the natural immortality of brutes does not in the least imply, that they are endued with any latent capacities of a rational or moral nature. And the economy of the universe might require, that there should be living creatures without any capacities of this kind. And all difficulties as to the manner how they are to be disposed of are so apparently and wholly founded in our ignorance, that it is wonderful they should be insisted upon by any, but such as are weak enough to think they are acquainted with the whole system of things. There is then absolutely nothing at all in this objection, which is so rhetorically urged, against the greatest part of the natural proofs or presumptions of the immortality of human minds: I say the greatest part; for it is less applicable to the following observation, which is more peculiar to mankind:

This objection is both (1) weak,

and (2) invidious.

And (3) there are arguments for human immortality not applicable to brutes.

[17.] III. That as it is evident our *present* powers and capacities of reason, memory, and affection, do not depend upon our gross body in the manner in which perception by

III. Death does not destroy our powers of reflection.

[11] [See Note C on "A Future Existence for the Brute Creation," at the end of this chapter.]

our organs of sense does; so they do not appear to depend upon it at all in any such manner, as to give ground to think, that the dissolution of this body will be the destruction of these our *present* powers of reflection, as it will of our powers of sensation; or to give ground to conclude, even that it will be so much as a suspension of the former.

Sensation.

Reflection.

Sensation not essential to reflection once ideas are gained.

[18.] Human creatures exist at present in two states of life and perception, greatly different from each other; each of which has its own peculiar laws, and its own peculiar enjoyments and sufferings. When any of our senses are affected or appetites gratified with the objects of them, we may be said to exist or live in a state of sensation. When none of our senses are affected or appetites gratified, and yet we perceive, and reason, and act; we may be said to exist or live in a state of reflection. Now it is by no means certain, that any thing which is dissolved by death, is any way necessary to the living being in this its state of reflection, after ideas are gained. For, though, from our present constitution and condition of being, our external organs of sense are necessary for conveying in ideas to our reflecting powers, as carriages, and levers, and scaffolds are in architecture: yet when these ideas are brought in, we are capable of reflecting in the most intense degree, and of enjoying the greatest pleasure and feeling the greatest pain, by means of that reflection, without any assistance from our senses; and without any at all, which we know of, from that body which will be dissolved by death. It does not appear then, that the relation of this gross body to the reflecting being is, in any degree, necessary to thinking; to our intellectual enjoyments or sufferings: nor, consequently, that the dissolution or alienation of the former by death, will be the destruction of those present powers, which render us capable of this state of reflection.

This confirmed by the facts of chronic disease.

Further, there are instances of moral diseases, which do not at all affect our present intellectual powers; and this affords a presumption, that those diseases will not destroy these present powers. Indeed, from the observations made above,[12] it appears, that there is no presumption, from their mutually affecting each other, that the dissolution of the body is the destruction of the living agent. And by the same reasoning, it must appear too, that there is no presumption, from their

[12] § 11 above.

mutually affecting each other, that the dissolution of the body is the destruction of our present reflecting powers: but instances of their not affecting each other, afford a presumption of the contrary. Instances of mortal diseases not impairing our present reflecting powers, evidently turn our thoughts even from imagining such diseases to be the destruction of them. Several things indeed greatly affect all our living powers, and at length suspend the exercise of them; as for instance drowsiness, increasing till it ends in sound sleep: and from hence we might have imagined it would destroy them, till we found by experience the weakness of this way of judging. But in the diseases now mentioned, there is not so much as this shadow of probability, to lead us to any such conclusion, as to the reflecting powers which we have at present. For in those diseases, persons the moment before death appear to be in the highest vigour of life. They discover apprehension, memory, reason, all entire; with the utmost force of affection; sense of a character, of shame and honour; and the highest mental enjoyments and sufferings, even to the last gasp: and these surely prove even greater vigour of life than bodily strength does. Now what pretence is there for thinking, that a progressive disease when arrived to such a degree, I mean that degree which is mortal, will destroy those powers, which were not impaired, which were not affected by it, during its whole progress quite up to that degree? And if death by diseases of this kind is not the destruction of our present reflecting powers, it will scarce be thought that death by any other means is.

No presumption that death even suspends the exercise of our reflective powers.

[19.] It is obvious that this general observation may be carried on further: and there appears so little connexion between our bodily powers of sensation, and our present powers of reflection, that there is no reason to conclude, that death, which destroys the former, does so much as suspend the exercise of the latter, or interrupt our *continuing* to exist in the like state of reflection which we do now. For suspension of reason, memory, and the affections which they excite, is no part of the idea of death, nor is implied in our notion of it. And our daily experiencing these powers to be exercised, without any assistance, that we know of, from those bodies, which will be dissolved by death; and our finding often, that the exercise of them is so lively to the last; these things afford a

to some fixed general laws of wisdom, upon every one in proportion to the degrees of his virtue. And though the advantages of that future natural state should not be bestowed, as these of the present in some measure are, by the will of the society; but entirely by His more immediate action, upon Whom the whole frame of nature depends: yet this distribution may be just as natural, as their being distributed here by the instrumentality of men. And indeed, though one were to allow any confused undetermined sense, which people please to put upon the word *natural*, it would be a shortness of thought scarce credible, to imagine, that no system or course of things can be so, but only what we see at present:[17] especially whilst the probability of a future life, or the natural immortality of the soul, is admitted upon the evidence of reason; because this is really both admitting and denying at once, a state of being different from the present to be natural.

Meaning of the word *natural*.

But the only distinct meaning of that word is, *stated*, *fixed*, or *settled*: since what is natural, as much requires and presupposes an intelligent agent to render it so, *i.e.* to effect it continually, or at stated times; as what is supernatural or miraculous does to effect it for once.[18] And from hence it must follow, that persons' notion of what is natural, will be enlarged in proportion to their greater knowledge of the works of God, and the dispensations of His Providence. Nor is there any absurdity in supposing, that there may be beings in the universe, whose capacities, and knowledge, and views, may be so extensive, as that the whole Christian dispensation may to them appear natural, *i.e.* analogous or conformable to God's dealings with other parts of His creation; as natural as the visible known course of things appears to us. For there seems scarce any other possible sense to be put upon the word, but that only in which it is here used; similar, stated, or uniform.

Thus a future life is credible, and this is enough for religion.

[24.] This credibility of a future life, which has been here insisted upon, how little soever it may satisfy our curiosity, seems to answer all the purposes of religion, in like manner as a demonstrative proof would. Indeed a proof, even a demonstrative one, of a future life, would not be a proof of religion. For, that we are to live hereafter, is just as reconcilable with the scheme of atheism, and as well to be

[17] See Part II. ii. 4 and iv. 2.

[18] [See Part I. ii. 4.]

accounted for by it, as that we are now alive is: and therefore nothing can be more absurd than to argue from that scheme, that there can be no future state. But as religion implies a future state, any presumption against such a state, is a presumption against religion. And the foregoing observations remove all presumptions of that sort, and prove, to a very considerable degree of probability, one fundamental doctrine of religion; which, if believed, would greatly open and dispose the mind seriously to attend to the general evidence of the whole.

NOTE B.

THE IMMATERIALITY OF THE SOUL.

The argument from the immaterial simplicity of the soul to its indestructibility and thence to its immortality is as old as Plato's *Phaedo*; and it has exercised a wide influence on human thought. Cicero puts it tersely in his *De Senectute* (c. xxi.): "Et cum simplex natura animi esset, neque haberet in se quidquam admixtum dispar sui atque dissimile, non posse eum dividi; quod si non possit, non posse interire." The argument was a favourite one with thinkers who inherited the teaching of Descartes. Thus Berkeley writes in his *Principles of Human Knowledge* (§ 141): "We have shewn that the soul is indivisible, incorporeal, unextended, and it is consequently incorruptible. Nothing can be plainer than that the motions, changes, decays, and dissolutions which we hourly see befall natural bodies (and which is what we mean by the *course of nature*) cannot possibly affect an active, simple, uncompounded substance: such a being therefore is indissoluble by the force of nature; that is to say—the soul of man is *naturally* immortal."

The form in which Butler had this argument in view was that in which it was expressed by Clarke in the passage quoted at p. 17 above. It is evident on reflection that the argument, positively applied, will not bear examination. It is not necessary to do more than refer to the trenchant and profound criticism of it given by Kant in his treatment of the "Second Paralogism" of Rational Psychology (*Kritik of Pure Reason*, ed. I.). But without entering upon the subtleties of the Critical Philosophy, we can see that such adjectives as "simple" or "composite," when

NOTE C.

A FUTURE EXISTENCE FOR THE BRUTE CREATION.

The question of a future life for the brute creation has often been discussed. Not to speak of the Greek speculations about transmigration of souls (cp. Plato, *Tim.* 76) and the Egyptian deification of animals, their future existence is explicitly asserted in the curious work entitled *The Book of the Secrets of Enoch*, which was written by an Egyptian Jew about the beginning of our era. In § 58 (Charles' edition) we read: "For as there is a special place for mankind for all the souls of men according to their number, so there is also of beasts. And not one soul shall perish which God has made until the great judgment. And every soul of beast shall bring a charge against man if he feeds them badly." This idea seems to have passed over into the creed of Islam. As Dr. Charles points out in his interesting note, it is the doctrine of the Koran, that irrational animals will be restored to life at the resurrection that they may be judged and punished for the injuries they had inflicted on each other in their earthly life. And this being done, they will be turned to dust. The question seems to have attracted a good deal of attention in England in the eighteenth century. Boswell, in his *Life of Johnson* (ch. xix.), tells of "an essay, written by Mr. Deane, a divine of the Church of England, maintaining the future life of brutes by an explication of certain parts of the Scriptures," the mention of which provoked the scathing ridicule of the terrible doctor. Pope sang of the "poor Indian" who

"thinks, admitted to yon equal sky,
His faithful dog shall bear him company";

and apparently many serious-minded contemporaries of the poet held a similar belief. Dr. Samuel Clarke, when pressed on the point, declared that "that man does not do any great honour either to God or to the Christian religion, who will contend that through a boundless eternity there shall never exist anything in the immense universe but what must needs partake either of the happiness or misery of mankind" (*Reply to Collins*). Even more explicit is John Wesley in a remarkable sermon on the text *Rom.* viii. 19-22, entitled *The Great Deliverance.* "The whole brute creation will then undoubtedly be restored, not only to the vigour, strength, and swiftness which they had at their creation, but to a far higher degree of each than they ever enjoyed. They will be restored, not only to that measure of understanding which they had in Paradise, but to a degree of it as much higher than that as the understanding of an elephant is beyond that of a worm. . . . May I be permitted to mention here a conjecture concerning the brute creation? What if it should then please the all-wise, the all-gracious Creator to raise them higher in the scale of beings? What if it should please Him, when He makes us 'equal to angels,' to make them what we are now—creatures capable of God; capable of knowing and loving and enjoying the Author of their Being?"

Here is a remarkable coincidence with Butler,[1] who, although (as is his wont) expressing himself very cautiously, seems distinctly to favour the opinion so confidently advocated by his great contemporary. It may be interesting to quote an equally confident dictum on the other side, laid down half a century before by one of the masters of Anglican theology, Bishop Pearson. In his *Exposition of the Creed* (Art. xi. § 9), he declares that the creatures "which are below us are neither capable of reward nor punishment for anything acted in this life, and therefore though they die, yet shall they never rise, because there is no reason for their resurrection." The reasoning may not seem quite conclusive to those who believe themselves to have observed traces of a moral faculty in the conduct of an intelligent dog; but the negative conclusion of Pearson is, for all that, more in accordance with the evidence than the positive conclusion of Wesley. It must not be forgotten that, as has been pointed out by Mr. Gladstone in his *Studies*, the life of the lower animals does not suggest the idea of unfulfilled purpose, as the life of man does. In the case of the beasts we cannot get beyond a verdict of "not proven" when their final extinction at death is asserted; but in the case of man there are distinct intimations of immortality in the facts of the moral life of which he is conscious, and which he feels to be the appropriate sphere of his personality.[2]

[1] In Colliber's *Free Thoughts concerning Souls* (1734), some space is devoted to the problem of the condition of brutes after death. Colliber was a writer whom Butler read (see *Anal.* Part II. i. 14 note).

[2] It is not without interest to observe that the late Archbishop Benson of Canterbury seems to have been convinced that the life of animals did not terminate at death. "No one will persuade me," he wrote in his diary, when recording the death of a favourite horse, "that [she] comes to an end here" (*Life*, vol. ii. p. 217; cp. vol. i. p. 612).

CHAPTER II.

Of the Government of God by Rewards and Punishments; and particularly of the latter.

Doctrine of a future practically important, if our future condition depend on our present behaviour.

[1.] THAT which makes the question concerning a future life to be of so great importance to us, is our capacity of happiness and misery. And that which makes the consideration of it to be of so great importance to us, is the supposition of our happiness and misery Hereafter, depending upon our actions Here. Without this indeed, curiosity could not but sometimes bring a subject, in which we may be so highly interested, to our thoughts; especially upon the mortality of others, or the near prospect of our own. But reasonable men would not take any further thought about Hereafter, than what should happen thus occasionally to rise in their minds, if it were certain that our future interest no way depended upon our present behaviour: whereas on the contrary, if there be ground, either from analogy or any thing else, to think it does; then there is reason also for the most active thought and solicitude, to secure that interest; to behave so as that we may escape that misery, and obtain that happiness in another life, which we not only suppose ourselves capable of, but which we apprehend also is put in our own power. And whether there be ground for this last apprehension, certainly would deserve to be most seriously considered, were there no other proof of a future life and interest, than that presumptive one, which the foregoing observations amount to.

Our present happiness or misery largely depends on ourselves.

[2.] Now in the present state, all which we enjoy, and a great part of what we suffer, *is put in our own power*.[1] For pleasure and pain are the consequences of our actions: and

[1] [Cp. Part II. v. 5 for more on this head. See also Part I. vii. 8.]

we are endued by the Author of our nature with capacities of foreseeing these consequences. We find by experience He does not so much as preserve our lives, exclusively of our own care and attention, to provide ourselves with, and to make use of, that sustenance, by which He has appointed our lives shall be preserved; and without which, He has appointed, they shall not be preserved at all. And in general we foresee, that the external things, which are the objects of our various passions, can neither be obtained nor enjoyed, without exerting ourselves in such and such manners: but by thus exerting ourselves, we obtain and enjoy these objects, in which our natural good consists; or by this means God gives us the possession and enjoyment of them. I know not, that we have any one kind or degree of enjoyment, but by the means of our own actions. And by prudence and care, we may, for the most part, pass our days in tolerable ease and quiet: or, on the contrary, we may, by rashness, ungoverned passion, wilfulness, or even by negligence, make ourselves as miserable as ever we please. And many do please to make themselves extremely miserable, *i.e.* to do what they know beforehand will render them so. They follow those ways, the fruit of which they know, by instruction, example, experience, will be disgrace, and poverty, and sickness, and untimely death. This every one observes to be the general course of things; though it is to be allowed, we cannot find by experience, that all our sufferings are owing to our own follies.

Suggested reasons why happiness is not distributed without regard to conduct.

[3.] Why the Author of Nature does not give His creatures promiscuously such and such perceptions, without regard to their behaviour; why He does not make them happy without the instrumentality of their own actions, and prevent their bringing any sufferings upon themselves; is another matter.[2] Perhaps there may be some impossibilities in the nature of i.

[2] [FitzGerald observes that "Butler here hints at several possible solutions of the old atheistical dilemma. God prevents not evil, either because He cannot, or because He will not. If He cannot, He is not Almighty. If He will not, He is not All-good. Butler shews us that neither conclusion can be safely drawn. The supposition that God cannot remove these evils does not necessarily imply any defect in power; because, for anything we know to the contrary, the removal of them might involve a contradiction, and not to be able to do what is self-contradictory and impossible in the notion of it, is plainly no limitation of power." (p. 42, *Analogy*, ed. W. Fitzgerald, Bishop of Cork, 1857.)]

ii. things, which we are unacquainted with.[3] Or less happiness, it may be, would upon the whole be produced by such a
iii. method of conduct, than is by the present. Or perhaps Divine goodness, with which, if I mistake not, we make very free in our speculations, may not be a bare single disposition to produce happiness;[4] but a disposition to make the good,
iv. the faithful, the honest man happy. Perhaps an infinitely perfect Mind may be pleased, with seeing His creatures behave suitably to the nature which He has given them; to the relations which He has placed them in to each other; and to that, which they stand in to Himself: that relation to Himself, which, during their existence, is even necessary, and which is the most important one of all: perhaps, I say, an infinitely perfect Mind may be pleased with this moral piety of moral agents, in and for itself; as well as upon account of its being essentially con-
v. ducive to the happiness of His creation. Or the whole end, for which God made, and thus governs the world, may be utterly beyond the reach of our faculties: there may be somewhat in it as impossible for us to have any conception of, as for a blind man to have a conception of colours. But however this be, it is certain matter of universal experience, that the general method of Divine administration is, forewarning us, or giving us capacities to foresee, with more or less clearness, that if we act so and so, we shall have such enjoyments, if so and so, such sufferings; and giving us those enjoyments, and making us feel those sufferings, in consequence of our actions.

The present method of distribution *natural*, *i.e.* due to the Governor of Nature.

[4.] "But all this is to be ascribed to the general course of Nature." True. This is the very thing which I am observing. It is to be ascribed to the general course of Nature: *i.e.* not surely to the words or ideas, *course of nature*; but to Him Who appointed it, and put things into it: or to a course of operation, from its uniformity or constancy, called natural;[5] and which necessarily implies an operating agent.[6] For when men find

[3] Part I. chap. vii. [8].

[4] [Cp. Part I. iii. 3 below.]

[5] Part I. i. 23.

[6] [The principle that observed uniformity of rule does not supersede the necessity of a Ruler seems obvious when stated; and yet it is frequently forgotten even in modern speculation. Aristotle found evidence of Intelligence in the Uniformities rather than in the Anomalies of Nature; and yet it is in "extraordinary" phenomena that theologians in every age have been prone to see most plainly the hand of God. It is not necessary to suppose that Butler was indebted to anyone for his broader view, but it is interesting to observe that it had been well stated a few years before by Clarke. "There is no such thing as what men commonly call the *course of*

themselves necessitated to confess an Author of Nature, or that God is the natural governor of the world; they must not deny this again, because His government is uniform; they must not deny that He does things at all, because He does them constantly; because the effects of His acting are permanent, whether His acting be so or not; though there is no reason to think it is not. In short, every man, in every thing he does, naturally acts upon the forethought and apprehension of avoiding evil or obtaining good: and if the natural course of things be the appointment of God, and our natural faculties of knowledge and experience are given us by Him; then the good and bad consequences which follow our actions, are His appointment,[7] and our foresight of those consequences, is a warning given us by Him, how we are to act.

Final cause of pleasure and pain, to influence conduct.

[5.] "Is the pleasure then, naturally accompanying every particular gratification of passion, intended to put us upon gratifying ourselves in every such particular instance, and as a reward to us for so doing?" No certainly. Nor is it to be said, that our eyes were naturally intended to give us the sight of each particular object, to which they do or can extend; objects which are destructive of them, or which, for any other reason, it may become us to turn our eyes from. Yet there is no doubt, but that our eyes were intended for us to see with. So neither is there any doubt, but that the foreseen pleasures and pains belonging to the passions, were intended, in general, to induce mankind to act in such and such manners.

Thus we are under God's natural government,

[6.] Now from this general observation, obvious to every one, that God has given us to understand, He has appointed satisfaction and delight to be the consequence of our acting in one manner, and pain and uneasiness of our acting in another, and of our not acting at all; and that we find the consequences, which we were beforehand informed of, uniformly to follow; we may learn, that we are at present

nature, or the *power of nature*. The course of nature, truly and properly speaking, is nothing else but the Will of God producing certain effects in a continued, regular, constant, and uniform manner; which course or manner of acting being in every moment perfectly *arbitrary*, is as easy to be *altered* at any time as to be preserved" (*Evidences of Natural and Revealed Religion*, Prop. xiv.). See Part II. v. 3 below.]

[7] [It must be remembered that several of the orthodox opponents of Deism, who preceded Butler, had regarded the doctrine that future rewards and punishments may be conceived as the *natural* consequences of human action in this world, as heretical, and had been at the pains of controverting it.]

actually under His government in the strictest and most proper sense; in such a sense, as that He rewards and punishes us for our actions. An Author of Nature being supposed, it is not so much a deduction of reason, as a matter of experience, that we are thus under His government: under His government, in the same sense, as we are under the government of civil magistrates. Because the annexing pleasure to some actions, and pain to others, in our power to do or forbear, and giving notice of this appointment beforehand to those whom it concerns; is the proper formal notion of government.[8] Whether the pleasure or pain which thus follows upon our behaviour, be owing to the Author of Nature's acting upon us every moment which we feel it; or to His having at once contrived and executed His own part in the plan of the world;[9] makes no alteration as to the matter before us. For if civil magistrates could make the sanctions of their laws take place, without interposing at all, after they had passed them; without a trial, and the formalities of an execution: if they were able to make their laws execute themselves, or every offender to execute them upon himself; we should be just in the same sense under their government then, as we are now; but in a much

which implies: a b c

This true, although there be no continuous administration from without,

[8] [He repeats this definition, Part I. iv. 2.]

[9] [Butler here seems to favour (though he does not explicitly adopt) the latter view, which was widely held in England in the eighteenth century, both by the Deists and by their orthodox opponents. It conceives the relation of the world to God as that of a machine to the mechanic who made it. Stress is laid on the *transcendence* of the Supreme, but His *immanence* in nature is overlooked or forgotten. It is, perhaps, the gravest blot on Paley's *Natural Theology* that he treats as adequate the analogy of the universe to a complicated piece of mechanism, set going at the beginning by the Great Artificer, Who thenceforward stands aloof from it. FitzGerald points out that Clarke had a truer conception of this great matter. But, without the aid of Clarke, Butler might have found teaching in the formularies of his own church which would have saved him from the somewhat unfortunate illustration which he here permits himself to use (although it is true that he only uses it in an argument *ad hominem*, and that he hints at a juster view in § 4 above). "It is not to be thought that God hath created all this whole universal world as it is; and thus once made, hath given it up to be ruled and used after our own wits and device, and so taketh no more charge thereof; as we see the shipwright, after he hath brought his ship to a perfect end, then delivereth he it to the mariners, and taketh no more care thereof. Nay, God hath not so created the world, that He is careless of it; but He still preserveth it by His goodness; He still stayeth it in His creation. For else, without His special goodness, it could not stand long in this condition" (*Homily for Rogation Week*, Part I.). See the article "Nature" in Hastings' *Bible Dictionary*.]

higher degree, and more perfect manner. Vain is the ridicule with which, one foresees, some persons will divert themselves, upon finding lesser pains considered as instances of Divine punishment. There is no possibility of answering or evading the general thing here intended, without denying all final causes. For final causes being admitted, the pleasures and pains now mentioned must be admitted too as instances of them. And if they are; if God annexes delight to some actions and uneasiness to others, with an apparent design to induce us to act so and so; then He not only dispenses happiness and misery, but also rewards and punishes actions. If, for example, the pain which we feel, upon doing what tends to the destruction of our bodies, suppose upon too near approaches to fire, or upon wounding ourselves, be appointed by the Author of Nature to prevent our doing what thus tends to our destruction; this is altogether as much an instance of His punishing our actions, and consequently of our being under His government, as declaring by a voice from heaven, that if we acted so, He would inflict such pain upon us, and inflicting it, whether it be greater or less.

and although particular instances may seem unconvincing.

Illustration.

[7.] Thus we find, that the true notion or conception of the Author of Nature, is that of a master or governor, prior to the consideration of His moral attributes. The fact of our case, which we find by experience, is, that He actually exercises dominion or government over us at present, by rewarding and punishing us for our actions, in as strict and proper a sense of these words, and even in the same sense, as children, servants, subjects, are rewarded and punished by those who govern them.

Thus the Author of Nature is our Governor, whether He govern morally or no.

[8.] And thus the whole analogy of Nature, the whole present course of things, most fully shews, that there is nothing incredible in the general doctrine of religion, that God will reward and punish men for their actions hereafter: nothing incredible, I mean, arising out of the notion of rewarding and punishing. For the whole course of Nature is a present instance of His exercising that government over us, which implies in it rewarding and punishing.

Hence, doctrine of future reward analogous to present experience.

Analogy between present and future punishments drawn out.

[9.] BUT as Divine punishment is what men chiefly object against, and are most unwilling to allow; it may be proper to mention some circumstances in the natural course of punishments at present, which are analogous to what religion teaches us concerning a future state of punishment; indeed so analogous, that as they add a further credibility to it, so they cannot but raise a most serious apprehension of it in those who will attend to them.

Ill consequences of imprudence are natural punishments.

[10.] It has been now observed, that such and such miseries naturally follow such and such actions of imprudence and wilfulness, as well as actions more commonly and more distinctly considered as vicious; and that these consequences, when they may be foreseen, are properly natural punishments annexed to such actions. For the general thing here insisted upon, is, not that we see a great deal of misery in the world, but a great deal which men bring upon themselves by their own behaviour, which they might have foreseen and avoided. Now the circumstances of these natural punishments, particularly deserving our attention, are such as these; That oftentimes they follow, or are

Points of analogy between these and *future* punishments.

i. inflicted in consequence of, actions, which procure many present advantages, and are accompanied with much present pleasure; for instance, sickness and untimely death is the consequence of intemperance, though accompanied with the
ii. highest mirth and jollity: That these punishments are often much greater, than the advantages or pleasures obtained by the actions, of which they are the punishments or
iii. consequences: That though we may imagine a constitution of nature, in which these natural punishments, which are in fact to follow, would follow, immediately upon such actions being done, or very soon after; we find on the contrary in our world, that they are often delayed a great while, sometimes even till long after the actions occasioning them are forgot; so that the constitution of nature is such, that delay of punishment is no sort nor degree of presumption
iv. of final impunity: That after such delay, these natural punishments or miseries often come, not by degrees, but suddenly, with violence, and at once; however, the chief misery often
v. does: That as certainty of such distant misery following such actions, is never afforded persons; so perhaps during the actions, they have seldom a distinct full expectation of its

following:[10] and many times the case is only thus, that they see in general, or may see, the credibility, that intemperance, suppose, will bring after it diseases; civil crimes, civil punishments; when yet the real probability often is, that they shall escape; but things notwithstanding take their destined course, and the misery inevitably follows at its appointed time, in very many of these cases. Thus also though youth may be vi.
alleged as an excuse for rashness and folly, as being naturally thoughtless, and not clearly foreseeing all the consequences of being untractable and profligate; this does not hinder, but that these consequences follow, and are grievously felt, throughout the whole course of mature life. Habits contracted even in that age, are often utter ruin: and men's success in the world, not only in the common sense of worldly success, but their real happiness and misery, depends, in a great degree, and in various ways, upon the manner in which they pass their youth; which consequences they for the most part neglect to consider, and perhaps seldom can properly be said to believe, beforehand. It requires also to be vii.
mentioned, that in numberless cases, the natural course of things affords us opportunities for procuring advantages to ourselves at certain times, which we cannot procure when we will; nor ever recall the opportunities, if we have neglected them.[11] Indeed the general course of nature is an example of this. If, during the opportunity of youth, persons are indocile and self-willed; they inevitably suffer in their future life, for want of those acquirements, which they neglected the natural season of attaining. If the husbandman lets his seed-time pass without sowing, the whole year is lost to him beyond recovery. In like manner, though after men have been guilty of folly and extravagance *up to a certain degree*, it is often in their power, for instance, to retrieve their affairs, to recover their health and character; at least in good measure: yet real reformation is, in many cases, of no avail at all towards preventing the miseries, poverty, sickness, infamy, naturally annexed to folly and extravagance *exceeding that degree*. There is a certain bound to imprudence and misbehaviour, which being transgressed, there remains no place for repentance in the natural course of things. It is further very much viii.

[10] See Part II. vi. 9.

[11] [Cp. Part I. v. 9.]

are despised, punishment follows in this life.

b, c examples of others; from the lesser inconveniences which
d they bring upon themselves; from the instructions of wise and virtuous men: after these have been long despised, scorned, ridiculed: after the chief bad consequences, temporal consequences, of their follies, have been delayed for a great while; at length they break in irresistibly, like an armed force: repentance is too late to relieve, and can serve only to aggravate, their distress:[15] the case is become desperate: and poverty and sickness, remorse and anguish, infamy and death, the effects of their own doings, overwhelm them, beyond possibility of remedy or escape. This is an account of what is in fact the general constitution of Nature.

Present punishment not always in proportion to guilt, but the connexion plain enough to shew future punishment to be credible despite objections;

[13.] It is not in any sort meant, that according to what appears at present of the natural course of things, men are always uniformly punished in proportion to their misbehaviour: but that there are very many instances of misbehaviour punished in the several ways now mentioned, and very dreadful instances too; sufficient to shew what the laws of the universe may admit; and, if thoroughly considered, sufficient fully to answer all objections against the credibility of a future state of punishments, from any imaginations,

such as

a that the frailty of our nature and external temptations, almost annihilate the guilt of human vices: as well as objections
b of another sort; from necessity; from suppositions, that the
c will of an infinite Being cannot be contradicted; or that
d He must be incapable of offence and provocation.[16]

Desirable to draw out this analogy to check the presumption of the sceptic.

[14.] Reflections of this kind are not without their terrors to serious persons, the most free from enthusiasm, and of the greatest strength of mind; but it is fit things be stated and considered as they really are. And there is, in the present age, a certain fearlessness, with regard to what may be hereafter under the government of God, which nothing but an universally acknowledged demonstration on the side of atheism can justify; and which makes it quite necessary, that men be reminded, and if possible made to feel, that there is no sort of ground for being thus presumptuous, even upon the most sceptical principles. For, may it not be said of any person upon his being born into the world, he may behave so, as to be of no service to it, but by being

15 [See Part I. iii. 5.]

16 See Part I. iv. and vi.

made an example of the woful effects of vice and folly? That he may, as any one may, if he will, incur an infamous execution, from the hands of civil justice; or in some other course of extravagance shorten his days; or bring upon himself infamy and diseases worse than death? So that it had been better for him, even with regard to the present world, that he had never been born. And is there any pretence of reason, for people to think themselves secure, and talk as if they had certain proof, that, let them act as licentiously as they will, there can be nothing analogous to this, with regard to a future and more general interest, under the providence and government of the same God?

state not an instance of *perfect* moral government.

government, which we experience ourselves under in the present state, taken alone, is allowed not to be the perfection of moral government. And yet this by no means hinders, but that there may be somewhat, be it more or less, truly moral in it. A righteous government may plainly appear to be carried on to some degree: enough to give us the apprehension that it shall be completed, or carried on to that degree of perfection which religion teaches us it shall; but which cannot appear, till much more of the Divine administration be seen, than can in the present life. And the design of this chapter is to inquire, how far this is the case: how far, over and above
α the moral nature[5] which God has given us, and our natural
β notion of Him as righteous Governor of those His creatures, to
γ whom He has given this nature;[6] I say how far besides this, the principles and beginnings of a moral government over the world may be discerned, notwithstanding and amidst all the confusion and disorder of it.

But the beginnings of such may be discerned.

Shaftesbury's argument for this,

[5.] Now one might mention here, what has been often urged with great force, that in general, less uneasiness and more satisfaction, are the natural consequences[7] of a virtuous than of a vicious course of life, in the present state, as an instance of a moral government established in Nature; an instance of it, collected from experience and present matter of fact. But it must be owned a thing of difficulty to weigh and balance pleasures and uneasinesses, each amongst themselves, and also against each other, so as to make an estimate with any exactness, of the overplus of happiness on the side of virtue.[8] And it is not impossible, that, amidst the infinite disorders of the world, there may be exceptions to the happi-
a ness of virtue; even with regard to those persons, whose course of life from their youth up has been blameless; and
b more with regard to those, who have gone on for some time in the ways of vice, and have afterwards reformed. For suppose an instance of the latter case; a person with his passions inflamed, his natural faculty of self-government impaired by habits of indulgence, and with all his vices about him, like so many harpies, craving for their accustomed grati-

unsatisfactory, for (i.) it is difficult to weigh pleasure against pain,

and (ii.) there may be exceptions to the rule.

[5] *Dissertation* II.

[6] Ch. vi. [§ 11].

[7] See Lord Shaftesbury's *Inquiry concerning Virtue*, Part II. [Book II., Part II., p. 99 ff.]

[8] [Butler repeats this important observation, Part II. vi. 3, and viii. 9.]

fication: who can say how long it might be, before such a person would find more satisfaction in the reasonableness and present good consequences of virtue, than difficulties and self-denial in the restraints of it? Experience also shews, that c men can, to a great degree, get over their sense of shame, so as that by professing themselves to be without principle, and avowing even direct villany, they can support themselves against the infamy of it. But as the ill actions of any one α will probably be more talked of, and oftener thrown in his way, upon his reformation; so the infamy of them will be much β more felt, after the natural sense of virtue and of honour is recovered. Uneasiness of this kind ought indeed to be put to the account of former vices:[9] yet it will be said, they are in part the consequences of reformation. Still I am far from allowing it doubtful, whether virtue, upon the whole, be happier than vice in the present world.[10] But if it were, yet the beginnings of a righteous administration may beyond all question be found in Nature, if we will attentively inquire after them. And,

Yet the beginnings of a moral administration may be traced.

[6.] I. In whatever manner the notion of God's moral government over the world might be treated, if it did not appear, whether He were in a proper sense our Governor at all: yet when it is certain matter of experience, that He does manifest Himself to us under the character of a Governor, in the sense explained;[11] it must deserve to be considered, whether there be not reason to apprehend, that He may be a righteous or moral Governor. Since it appears to be fact, that God does govern mankind by the method of rewards and punishments, according to some settled rules of distribution; it is surely a question to be asked, What presumption is there against His finally rewarding and punishing them according to this particular rule, namely, as they act reasonably or unreasonably, virtuously or viciously? since rendering men happy or miserable by this rule, certainly falls in, much more falls in, with our natural apprehensions and sense of things, than doing so by any other rule whatever: since rewarding and punishing actions by any other rule, would appear much harder to be accounted for, by minds formed as He has formed ours. Be the evidence of religion then more or less clear, the expectation

I. It is *a priori* probable that God's natural government, which is a fact, should be moral.

[9] [See above, p. 44.]

[10] [Cp. Serm. xv. 16: "Virtue is demonstrably the happiness of man."]

[11] Ch. II.

which it raises in us, that the righteous shall, upon the whole, be happy, and the wicked miserable, cannot, however, possibly be considered as absurd or chimerical; because it is no more than an expectation, that a method of government already begun, shall be carried on, the method of rewarding and punishing actions; and shall be carried on by a particular rule, which unavoidably appears to us at first sight more natural than any other, the rule which we call distributive justice.[12] Nor,

II. Natural government involves a moral element, since it involves the rewarding of prudence which is a virtue.

[7.] II. Ought it to be entirely passed over, that tranquillity, satisfaction, and external advantages, being the natural consequences of prudent management of ourselves, and our affairs; and rashness, profligate negligence, and wilful folly, bringing after them many inconveniences and sufferings; these afford instances of a right constitution of Nature: as the correction of children, for their own sakes, and by way of example, when they run into danger or hurt themselves, is a part of right education. And thus, that God governs the world by general fixed laws, that He has endued us with capacities of reflecting upon this constitution of things, and foreseeing the good and bad consequences of our behaviour; plainly implies some sort of moral government: since from such a constitution of things it cannot but follow, that prudence and imprudence, which are of the nature of virtue and vice,[13] must be, as they are, respectively rewarded and punished.

III. It is essential to society that vice should be punished, as prejudicial to its life;

[8.] III. From the natural course of things, vicious actions are, to a great degree, actually punished as mischievous to society; and besides punishment actually inflicted upon this account, there is also the fear and apprehension of it in those persons, whose crimes have rendered them obnoxious to it, in case of a discovery; this state of fear being itself often a very considerable punishment. The natural fear and apprehension of it too, which restrains from such crimes, is a declaration of Nature against them. It is necessary to the very being of society, that vices destructive of it, should be punished *as being so*; the vices of falsehood, injustice, cruelty: which punishment therefore is as natural as society; and so is an instance of a kind of moral government, naturally established, and actually taking place. And, since the certain natural

[12] [See below, Part I. vi. 9.]

[13] See *Dissertation II.* [§ 6].

course of things is the conduct of Providence or the government of God, though carried on by the instrumentality of men; the observation here made amounts to this, that mankind find themselves placed by Him in such circumstances, as that they are unavoidably accountable for their behaviour, and are often punished, and sometimes rewarded under His government, in the view of their being mischievous, or eminently beneficial to society.

and what actually happens is by God's disposition.

[9.] If it be objected that good actions, and such as are beneficial to society, are often punished, as in the case of persecution and in other cases; and that ill and mischievous actions are often rewarded: it may be answered distinctly; first, that this is in no sort necessary, and consequently not natural, in the sense in which it is necessary, and therefore natural, that ill or mischievous actions should be punished: and in the next place, that good actions are never punished, considered as beneficial to society, nor ill actions rewarded, under the view of their being hurtful to it.[14] So that it stands good, without any thing on the side of vice to be set over against it, that the Author of Nature has as truly directed, that vicious actions, considered as mischievous to society, should be punished, and put mankind under a necessity of thus punishing them; as He has directed and necessitated us to preserve our lives by food.

Objection: Good actions often punished and bad ones rewarded.

Answer: a

b

[10.] IV. In the natural course of things, virtue *as such* is actually rewarded, and vice *as such* punished: which seems to afford an instance or example, not only of government, but of moral government, begun and established; moral in the strictest sense; though not in that perfection of degree, which religion teaches us to expect. In order to see this more clearly, we must distinguish between actions themselves, and that quality ascribed to them, which we call virtuous or vicious. The gratification itself of every natural passion must be attended with delight: and acquisitions of fortune, however made, are acquisitions of the means or materials of enjoyment. An action then, by which any natural passion is gratified or fortune acquired, procures delight or advantage; abstracted from all consideration of the morality of such

As a fact, virtue and vice are rewarded and punished *as such*.

(Explanatory distinction.)

[14] [As FitzGerald observes, Mandeville in his *Fable of the Bees* (1714) had maintained the contrary, arguing in favour of the paradox that "private vices are public benefits."]

action. Consequently, the pleasure or advantage in this case, is gained by the action itself, not by the morality, the virtuousness or viciousness of it; though it be, perhaps, virtuous or vicious. Thus, to say such an action or course of behaviour, procured such pleasure or advantage, or brought on such inconvenience and pain, is quite a different thing from saying, that such good or bad effect was owing to the virtue or vice of such action or behaviour. In one case, an action abstracted from all moral consideration, produced its effect: in the other case, for it will appear that there are such cases, the morality of the action, the action under a moral consideration, *i.e.* the virtuousness or viciousness of it, produced the effect. Now I say virtue as such, naturally procures considerable advantages to the virtuous, and vice as such, naturally occasions great inconvenience and even misery to the vicious, in very many instances. The immediate effects of virtue and vice upon the mind and temper, are to be mentioned as instances of it.[15] Vice as such is naturally attended with some sort of uneasiness, and, not uncommonly, with great disturbance and apprehension. That inward feeling, which, respecting lesser matters, and in familiar speech, we call being vexed with oneself, and in matters of importance and in more serious language, remorse; is an uneasiness naturally arising from an action of a man's own, reflected upon by himself as wrong, unreasonable, faulty, *i.e.* vicious in greater or less degrees: and this manifestly is a different feeling from that uneasiness, which arises from a sense of mere loss or harm. What is more common, than to hear a man lamenting an accident or event, and adding—but however he has the satisfaction that he cannot blame himself for it; or on the contrary, that he has the uneasiness of being sensible it was his own doing? Thus also the disturbance and fear, which often follow upon a man's having done an injury, arise from a sense of his being blameworthy; otherwise there would, in many cases, be no ground of disturbance, nor any reason to fear resentment or shame. On the other hand, inward security and peace, and a mind open to the several gratifications of life, are the natural attendants of innocence and virtue. To which must be

This is proved (i) by the facts of our moral life:

(*a*) the sense of well or ill-doing,

[15] [This argument had been pressed by Clarke (*Evidences*, Prop. iv. p. 255).]

added the complacency, satisfaction, and even joy of heart, which accompany the exercise, the real exercise, of gratitude, friendship, benevolence.

(*b*) the presages of conscience

[11.] And here, I think, ought to be mentioned, the fears of future punishment, and peaceful hopes of a better life, in those who fully believe, or have any serious apprehension of religion: because these hopes and fears are present uneasiness and satisfaction to the mind, and cannot be got rid of by great part of the world, even by men who have thought most thoroughly upon that subject of religion. And no one can say, how considerable this uneasiness and satisfaction may be, or what upon the whole it may amount to.[16]

(ii) by the facts of our social life:

our love of good and dislike of bad men,

[12.] In the next place comes in the consideration, that all honest and good men are disposed to befriend honest good men as such, and to discountenance the vicious as such, and do so in some degree;[17] indeed in a considerable degree: from which favour and discouragement cannot but arise considerable advantage and inconvenience. And though the generality of the world have little regard to the morality of their own actions, and may be supposed to have less to that of others, when they themselves are not concerned; yet let any one be known to be a man of virtue, somehow or other he will be favoured, and good offices will be done him, from regard to his character, without remote views, occasionally, and in some low degree, I think, by the generality of the world, as it happens to come in their way.[18] Public honours too and advantages are the natural consequences, are sometimes at least the consequences in fact, of virtuous actions;

honour,

[16] [These arguments in favour of the thesis that virtue and vice are rewarded as such, are put very clearly by Cumberland (1632-1718), in a passage to which Hallam considered Butler to be indebted: "Talia autem effecta sunt tum internae illae quae nobilissimas quasque ad bonum publicum collimantes actiones comitantur, deliciae mentis ac e contra furiae illae, seu metus, et aegritudines animi quae flagitiosos infectantur; tum etiam extrinsecus adventantes poenae ac mercedes ab aliis rationalibus" (*De Legibus Naturae*, v. 22).]

[17] [See, for the reasons of this, Serm. xiii. 7.]

[18] [In an autograph fragment of Butler's (Brit. Mus. Add. MS. 9815) he shrewdly says: "Good men surely are not treated in this world as they deserve, yet 'tis seldom, very seldom their goodness which makes them disliked, even in cases where it may seem to be so: but 'tis some behaviour or other, which, however excusable, perhaps infinitely overbalanced by their virtues, yet is offensive, possibly wrong; however such, it may be, as would pass off very well in a man of the world" (Steere's *Remains of Butler*, p. 10).]

of eminent justice, fidelity, charity, love to our country, considered in the view of being virtuous. And sometimes even death itself, often infamy and external inconveniences, are the public consequences of vice as vice. For instance, the sense which mankind have of tyranny, injustice, oppression, additional to the mere feeling or fear of misery, has doubtless been instrumental in bringing about revolutions, which make a figure even in the history of the world. For it is plain, men resent injuries as implying faultiness, and retaliate, not merely under the notion of having received harm, but of having received wrong; and they have this resentment in behalf of others, as well as of themselves. So likewise even the generality are, in some degree, grateful and disposed to return good offices, not merely because such an one has been the occasion of good to them, but under the view, that such good offices implied kind intention and good desert in the doer. To all this may be added two or three particular things, which many persons will think frivolous; but to me nothing appears so, which at all comes in towards determining a question of such importance, as, whether there be, or be not, a moral institution of government, in the strictest sense moral, *visibly* established and begun in Nature. The particular things are these: That in domestic government, which is doubtless natural, children and others also are very generally punished for falsehood and injustice and ill-behaviour, as such, and rewarded for the contrary; which are instances where veracity, and justice, and right behaviour as such, are naturally enforced by rewards and punishments, whether more or less considerable in degree: That, though civil government be supposed to take cognizance of actions in no other view than as prejudicial to society, without respect to the immorality of them; yet as such actions are immoral, so the sense which men have of the immorality of them, very greatly contributes, in different ways, to bring offenders to justice: and that entire absence of all crime and guilt in the moral sense, when plainly appearing, will almost of course procure, and circumstances of aggravated guilt prevent, a remission of the penalties annexed to civil crimes, in many cases, though by no means in all.

shame, resentment, gratitude; illustrated by (*a*) domestic and (*b*) civil government.

Summary of Argument IV.

[13.] Upon the whole then, besides the good and bad effects of virtue and vice upon men's own minds, the course of the world does, in some measure, turn upon the approbation and disapprobation of them as such, in others. The sense of well and ill doing, the presages of conscience, the love of good characters and dislike of bad ones, honour, shame, resentment, gratitude; all these, considered in themselves, and in their effects, do afford manifest real instances of virtue as such naturally favoured, and of vice as such discountenanced, more or less, in the daily course of human life; in every age, in every relation, in every general circumstance of it. That God has given us a moral nature,[19] may most justly be urged as a proof of our being under His moral government: but that He has placed us in a condition, which gives this nature, as one may speak, scope to operate, and in which it does unavoidably operate; *i.e.* influence mankind to act, so as thus to favour and reward virtue, and discountenance and punish vice; this is not the same, but a further, additional proof of His moral government: for it is an instance of it. The first is a proof, that He will finally favour and support virtue effectually: the second is an example of His favouring and supporting it at present, in some degree.

Thus the *a priori* argument from our having a moral faculty is confirmed *a posteriori* by our exercise of the same.

[14.] If a more distinct inquiry be made, whence it arises, that virtue as such is often rewarded, and vice as such is punished, and this rule never inverted: it will be found to proceed, in part, immediately from the moral nature itself, which God has given us; and also in part, from His having given us, together with this nature, so great a power over each other's happiness and misery. For *first*, it is certain, that peace and delight, in some degree and upon some occasions, is the necessary and present effect of virtuous practice; an effect arising immediately from that constitution of our nature. We are so made, that well-doing as such gives us satisfaction, at least, in some instances; ill-doing as such, in none. And *secondly*, from our moral nature, joined with God's having put our happiness and misery in many respects in each other's power, it cannot but be, that vice as such, some kinds and instances of it at least, will be infamous, and men will be disposed to punish it as in itself detestable; and the villain will by no means be able always to avoid feeling that

Virtue never punished as such, or vice rewarded as such.

This prevented (*a*) by our moral faculty;

(*b*) by the tendencies of our social life.

[19] See *Dissertation II.*

infamy, any more than he will be able to escape this further punishment, which mankind will be disposed to inflict upon him, under the notion of his deserving it. But there can be nothing on the side of vice, to answer this; because there is nothing in the human mind contradictory, as the logicians speak, to virtue. For virtue consists in a regard to what is right and reasonable, as being so; in a regard to veracity, justice, charity, in themselves: and there is surely no such thing, as a like natural regard to falsehood, injustice, cruelty. If it be thought, that there are instances of an approbation of vice, as such, in itself, and for its own sake, (though it does not appear to me, that there is any such thing at all; but supposing there be,) it is evidently monstrous:[20] as much so, as the most acknowledged perversion of any passion whatever. Such instances of perversion then being left out as merely imaginary, or, however, unnatural; it must follow, from the frame of our nature, and from our condition, in the respects now described, that vice cannot at all be, and virtue cannot but be, favoured as such by others, upon some occasions, and happy in itself, in some degree. For what is here insisted upon, is not the degree in which virtue and vice are thus distinguished, but only the thing itself, that they are so in some degree; though the whole good and bad effect of virtue and vice as such, is not inconsiderable in degree. But that they must be thus distinguished in some degree, is in a manner necessary: it is matter of fact of daily experience, even in the greatest confusion of human affairs.

Objective definition of virtue.

Perversions of the moral faculty.

Certainly reward is not always in proportion to merit,

[15.] It is not pretended but that in the natural course of things, happiness and misery appear to be distributed by other rules, than only the personal merit and demerit of characters. for: i. They may sometimes be distributed by way of mere discipline. ii. There may be the wisest and best reasons, why the world should be governed by general laws, from whence such promiscuous distribution perhaps must follow;[21] and also

[20] [Shaftesbury in the same way compares a man of perverted nature to a monstrous birth. "Nor are they less Monsters who are mis-shapen or distorted in an inward part" (*Works*, II. 136).]

[21] [Butler repeats this observation, Part I. vii. 8, and again in *Public Sermons*, iii. § 19. A few years later Berkeley made a similar remark in *Siris* (§ 256): "General rules are necessary to make the world intelligible; and from the constant observations of such rules, natural evils will sometimes unavoidably ensue: things will be produced in a slow length of time, and arrive at different degrees of perfection." Cp. Arist. *Nic. Eth.* V. x. 4.]

why our happiness and misery should be put in each other's iii.
power, in the degree which they are. And these things, as in general they contribute to the rewarding virtue and punishing vice, as such: so they often contribute also, not to the inversion of this, which is impossible; but to the rendering persons prosperous, though wicked; afflicted, though righteous; and, which is worse, to the *rewarding some actions*, though vicious, and *punishing other actions*, though virtuous. But all this cannot drown the voice of Nature in the conduct of Providence, plainly declaring itself for virtue, by way of distinction from vice, and preference to it. For our being so constituted as that virtue and vice are thus naturally favoured and discountenanced, rewarded and punished respectively as such, is an intuitive proof of the intent of Nature, that it should be so:[22] otherwise the constitution of our mind, from which it thus immediately and directly proceeds, would be absurd. But it cannot be said, because virtuous actions are sometimes punished, and vicious actions rewarded, that Nature intended it. For, though this great disorder is brought about, as all actions are done, by means of some

But the general tendency of Nature is to reward virtue.

natural passion; yet *this may be*, as it undoubtedly is, iv.
brought about by the perversion of such passion, implanted in us for other, and those very good purposes. And indeed these other and good purposes, even of every passion, may be clearly seen.[23]

Thus Argument IV. proves the Governor of Nature to be on the side of virtue.

[16.] We have then a declaration, in some degree of present effect, from Him Who is supreme in Nature, which side He is of, or what part He takes: a declaration for virtue, and against vice. So far therefore as a man is true to virtue, to veracity and justice, to equity and charity, and the right of the case, in whatever he is concerned; so far he is on the side of the Divine administration, and cooperates with it: and from hence, to such a man, arises naturally a secret satisfaction and sense of security, and implicit hope of somewhat further. And,

The tendencies of virtue, as yet unrealised, indicate a moral constitution of Nature.

[17.] V. This hope is confirmed by the necessary tendencies of virtue, which, though not of present effect, yet are at present discernible in Nature; and so afford an instance of somewhat moral in the essential constitution of it. There is, in the nature of things, a tendency in virtue and vice to produce the

[22] [Cp. Introd. § 10.]

[23] [Cp. Serm. viii. §§ 16, 17.]

be considered as the means of security from opposite power, or of obtaining other advantages. And it has this tendency, by rendering public good, an object and end, to every member of the society; by putting every one upon consideration and diligence, recollection and self-government, both in order to see what is the most effectual method, and also in order to perform their proper part, for obtaining and preserving it;[25] by uniting a society within itself, and so increasing its strength; and, which is particularly to be mentioned, uniting it by means of veracity and justice. For as these last are principal bonds of union, so benevolence or public spirit, undirected, unrestrained by them, is, nobody knows what.[26]

But, from analogy, for the actual triumph of virtue

[20.] And suppose the invisible world, and the invisible dispensations of Providence, to be, in any sort, analogous to what appears: or that both together make up one uniform scheme, the two parts of which, the part which we see, and that which is beyond our observation, are analogous to each other: then, there must be a like natural tendency in the derived power, throughout the universe, under the direction of virtue, to prevail in general over that, which is not under its direction; as there is in reason, derived reason in the universe, to prevail over brute force. But then, in order to the prevalence of virtue, or that it may actually produce, what it has a tendency to produce; the like concurrences

the like conditions must be fulfilled.

i. are necessary, as are, to the prevalence of reason. There must be some proportion, between the natural power or force which is, and that which is not, under the direction
ii. of virtue: there must be sufficient length of time; for the complete success of virtue, as of reason, cannot, from the
iii. nature of the thing, be otherwise than gradual: there must be, as one may speak, a fair field of trial, a stage large and extensive enough, proper occasions and opportunities, for the virtuous to join together,[27] to exert themselves against lawless force, and to reap the fruit of their united labours.

Of these conditions (i.) is (perhaps) satisfied.

Now indeed it is to be hoped, that the disproportion between the good and bad, even here on earth, is not so great, but that the former have natural power sufficient to their prevailing to a considerable degree, if circumstances would permit this

[25] [Compare his definition of the "sum of morals" in Serm. ix. 8.]

[26] [Cp. *Dissertation II.*, "On Virtue," § 8; and § 3 above.]

[27] [Cp. *Public Sermons*, I. § 15.]

power to be united. For, much less, very much less, power under the direction of virtue, would prevail over much greater not under the direction of it. However, good men over the face of the earth cannot unite; as for other reasons, so because they cannot be sufficiently ascertained of each other's characters. And the known course of human things, the scene we are now passing through, particularly the shortness of life, denies to virtue its full scope in several other respects. The natural tendency which we have been considering, though real, is *hindered* from being carried into effect in the present state: but these hindrances may be removed in a future one. Virtue, to borrow the Christian allusion, is militant here; and various untoward accidents contribute to its being often overborne: but it may combat with greater advantage hereafter, and prevail completely, and enjoy its consequent rewards, in some future states.[28] Neglected as it is, perhaps unknown, perhaps despised and oppressed here; there may be scenes in eternity, lasting enough, and in every other way adapted, to afford it a sufficient sphere of action; and a sufficient sphere for the natural consequences of it to follow in fact. If the soul be naturally immortal, and this state be a progress towards a future one, as childhood is towards mature age; good men may naturally unite, not only amongst themselves, but also with other orders of virtuous creatures, in that future state. For virtue, from the very nature of it, is a principle and bond of union, in some degree, amongst all who are endued with it, and known to each other; so as that by it, a good man cannot but recommend himself to the favour and protection of all virtuous beings, throughout the whole universe, who can be acquainted with his character, and can any way interpose in his behalf in any part of his duration. And one might add, that suppose all this advantageous tendency of virtue to become effect, amongst one or more orders of creatures, in any distant scenes and periods, and to be seen by any orders of vicious creatures, throughout the universal kingdom of God; this happy effect of virtue

But (ii.) and (iii.) are not.

Thus the tendency of virtue is *hindered* here.

The hindrances may be removed hereafter.

The happy tendency of virtue in the future life.

[28] [In ch. ii. § 10, note [13], he had pointed out that reason, without the aid of revelation, is incompetent to determine whether or not probation is terminated by death; and he is careful here not to assume that it *is* thus terminated. None the less, his language suggests that he did not think that the state consequent on death would be one of complete security, unexposed to temptation and trial.]

suppose them come to pass, and then, the dominion and preeminence promised must naturally follow, to a very considerable degree.

This tendency of virtue to prevail coherent with the general system of religion.

[22.] Consider now the general system of religion: that the government of the world is uniform, and one, and moral; that virtue and right shall finally have the advantage, and prevail over fraud and lawless force, over the deceits, as well as the violence of wickedness, under the conduct of one supreme governor: and from the observations above made, it will appear, that God has, by our reason, given us to see a peculiar connexion in the several parts of this scheme, and a tendency towards the completion of it, arising out of the very nature of virtue; which tendency is to be considered as somewhat moral in the essential constitution of things. If any one should think all this to be of little importance; I desire him to consider, what he would think, if vice had, essentially and in its nature, these advantageous tendencies; or if virtue had essentially the direct contrary ones.

Objection: The tendency may never be *perfectly* realised, as religion teaches.

[23.] But it may be objected, that, notwithstanding all these natural effects and these natural tendencies of virtue; yet things may be now going on throughout the universe, and may go on hereafter, in the same mixed way as here at present upon earth: virtue sometimes prosperous, sometimes depressed; vice sometimes punished, sometimes successful.[30]

Answer: (i.) This chap. does not *prove* the doctrine of retribution, but suggests confirmations of its truth.

The answer to which is, that it is not the purpose of this chapter, nor of this treatise, properly to prove God's perfect moral government over the world, or the truth of Religion; but to observe what there is in the constitution and course of Nature, to confirm the proper proof of it, supposed to be known: and that the weight of the foregoing observations to this purpose may be thus distinctly proved. Pleasure and pain are indeed to a certain degree, say to a very high degree, distributed amongst us without any apparent regard to the merit or demerit of characters. And were there nothing else concerning this matter discernible in the constitution and course of Nature; there would be no ground from the constitution and course of Nature to hope or to fear, that men would be rewarded or punished hereafter according to their deserts: which, however, it is to be remarked, implies, that

[30] [This is, in substance, the objection urged a few years later by Hume in his essay *Of a Providence and a Future State.*]

even then there would be no ground from appearances to think, that vice upon the whole would have the advantage, rather than that virtue would. And thus the proof of a future state of retribution would rest upon the usual known arguments for it: which are I think plainly unanswerable; and would be so, though there were no additional confirmation of them from the things above insisted on. But these things are a very strong confirmation of them. For,

(ii.) No ground to think that vice will ever prevail.

[24.] First, They shew, that the Author of Nature is not indifferent to virtue and vice. They amount to a declaration from Him, determinate and not to be evaded, in favour of one, and against the other; such a declaration, as there is nothing to be set over against or answer, on the part of vice. So that were a man, laying aside the proper proof of Religion, to determine from the course of Nature only, whether it were most probable, that the righteous or the wicked would have the advantage in a future life; there can be no doubt, but that he would determine the probability to be, that the former would. The course of Nature then, in the view of it now given, furnishes us with a real practical proof of the obligations of Religion.[31]

We have proved (1) God is not indifferent to virtue and vice.

[25.] Secondly, When, conformably to what Religion teaches us, God shall reward and punish virtue and vice as such, so as that every one shall, upon the whole, have his deserts; this distributive justice will not be a thing different in *kind*, but only in *degree*, from what we experience in His present government. It will be that in *effect*, toward which we now see a *tendency*. It will be no more than the *completion* of that moral government, the *principles and beginning* of which have been shewn, beyond all dispute, discernible in the present constitution and course of Nature. And from hence it follows,

(2) The distributive justice of which religion tells analogous to what we see, only more perfect.

[26.] Thirdly, That, as under the natural government of God, our experience of those kinds and degrees of happiness and misery, which we do experience at present, gives just ground to hope for, and to fear, higher degrees and other kinds of both in a future state, supposing a future state admitted: so under His moral government, our experience, that virtue and vice are, in the manners above mentioned, actually rewarded and punished at present, in a certain degree, gives just ground

(3) Such greater perfection of moral government analogous to higher degrees of reward and punishment in future under God's natural government.

[31] [Cp. Introd. § 10 note.]

to hope and to fear, that they *may be* rewarded and punished in a higher degree hereafter. It is acknowledged indeed that this alone is not sufficient ground to think, that they *actually will be* rewarded and punished in a higher degree, rather than in a lower: but then,

(4) The essential tendencies of virtue and vice justify us in expecting it.

[27.] Lastly, There is sufficient ground to think so, from the good and bad tendencies of virtue and vice. For these tendencies are essential, and founded in the nature of things: whereas the hindrances to their becoming effect are, in numberless cases, not necessary, but artificial only. Now it may be much more strongly argued, that these tendencies, as well as the actual rewards and punishments, of virtue and vice, which arise directly out of the nature of things, will remain hereafter, than that the accidental hindrances of them will. And if these hindrances do not remain; those rewards and punishments cannot but be carried on much further towards the perfection of moral government: *i.e.* the tendencies of virtue and vice will become effect: but when, or where, or in what particular way, cannot be known at all, but by revelation.

Summary.

[28.] Upon the whole: there is a kind of moral government
§ 7. implied in God's natural government;[32] virtue and vice are naturally rewarded and punished as beneficial and mischievous
§ 8. to society;[33] and rewarded and punished directly as virtue
§§ 10-15. and vice.[34] The notion then of a moral scheme of government is not fictitious, but natural; for it is suggested to our thoughts by the constitution and course of Nature: and the execution of this scheme is actually begun, in the instances here
§ 16. mentioned. And these things are to be considered as a declaration of the Author of Nature, for virtue, and against vice: they give a credibility to the supposition of their being rewarded and punished hereafter; and also ground to hope and to fear, that they may be rewarded and punished in higher degrees than they are here. And as all this is confirmed, so the argument for Religion, from the constitution and course of Nature, is
§§ 17-21. carried on further, by observing, that there are natural tendencies, and, in innumerable cases, only artificial hindrances, to this moral scheme's being carried on much further towards perfection, than it is at present.[35] The notion then of a moral scheme of government, much more perfect than what is seen, is

[32] § 7 above.
[33] *Ibid.*
[34] § 8 above.
[35] § 17, etc.

not a fictitious, but a natural notion; for it is suggested to our thoughts, by the essential tendencies of virtue and vice. And these tendencies are to be considered as intimations, as implicit promises and threatenings, from the Author of Nature, of much greater rewards and punishments to follow virtue and vice, than do at present. And indeed, every *natural* tendency, which is to continue, but which is hindered from becoming effect by only *accidental* causes, affords a presumption, that such tendency will, some time or other, become effect: a presumption in degree proportionable to the length of the duration, through which such tendency will continue. And from these things together, arises a real presumption, that the moral scheme of government established in Nature, shall be carried on much further towards perfection hereafter; and, I think, a presumption that it will be absolutely completed. But from these things, joined with the moral nature which God has given us, considered as given us by Him, arises a practical proof[36] that it will be completed: a proof from fact: and therefore a distinct one from that, which is deduced from the eternal and unalterable relations, the fitness and unfitness of actions.

§ 22.

§§ 25, 26.

§ 27.

§ 13.

A practical proof.

[36] See this proof drawn out briefly, ch. vi. [§ 11. Cp. also what he says about this 'practical proof' in Part II. viii. 11.]

CHAPTER IV.

Of a State of Probation, as implying Trial, Difficulties and Danger.

A state of probation implies trial, difficulties, and danger.

[1.] THE general doctrine of Religion, that our present life is a state of probation for a future one, comprehends under it several particular things, distinct from each other. But the first and most common meaning of it seems to be, that our future interest is now depending, and depending upon ourselves; that we have scope and opportunities here, for that good and bad behaviour, which God will reward and punish hereafter; together with temptations to one, as well as inducements of reason to the other. And this is, in a great measure, the same with saying, that we are under the moral government of God, and to give an account of our actions to Him. For the notion of a future account and general righteous judgment, implies some sort of temptations to what is wrong: otherwise there would be no moral possibility of doing wrong, nor ground for judgment, or discrimination. But there is this difference, that the word *probation* is more distinctly and particularly expressive of allurements to wrong, or difficulties in adhering uniformly to what is right, and of the danger of miscarrying by such temptations, than the words *moral government.* A state of probation then, as thus particularly implying in it trial, difficulties and danger, may require to be considered distinctly by itself.

Under God's Natural Government we are in a state of probation as regards our present interest,

[2.] And as the moral government of God, which Religion teaches us, implies, that we are in a state of trial with regard to a future world: so also His natural government over us implies, that we are in a state of trial, in the like sense, with regard to the present world. Natural government by rewards and punishments, as much implies natural trial, as moral government does moral trial. The natural government of God here meant[1] consists in His annexing pleasure to some actions, and pain to others, which are in our power to do or forbear, and in giving us notice of such appointment beforehand. This necessarily implies, that He has made our happiness and misery, or our interest, to depend in part upon ourselves. And so far as men have temptations to any course of action which will probably occasion them greater temporal inconvenience and uneasiness, than satisfaction; so far their temporal interest is in danger from themselves, or they are in a state of trial with respect to it. Now people often blame others, and even themselves, for their misconduct in their temporal concerns. And we find many are greatly wanting to themselves, and miss of that natural happiness, which they might have obtained in the present life: perhaps every one does in some degree. But many run themselves into great inconvenience, and into extreme distress and misery: not through incapacity of knowing better, and doing better for themselves, which would be nothing to the present purpose; but through their own fault. And these things necessarily imply temptation, and danger of miscarrying, in a greater or less degree, with respect to our worldly interest or happiness. Every one too, without having Religion in his thoughts, speaks of the hazards which young people run, upon their setting out in the world: hazards from other causes, than merely their ignorance, and unavoidable accidents. And some courses of vice, at least, being contrary to men's worldly interest or good; temptations to these must at the same time be temptations to forego our present and our future interest. Thus in our natural or temporal capacity, we are in a state of trial, *i.e.* of difficulty and danger, analogous, or like to our moral and religious trial.

like to our state of probation under God's Moral Government as regards our future interest.

[3.] This will more distinctly appear to any one, who thinks it worth while, more distinctly, to consider, what it is which constitutes our trial in both capacities, and to observe, how mankind behave under it.

(i.) The same *causes* of trial in both cases, are either (*a*) external circumstances,

[4.] And that which constitutes this our trial, in both these capacities, must be somewhat either in our external circumstances, or in our nature. For, on the one hand, persons may be betrayed into wrong behaviour upon surprise, or overcome

[1] Ch. ii. [§ 6].

upon any other very singular and extraordinary external occasions; who would, otherwise, have preserved their character of prudence and of virtue: in which cases, every one, in speaking of the wrong behaviour of these persons, would impute it to such particular external circumstances.

or (*b*) internal passions,

And on the other hand, men who have contracted habits of vice and folly of any kind, or have some particular passions in excess, will seek opportunities, and, as it were, go out of their way, to gratify themselves in these respects, at the expense of their wisdom and their virtue; led to it, as every one would say, not by external temptations, but by such

which last are distinct from self-love.

habits and passions. And the account of this last case is, that particular passions are no more coincident with prudence, or that reasonable self-love, the end of which is our worldly interest,[2] than they are with the principle of virtue and religion; but often draw contrary ways to one, as well as to the other: and so such particular passions are as much temptations, to act imprudently with regard to our worldly interest, as to act viciously.[3] However, as when we say, men are misled by external circumstances of temptation; it cannot but be

(*a*) and (*b*) always imply each other.

understood, that there is somewhat within themselves, to render those circumstances temptations, or to render them susceptible of impressions from them: so when we say, they are misled by passions; it is always supposed, that there are occasions, circumstances, and objects, exciting these passions, and affording means for gratifying them. And therefore, temptations from within, and from without, coincide, and mutually imply each other. Now the several external objects of the appetites, passions, and affections, being present to the senses, or offering themselves to the mind, and so exciting emotions suitable to their nature; not only in cases where they can be gratified consistently with innocence and prudence, but also in cases where they cannot, and yet can be gratified imprudently and viciously: this as really puts them in danger of voluntarily foregoing their present interest or good, as their

[2] [Here, for the moment, he seems to confine the sphere of prudence to the present life, and to our worldly interest; but in the larger sense of the word (*Dissertation* II., "On Virtue," § 16) it includes the future as well. He explains (Serm. iii. § 8) that it is only when the future is thus taken into view that self-love and conscience are coincident in their dictates. See note to Part I. v. 13 below.]

[3] See Serm. xi. § 4 ff., Serm. i. § 7 note, and Preface, § 36; [cp. also Serm. ii. § 11].

future; and as really renders self-denial necessary to secure one, as the other: *i.e.* we are in a like state of trial with respect to both, by the very same passions, excited by the very same means. Thus mankind having a temporal interest depending upon themselves, and a prudent course of behaviour being necessary to secure it; passions inordinately excited, whether by means of example, or by any other external circumstance, towards such objects, at such times, or in such degrees, as that they cannot be gratified consistently with worldly prudence; are temptations, dangerous, and too often successful temptations, to forego a greater temporal good for a less; *i.e.* to forego what is, upon the whole, our temporal interest, for the sake of a present gratification. This is a description of our state of trial in our temporal capacity. Substitute now the word *future* for *temporal*, and *virtue* for *prudence*; and it will be just as proper a description of our state of trial in our religious capacity; so analogous are they to each other.

The same form of words describes our trial in both capacities.

[5.] If, from consideration of this our like state of trial in both capacities, we go on to observe further, how mankind behave under it; we shall find there are some, who have so little sense of it, that they scarce look beyond the passing day: they are so taken up with present gratifications, as to have, in a manner, no feeling of consequences, no regard to their future ease or fortune in this life; any more than to their happiness in another. Some appear to be blinded and deceived by inordinate passion, in their worldly concerns, as much as in Religion.[4] Others are, not deceived, but, as it were, forcibly carried away by the like passions, against their better judgment, and feeble resolutions too of acting better.[5] And there are men, and truly they are not a few, who shamelessly avow, not their interest, but their mere will and pleasure, to be their law of life: and who, in open defiance of every thing that is reasonable, will go on in a course of

(ii) Trial has the same *effects* in both cases upon different types of man;

(*a*) the careless;

(*b*) he who is blinded by passion;

(*c*) the weak;

(*d*) the deliberate profligate.

4 [Cicero speaks in like terms of this *blinding* power of passion: "At vero eos et accusamus et iusto odio dignissimos ducimus, qui blanditiis praesentium uoluptatum deleniti atque corrupti quos dolores et quas molestias excepturi sint *occaecati cupiditate* non prouident" (*De Fin.* I. x. 33).]

5 [This is the man whom Ovid describes in the oft-quoted words, "Video meliora proboque: deteriora sequor." He is the ἀκρατής, the 'incontinent' man of Aristotle's *Ethics*, distinguished by Aristotle as by Butler from the ἀκόλαστος or deliberate profligate, who recognises no law save that of his own passions.]

vicious extravagance, foreseeing, with no remorse and little fear, that it will be their temporal ruin; and some of them, under the apprehension of the consequences of wickedness in another state. And to speak in the most moderate way, human creatures are not only continually liable to go wrong voluntarily, but we see likewise that they often actually do so, with respect to their temporal interests, as well as with respect to Religion.

As our trials in both cases have the same causes and the same effects they are analogous.

[6.] Thus our difficulties and dangers, or our trials, in our temporal and our religious capacity, as they proceed from the same causes, and have the same effect upon men's behaviour, are evidently analogous, and of the same kind.

(iii) The dangers in both cases increased by like causes; *e.g.* in our temporal capacity,

[7.] It may be added, that as the difficulties and dangers of miscarrying in our religious state of trial, are greatly increased, and one is ready to think, in a manner wholly *made*, by the ill behaviour of others; by a wrong education,
a wrong in a moral sense, sometimes positively vicious; by
b general bad example; by the dishonest artifices which are got into business of all kinds; and, in very many parts of
c the world, by religion's being corrupted into superstitions, which indulge men in their vices: so in like manner, the

and in our future capacity.

difficulties of conducting ourselves prudently in respect to our present interest, and our danger of being led aside from
a pursuing it, are greatly increased, by a foolish education; and, after we come to mature age, by the extravagance and
b carelessness of others, whom we have intercourse with; and by
c mistaken notions, very generally prevalent, and taken up from common opinion, concerning temporal happiness, and wherein it consists. And persons, by their own negligence

In both capacities, each wrong step makes it harder to see or to keep the right path.

and folly in their temporal affairs, no less than by a course of vice, bring themselves into new difficulties; and, by habits of indulgence, become less qualified to go through them: and one irregularity after another, embarrasses things to such a degree, that they know not whereabout they are; and often makes the path of conduct so intricate and perplexed, that it is difficult to trace it out; difficult even to determine what is the prudent or the moral part.[6] Thus, for instance, wrong

[6] [Butler strongly holds that, as a rule, the right course is immediately evident to any honest conscience (see Serm. iii. § 4); but he recognises here, with his never-failing common sense, that there may be exceptional cases. See also Part II. vi. §§ 13 and 18.]

behaviour in one stage of life, youth; wrong, I mean, considering ourselves only in our temporal capacity, without taking in religion; this, in several ways, increases the difficulties of right behaviour in mature age; *i.e.* puts us into a more disadvantageous state of trial in our temporal capacity.

In neither capacity are we in the best position, to win either happiness or virtue.

[8.] We are an inferior part of the creation of God. There are natural appearances of our being in a state of degradation.[7] And we certainly are in a condition, which *does not seem*, by any means, the most advantageous we could imagine or desire, either in our natural or moral capacity, for securing either our present or future interest. However, this condition, low and careful and uncertain as it is, does not afford any just ground of complaint. For, as men may manage their temporal affairs with prudence, and so pass their days here on earth in tolerable ease and satisfaction, by a moderate degree of care: so likewise with regard to religion, there is no more required than what they are well able to do, and what they must be greatly wanting to themselves, if they neglect. And for persons to have that put upon them, which they are well able to go through, and no more, we naturally consider as an equitable thing: supposing it done by proper authority. Nor have we any more reason to complain of it, with regard to the Author of Nature, than of His not having given us other advantages, belonging to other orders of creatures.

But the position is not impossible;

hence, there is no injustice in this.

Thus our *religious* analogous to our *worldly* state, in that each is a state of probation.

[9.] But the thing here insisted upon is, that the state of trial, which Religion teaches us we are in, is rendered credible, by its being throughout uniform and of a piece with the general conduct of Providence towards us, in all other respects within the compass of our knowledge. Indeed if mankind, considered in their natural capacity, as inhabitants of this world only, found themselves, from their birth to their death, in a settled state of security and happiness, without any solicitude or thought of their own: or if they were in no danger of being brought into inconveniences and distress, by carelessness, or the folly of passion, through bad example, the treachery of others, or the deceitful appearances of things: were this our

[7] Part II. ch. v. [§ 10. It is worth while to compare also the grave and stately passage about the disappointments and miseries of the world in Serm. vi. §§ 10, 11. If it be objected that Butler's tone is too deeply tinged with melancholy, it can only be answered that his view of life in this regard is, in a remarkable degree, that of the New Testament itself].

CHAPTER V.

Of a State of Probation, as intended for Moral Discipline and Improvement.[1]

How we come to be in this dangerous world, we know not (though two considerations lessen the difficulties);

[1.] FROM the consideration of our being in a probation-state, of so much difficulty and hazard, naturally arises the question, how we came to be placed in it? But such a general inquiry as this would be found involved in insuperable difficulties. For, though some of these difficulties would be
a lessened by observing, that all wickedness is voluntary, as is
b implied in its very notion; and that many of the miseries of life have apparent good effects: yet, when we consider other circumstances belonging to both, and what must be the consequence of the former in a life to come; it cannot but be acknowledged plain folly and presumption, to pretend to give an account of the whole reasons of this matter: the whole reasons of our being allotted a condition, out of which so much wickedness and misery, so circumstanced, would in
a fact arise. Whether it be not beyond our faculties, not only to find out, but even to understand, the whole account of this; or, though we should be supposed capable of under-
b standing it, yet, whether it would be of service or prejudice to us to be informed of it, is impossible to say.[2] But as our present condition can in no wise be shewn inconsistent with the perfect moral government of God: so Religion teaches us we were placed in it, that we might qualify ourselves, by the

but *one* reason was to discipline us

[1] [The germ of this chapter may be traced in Serm. xv. "On the Ignorance of Man" (§ 9), a sermon which indeed contains the main thoughts of the *Analogy*.]

[2] [Butler refuses to consider the problem of the origin of evil, as to which there had been much speculation, by Archbishop King and others, in his day. He doubts whether we could understand the solution if we discovered it, or whether it would be of any service to us if we did. Compare what he says in Serm. xv. § 8.]

practice of virtue, for another state which is to follow it. And this, though but a partial answer, a very partial one indeed, to the inquiry now mentioned; yet, is a more satisfactory answer to another, which is of real, and of the utmost importance to us to have answered: the inquiry, What is our business here? The known end then, why we are placed in a state of so much affliction, hazard, and difficulty, is, our improvement in virtue and piety, as the requisite qualification for a future state of security and happiness.

for a future state.

[2.] Now the beginning of life, considered as an education for mature age in the present world, appears plainly, at first sight, analogous to this our trial for a future one: the former being in our temporal capacity, what the latter is in our religious capacity. But some observations common to both of them, and a more distinct consideration of each, will more distinctly shew the extent and force of the analogy between them; and the credibility, which arises from hence, as well as from the nature of the thing, that the present life was intended to be a state of discipline for a future one.

That this life disciplines us for the next, analogous to youth being a discipline for maturity.

[3.] I. Every species of creatures is, we see, designed for a particular way of life; to which, the nature, the capacities, temper, and qualifications of each species, are as necessary as their external circumstances. Both come into the notion of such state, or particular way of life, and are constituent parts of it. Change a man's capacities or character to the degree, in which it is conceivable they may be changed; and he would be altogether incapable of a human course of life, and human happiness; as incapable, as if, his nature continuing unchanged, he were placed in a world, where he had no sphere of action, nor any objects to answer his appetites, passions, and affections of any sort. "One thing is set over against another,"[3] as an ancient writer expresses it. Our nature corresponds to our external condition. Without this correspondence, there would be no possibility of any such thing as human life and human happiness: which life and happiness are, therefore, a *result* from our nature and condition jointly:[4] meaning by human life, not living in the

I. There must be a correspondence between faculty and environment: therefore certain capacities necessary for life in the future state.

[3] [*Ecclus.* xlii. 24, a verse which he also quotes in Serm. vi. § 1. It might serve as a motto for the *Analogy.*]

[4] [In this remarkable paragraph Butler speaks with the voice of modern science. Organ and environment, faculty and its sphere of

thought and intention, *i.e.* inward act: for such intention is an act. Resolutions also to do well are properly acts. And endeavouring to enforce upon our own minds a practical sense of virtue, or to beget in others that practical sense of it, which a man really has himself, is a virtuous act. All these, therefore, may and will contribute towards forming good habits.

But passive impressions grow *weaker* by repetition.

But going over the theory of virtue in one's thoughts, talking well, and drawing fine pictures, of it; this is so far from necessarily or certainly conducing to form a habit of it, in him who thus employs himself, that it may harden the mind in a contrary course,[7] and render it gradually more insensible, *i.e.* form a habit of insensibility, to all moral considerations. For, from our very faculty of habits, passive impressions, by
e.g. being repeated, grow weaker.[8] Thoughts, by often passing
α through the mind, are felt less sensibly: being accustomed
β to danger, begets intrepidity, *i.e.* lessens fear; to distress,
γ lessens the passion of pity; to instances of others' mortality, lessens the sensible apprehension of our own.

Thus the active habit grows stronger while the passive impression grows weaker.

And from these two observations together; that practical habits are formed and strengthened by repeated acts, and that passive impressions grow weaker by being repeated upon us; it must follow, that active habits may be gradually forming and strengthening, by a course of acting upon such and such motives and excitements, whilst these motives and excitements themselves are, by proportionable degrees, growing less sensible, *i.e.* are continually less and less sensibly felt, even as the active habits strengthen. And experience confirms this: for active principles,

[7] [So Tennyson speaks in *The Brook* of:

"... those
Who dabbling in the fount of fictive tears,
And nursed by mealy-mouth'd philanthropies,
Divorce the Feeling from her mate the Deed."]

[8] [Dugald Stewart, who questions, though seemingly on insufficient grounds, the truth of this law as regards *moral* impressions (*Works*, vi. 304 n.), gives a good illustration of it elsewhere (vi. 127), derived from "the effects produced by an immoderate use of strong liquors, which, at the same time that it confirms the active habit of intemperance, deadens and destroys the sensibility of the palate." The law is, indeed, as Höffding has pointed out, a consequence of the law of the persistence of energy. "For the more energy an individual expends on the one kind of reaction, the less can he expend on the other. This truth is strikingly illustrated in Saxo's well-known tale of the different effects which the news of the murder of Regner Lodbrog produced on his sons: he in whom the emotion was weakest had the greatest energy for action" (*Psychology*, p. 99). With Butler's doctrine of habits it is worth while to compare Aristotle's brief treatment of the same subject (*Nic. Eth.* II. i. 3 ff.).]

at the very time that they are less lively in perception than they were, are found to be, somehow, wrought more thoroughly into the temper and character, and become more effectual in influencing our practice. The three things just mentioned *e.g.* may afford instances of it. Perception of danger is a natural *α* excitement of passive fear, and active caution: and by being inured to danger, habits of the latter are gradually wrought, at the same time that the former gradually lessens. Perception *β* of distress in others is a natural excitement, passively to pity, and actively to relieve it: but let a man set himself to attend to, inquire out, and relieve distressed persons, and he cannot but grow less and less sensibly affected with the various miseries of life, with which he must become acquainted; when yet, at the same time, benevolence, considered not as a passion, but as a practical principle[9] of action, will strengthen: and whilst he passively compassionates the distressed less, he will acquire a greater aptitude actively to assist and befriend them. So also at the same time that the daily instances of men's *γ* dying around us give us daily a less sensible passive feeling or apprehension of our own mortality, such instances greatly contribute to the strengthening a practical regard to it in serious men; *i.e.* to forming a habit of acting with a constant view to it. And this seems again further to shew, that passive impressions made upon our minds by admonition, experience, example, though they may have a remote efficacy, and a very great one, towards forming active habits, yet, can have this efficacy no otherwise than by inducing us to such a course of action: and that it is not being affected so and so, but acting, which forms those habits: only it must be always remembered, that real endeavours to enforce good impressions upon ourselves are a species of virtuous action. Nor do we know how far it is possible, in the nature of things, that effects should be wrought in us at once, equivalent to habits, *i.e.* what is wrought by use and exercise.[10] However, the thing insisted upon is, not what may be possible, but what is in fact the appointment of Nature: which is, that active habits are to be formed by exercise. Their

Passive impressions can only form a habit by inducing action.

Resolutions are actions.

The effects of habit *may* be wrought suddenly, but, as a rule, are due to repetition.

[9] [He distinguishes at § 20 in like manner between self-love as an *active principle* and as a *desire*.]

[10] [As FitzGerald points out, the answer to the problems suggested by what is called a death-bed repentance would depend on what could be ascertained on this point.]

progress may be so gradual, as to be imperceptible in its steps: it may be hard to explain the faculty, by which we are capable of habits, throughout its several parts; and to trace it up to its original, so as to distinguish it from all others in our mind: and it seems as if contrary effects were to be ascribed to it. But the thing in general, that our nature is formed to yield, in some such manner as this, to use and exercise, is matter of certain experience.

Practical principles grow stronger by exercise,

[5.] Thus, by accustoming ourselves to any course of action, we get an aptness to go on, a facility, readiness, and often pleasure, in it. The inclinations which rendered us averse to it grow weaker: the difficulties in it, not only the imaginary but the real ones, lessen: the reasons for it offer themselves of course to our thoughts upon all occasions: and the least glimpse of them is sufficient to make us go on, in a course of action, to which we have been accustomed. And practical principles appear to grow stronger, absolutely in themselves, by exercise; as well as relatively, with regard to contrary principles; which, by being accustomed to submit, do so habitually, and of course.[11] And thus a new character, in several respects, may be formed; and many habitudes of life, not given by Nature, but which Nature directs us to acquire.

(*a*) absolutely, (*b*) by the weakening of contrary principles.

III. We need improvement

[6.] III. Indeed we may be assured, that we should never have had these capacities of improving by experience, acquired knowledge, and habits, had they not been necessary, and intended to be made use of. And accordingly we find them so necessary, and so much intended, that without them we should be utterly incapable of that, which was the end for which we were made, considered in our temporal capacity only: the employments and satisfactions of our mature state of life.

before we are qualified for maturity in the present life.

[7.] Nature does in no wise qualify us wholly, much less at once, for this mature state of life. Even maturity of understanding, and bodily strength, are not only arrived to gradually, but are also very much owing to the continued exercise of our powers of body and mind from infancy. But if we suppose a person brought into the world with both these in maturity, as far as this is conceivable; he would plainly at first be as unqualified for the human life of mature age,

[11] [Cp. p. 89 below.]

as an idiot. He would be in a manner distracted, with astonishment, and apprehension, and curiosity, and suspense: nor can one guess, how long it would be, before he would be familiarized to himself and the objects about him enough, even to set himself to any thing. It may be questioned too, whether the natural information of his sight and hearing would be of any manner of use at all to him in acting, before experience.[12] And it seems, that men would be strangely headstrong and self-willed, and disposed to exert themselves with an impetuosity, which would render society insupportable, and the living in it impracticable; were it not for some acquired moderation and self-government, some aptitude, and readiness in restraining themselves, and concealing their sense of things. Want of every thing of this kind which is learnt would render a man as uncapable of society, as want of language would; or as his natural ignorance of any of the particular employments of life would render him uncapable of providing himself with the common conveniences, or supplying the necessary wants of it. In these respects, and probably in many more, of which we have no particular notion, mankind is left, by Nature, an unformed, unfinished creature; utterly deficient and unqualified, before the acquirement of knowledge, experience, and habits, for that mature state of life, which was the end of his creation, considering him as related only to this world.

Youth is a state suitable to our discipline for maturity.

[8.] But then, as Nature has endued us with a power of supplying those deficiencies, by acquired knowledge, experience, and habits: so likewise we are placed in a condition, in infancy, childhood, and youth, fitted for it; fitted for our acquiring those qualifications of all sorts, which we stand in need of in mature age. Hence children, from their very birth, are daily growing acquainted with the objects about them, with the scene in which they are placed, and to have a future part; and learning somewhat or other, necessary to the performance of it. The subordinations, to which they are accustomed in domestic life, teach them self-government in common behaviour abroad, and prepare them for

[12] [This question had been raised by Molyneux (Locke, *Essay* II. ix. 8), and is fully discussed by Berkeley (*New Theory of Vision*, §§ 132 ff.). It cannot be said that the experiments which have since then been made by Cheselden and others on persons born blind, who have been couched for cataract, are decisive as to the true answer.]

subjection and obedience to civil authority. What passes before their eyes, and daily happens to them, gives them experience, caution against treachery and deceit, together with numberless little rules of action and conduct, which we could not live without; and which are learnt so insensibly and so perfectly, as to be mistaken perhaps for instinct: though they are the effect of long experience and exercise; as much so as language, or knowledge in particular business, or the qualifications and behaviour belonging to the several ranks and professions. Thus the beginning of our days is adapted to be, and is, a state of education in the theory and practice of mature life. We are much assisted in it by example, instruction, and the care of others; but a great deal is left to ourselves to do. And of this, as part is done easily and of course; so part requires diligence and care, the voluntary foregoing many things which we desire, and setting ourselves to what we should have no inclination to, but for the necessity oı expedience of it. For, that labour and industry, which the station of so many absolutely requires, they would be greatly unqualified for, in maturity; as those in other stations would be, for any other sorts of application; if both were not accustomed to them in their youth. And according as persons behave themselves, in the general education which all go through, and in the particular ones adapted to particular employments; their character is formed, and made appear; they recommend themselves more or less; and are capable of, and placed in, different stations in the society of mankind.

So the present life is a discipline for the future.

[9.] The former part of life then is to be considered as an important opportunity, which Nature puts into our hands; and which, when lost, is not to be recovered.[13] And our being placed in a state of discipline throughout this life, for another world, is a providential disposition of things, exactly of the same kind, as our being placed in a state of discipline during childhood, for mature age. Our condition in both respects is uniform and of a piece, and comprehended under one and the same general law of Nature.

If we did not understand *how*, this

[10.] And if we were not able at all to discern, how or in what way the present life could be our preparation for another;

[13] [Cp. p. 41 above.]

this would be no objection against the credibility of its being so. For we do not discern, how food and sleep contribute to the growth of the body; nor could have any thought that they would, before we had experience. Nor do children at all think, on the one hand, that the sports and exercises, to which they are so much addicted, contribute to their health and growth; nor, on the other, of the necessity which there is for their being restrained in them: nor are they capable of understanding the use of many parts of discipline, which nevertheless they must be made to go through, in order to qualify them for the business of mature age. Were we not able then to discover, in what respects the present life could form us for a future one; yet nothing would be more supposable than that it might, in some respects or other, from the general analogy of Providence. And this, for ought I see, might reasonably be said, even though we should not take in the consideration of God's moral government over the world. But,

would be no objection against its credibility.

[11.] IV. Take in this consideration, and consequently, that the character of virtue and piety is a necessary qualification for the future state; and then we may distinctly see, how, and in what respects, the present life may be a preparation for it: since we *want, and are capable of improvement in that character, by moral and religious habits*; and *the present life is fit to be a state of discipline for such improvement*: in like manner as we have already observed, how, and in what respects, infancy, childhood, and youth, are a necessary preparation, and a natural state of discipline, for mature age.

IV. Most of all, we need *moral* improvement;

[12] Nothing which we at present see would lead us to the thought of a solitary unactive state hereafter: but, if we judge at all from the analogy of Nature, we must suppose, according to the Scripture account of it, that it will be a community.[14] And there is no shadow of anything unreasonable in conceiving, though there be no analogy for it, that this community will be, as the Scripture represents it, under the more immediate, or, if such an expression may be used, the more sensible government of God. Nor is our ignorance, what will be the employments of this happy community, nor our consequent ignorance, what particular scope or occasion there will be for the exercise of veracity, justice, and charity, amongst the

for, under God's moral government, the qualification for happiness hereafter must be virtue.

[14] [Cp. Part I. i. 23.]

members of it with regard to each other; any proof, that there will be no sphere of exercise for those virtues. Much less, if that were possible, is our ignorance any proof, that there will be no occasion for that frame of mind, or character, which is formed by the daily practice of those particular virtues here, and which is a result from it.[15] This at least must be owned in general, that, as the government established in the universe is moral, the character of virtue and piety must, in some way or other, be the condition of our happiness, or the qualification for it.

Our need of moral discipline due

(i) to the power of the passions;

(ii) to our original deficiency in moral strength.

As to (i), Passions

must be felt,

and therefore tend to break out.

[13.] Now from what is above observed, concerning our natural power of habits, it is easy to see, that we are *capable* of moral improvement by discipline. And how greatly we *want* it, need not be proved to any one who is acquainted with the great wickedness of mankind; or even with those imperfections, which the best are conscious of. But it is not perhaps distinctly attended to by every one, that the occasion which human creatures have for discipline, to improve in them this character of virtue and piety, is to be traced up higher than to excess in the passions, by indulgence and habits of vice. Mankind, and perhaps all finite creatures, from the very constitution of their nature, before habits of virtue, are deficient, and in danger of deviating from what is right; and therefore stand in need of virtuous habits, for a security against this danger. For, together with the general principle of moral understanding, we have in our inward frame various affections towards particular external objects. These affections are naturally, and of right, subject to the government of the moral principle, as to the occasions upon which they may be gratified; as to the times, degrees, and manner, in which the objects of them may be pursued; but then the principle of virtue can neither excite them, nor prevent their being excited. On the contrary, they are naturally felt, when the objects of them are present to the mind, not only before all consideration, whether they can be obtained by lawful means, but after it is found they cannot. For the natural objects of affection continue so; the necessaries, conveniences, and pleasures of life, remain naturally desirable; though they cannot be obtained innocently: nay, though they cannot possibly be obtained at all.

15 [Cp. p. 96 below, where he makes a similar remark about the virtue of patience.]

And when the objects of any affection whatever cannot be obtained without unlawful means; but may be obtained by them: such affection, though its being excited, and its continuing some time in the mind, be as innocent as it is natural and necessary; yet cannot but be conceived to have a tendency to incline persons to venture upon such unlawful means: and therefore must be conceived as putting them in some danger of it. Now what is the general security against this danger, against their actually deviating from right? As the danger is, so also must the security be, from within: from the practical principle of virtue.[16] And the strengthening or improving this principle, considered as practical, or as a principle of action, will lessen the danger, or increase the security against it. And this moral principle is capable of improvement, by proper discipline and exercise: by recollecting the practical impressions which example and experience have made upon us: and, instead of following humour and mere inclination, by continually attending to the equity and right of the case, in whatever we are engaged, be it in greater or less matters; and accustoming ourselves always to act upon it; as being itself the just and natural motive of action; and as this moral course of behaviour must necessarily, under Divine government, be our final interest. Thus the principle of virtue, improved into a habit, of which improvement we are thus capable, will plainly be, in proportion to the strength of it, a security against the danger which finite creatures are in, from the very nature of propension, or particular affections. This way of putting the matter, supposes particular affections to remain in a future

They can only be held in check by conscience, which needs to be improved by discipline into a virtuous habit.

[16] It may be thought, that a sense of interest would as effectually restrain creatures from doing wrong. But if by a *sense of interest* is meant a speculative conviction or belief, that such and such indulgence would occasion them greater uneasiness, upon the whole, than satisfaction; it is contrary to present experience to say, that this sense of interest is sufficient to restrain them from thus indulging themselves. And if by a *sense of interest* is meant a practical regard to what is upon the whole our happiness; this is not only coincident with the principle of virtue or moral rectitude, but is a part of the idea itself. And it is evident this reasonable self-love wants to be improved, as really as any principle in our nature. For we daily see it overmatched, not only by the more boisterous passions, but by curiosity, shame, love of imitation, by any thing, even indolence: especially if the interest, the temporal interest, suppose, which is the end of such self-love, be at a distance. So greatly are profligate men mistaken, when they affirm they are wholly governed by interestedness and self-love. And so little cause is there for moralists to disclaim this principle. See Part I. iv. 4.

This holds whether passions remain in the future state, or not.

state; which it is scarce possible to avoid supposing.[17] And if they do; we clearly see, that acquired habits of virtue and self-government may be necessary for the regulation of them. However, though we were not distinctly to take in this supposition, but to speak only in general; the thing really comes to the same. For habits of virtue, thus acquired by discipline, are improvement in virtue: and improvement in virtue must be advancement in happiness, if the government of the universe be moral.

(ii) The Fall is made conceivable

[14.] From these things we may observe, and it will further shew this our natural and original need of being improved by discipline, how it comes to pass, that creatures made upright fall; and that those who preserve their uprightness, by so doing, raise themselves to a more secure state of virtue. To say that the former is accounted for by the nature of liberty, is to say no more, than that an event's actually happening is accounted for by a mere possibility of its happening. But it seems distinctly conceivable from the very nature of particular affections or propensions. For, suppose creatures intended for such a particular state of life, for which such propensions were necessary: suppose them endued with such propensions, together with moral understanding, as well including a practical sense of virtue, as a speculative perception of it;[18] and that all these several principles, both natural and moral, forming an inward constitution of mind, were in the most exact proportion possible; *i.e.* in a proportion the most exactly adapted to their intended state of life; such creatures would be made upright, or finitely perfect.[19] Now particular propensions, from their very nature, must be felt, the objects of them being present; though they cannot be gratified at all, or not with the allowance of the moral principle. But if they can be gratified without its allowance, or by contradicting it; then they must be conceived to have some tendency in how low a degree soever, yet some tendency, to induce persons to such forbidden gratification. This tendency, in some one particular propension, may be

by the nature of the passions,

for, even in the case of a finitely perfect being, they must be felt,

and therefore they have a tendency to break out,

[17] [Cp. Serm. xiv. § 10: "When we shall have put off this mortal body, when we shall be divested of sensual appetites . . . we must have faculties of perception, though not sensitive ones; and pleasure or uneasiness from our perceptions, as now we have."]

[18] [Cp. Butler's definition of the moral faculty in *Dissertation* II. "On Virtue" (§ 1), and the note there.]

[19] [Cp. Serm. iii. § 2 note, for another description of a "finitely perfect" creature.]

increased, by the greater frequency of occasions naturally exciting it, than of occasions exciting others. The least voluntary indulgence in forbidden circumstances, though but in thought, will increase this wrong tendency; and may increase it further, till, peculiar conjunctures perhaps conspiring, it becomes effect; and danger of deviating from right, ends in actual deviation from it: a danger necessarily arising from the very nature of propension; and which therefore could not have been prevented, though it might have been escaped, or got innocently through. The case would be, as if we were to suppose a straight path marked out for a person, in which such a degree of attention would keep him steady: but if he would not attend in this degree, any one of a thousand objects, catching his eye, might lead him out of it. Now it is impossible to say, how much even the first full overt act of irregularity might disorder the inward constitution; unsettle the adjustments, and alter the proportions, which formed it, and in which the uprightness of its make consisted: but repetition of irregularities would produce habits. And thus the constitution would be spoiled; and creatures made upright, become corrupt and depraved in their settled character, proportionably to their repeated irregularities in occasional acts. But, on the contrary, these creatures might have improved and raised themselves, to a higher and more secure state of virtue, by the contrary behaviour: by steadily following the moral principle, supposed to be one part of their nature: and thus withstanding that unavoidable danger of defection, which necessarily arose from propension, the other part of it. For, by thus preserving their integrity for some time, their danger would lessen; since propensions, by being inured to submit, would do it more easily and of course: and their security against this lessening danger would increase; since the moral principle would gain additional strength by exercise: both which things are implied in the notion of virtuous habits. Thus then vicious indulgence is not only criminal in itself, but also depraves the inward constitution and character. And virtuous self-government is not only right in itself, but also improves the inward constitution or character: and may improve it to such a degree, that though we should suppose it impossible, for particular affections to be absolutely coincident with the moral

which every slightest indulgence increases.

Illustration.

The *first* irregular indulgence might disorder the man's whole constitution.

On the other hand, resistance would strengthen character:

(*a*) by weakening the passions,

(*b*) by strengthening conscience.

Thus, the highest grade of moral strength gained by

out some thought and care; and the opportunities which we have, or imagine we have, of avoiding what we dislike, or obtaining what we desire, by unlawful means, when we either cannot do it at all, or at least not so easily, by lawful ones; these things, *i.e.* the snares and temptations of vice, are what render the present world peculiarly fit to be a state of discipline, to those who will preserve their integrity: because they render being upon our guard, resolution, and the denial of our passions, necessary in order to that end. And the exercise of such particular recollection, intention of mind, and self-government, in the practice of virtue, has, from the make of our nature, a peculiar tendency to form habits of virtue; as implying, not only a real, but also a more continued, and a more intense exercise of the virtuous principle; or a more constant and a stronger effort of virtue exerted into act. Thus suppose a person to know himself to be in particular danger, for some time, of doing any thing wrong, which yet he fully resolves not to do; continued recollection, and keeping upon his guard, in order to make good his resolution, is a *continued* exerting of that act of virtue in a *high degree*, which need have been, and perhaps would have been, only *instantaneous* and *weak*, had the temptation been so. It is indeed ridiculous to assert, that self-denial is essential to virtue and piety: but it would have been nearer the truth, though not strictly the truth itself, to have said, that it is essential to discipline and improvement.[22] For though actions materially virtuous, which have no sort of difficulty, but are perfectly agreeable to our particular inclinations, may possibly be done only from these particular inclinations, and so may not be any exercise of the principle of virtue, *i.e.* not be virtuous actions at all; yet, on the contrary, they may be an exercise of that principle: and when they are, they have a tendency to form and fix

The snares of vice peculiarly fit the world to be a state of discipline, because they demand continued resolution and self-control, which form habits of virtue.

Self-denial essential to improvement in virtue,

for though (α) *materially* virtuous actions may not beget virtuous habits,

(β) *formally* virtuous actions do.

[22] [The distinction between actions *formally* and *materially* virtuous is that between actions objectively right, done from the right motive, and actions objectively right, done from a motive without moral value. It is plain that actions of either class may be entirely pleasurable to the actor, and yet that pleasure may not be the motive of the action. Thus the relation between virtue and self-denial is not fixed. The extreme Stoical view that pleasurable actions must be wrong—that where there is no self-denial, there is no virtue—and the extreme Aristotelian view that where there *is* self-denial, there is no virtue (the habit of virtue not having been perfectly formed, as is explained in the *Nicomachean Ethics*, II. iii. I), are both ruled out of court by Butler's sober common sense.]

the habit of virtue. But when the exercise of the virtuous principle is more continued, oftener repeated, and more intense; as it must be in circumstances of danger, temptation, and difficulty, of any kind and in any degree; this tendency is increased proportionably, and a more confirmed habit is the consequence.

The moral strength may be overtaxed:

[17.] This undoubtedly holds to a certain length: but how far it may hold, I know not. Neither our intellectual powers, nor our bodily strength, can be improved beyond such a degree: and both may be over-wrought. Possibly there may be somewhat analogous to this, with respect to the moral character; which is scarce worth considering. And I mention it only, lest it should come into some persons' thoughts, not as an exception to the foregoing observations, which perhaps it is; but as a confutation of them, which it is not. And there may be several other exceptions. Observations of this kind cannot be supposed to hold minutely, and in every case. It is enough that they hold in general. And these plainly hold so far, as that from them may be seen distinctly, which is all that is intended by them, that *the present world is peculiarly fit to be a state of discipline, for our improvement in virtue and piety*: in the same sense as some sciences, by requiring and engaging the attention, not to be sure of such persons as will not, but of such as will, set themselves to them; are fit to form the mind to habits of attention.

this would be an exceptional case.

Hence, the present world is peculiarly fitted to discipline us *in virtue*.

Objection (i) Most men use the present world for discipline *in vice*.

[18.] Indeed the present state is so far from proving, in event, a discipline of virtue to the generality of men, that, on the contrary, they seem to make it a discipline of vice.[23] And the viciousness of the world is, in different ways, the great temptation, which renders it a state of virtuous discipline, in the degree it is, to good men. The whole end, and the whole occasion, of mankind's being placed in such a state as the present, is not pretended to be accounted for. That which appears amidst the general corruption, is, that there are some persons, who, having within them the principle of amendment and recovery, attend to and follow the notices of virtue and religion, be they more clear or more obscure, which are afforded them; and that the present world is, not only an exercise of

Answer: (*a*) This alters not (but rather enhances) its fitness to discipline the well-disposed in virtue.

[23] [Cp. Aristotle, *Nic. Eth.* II. i. 6, *ἐκ τῶν αὐτῶν καὶ διὰ τῶν αὐτῶν καὶ γίνεται πᾶσα ἀρετὴ καὶ φθείρεται*, viz.: "Every virtue is produced and destroyed from and by the same things."]

of it; nor consequently can he fail of obtaining that happiness, which this constitution and relation necessarily suppose connected with that character.

The present world also fit to discipline us in the *passive* virtues,

[20.] These several observations, concerning the active principle of virtue and obedience to God's commands, are applicable to passive submission or resignation to His will:[27] which is another essential part of a right character, connected with the former, and very much in our power to form ourselves to. It may be imagined, that nothing but afflictions can give occasion for, or require this virtue; that it can have no respect to, nor be any way necessary to qualify for, a state of perfect happiness: but it is not experience which can make us think thus. Prosperity itself, whilst anything supposed desirable is not ours, begets extravagant and unbounded thoughts. Imagination is altogether as much a source of discontent, as any thing in our external condition. It is indeed true, that there can be no scope for patience, when sorrow shall be no more:[28] but there may be need of a temper of mind, which shall have been formed by patience. For, though self-love, considered merely as an active principle[29] leading us to pursue our chief interest, cannot but be uniformly coincident with the principle of obedience to God's commands, our interest being rightly understood; because this obedience, and the pursuit of our own chief interest, must be in every case one and the same thing: yet it may be questioned, whether self-love, considered merely as the desire of our own interest or happiness, can, from its nature, be thus absolutely and uniformly coincident with the will of God;[30] any more than particular affections

e.g. patient submission to God's Will, which is needed not only in adversity, but in prosperity;

and even in view of a happy future.

Self-love (not [*a*] as an *active principle*, but)

[*b*] as the *desire* of happiness, cannot always coincide with God's Will:

27 [Mr. Gladstone justly observes that in Serm. xiv. (§§ 3 ff.) a much larger scope is given to the virtue of resignation.]

28 [Cicero follows out this thought, in the endeavour to prove that the happiness of the future state will consist solely in contemplation. "Si nobis, cum ex hac vita migrassemus, in beatorum insulis immortale aevum, ut fabulae ferunt, degere liceret, quid opus esset eloquentia, cum iudicia nulla fierent? aut ipsis etiam virtutibus? Nec enim fortitudine egeremus, nullo proposito aut labore aut periculo; nec iustitia, cum esset nihil quod appeteretur alieni; nec temperantia, quae regeret eas quae nullae essent libidines: ne prudentia quidem egeremus, nullo delectu proposito bonorum et malorum. Una igitur essemus beati cognitione naturae et scientia qua sola etiam deorum est vita laudanda" (*Fragm. Hortensii dialogi* ap. Augustin. *de Trin.* xiv. 9. 12).]

29 [Cp. note 16 above.]

30 [Cp. his observations in Serm. iii. §§ 8, 9: "Duty and interest are perfectly coincident; for the most part in this world, but entirely and in every instance if we take in the future and the whole; this being implied in the notion of a good and perfect administration of things." See also the editor's note on "Conscience and Self-Love," appended to Serm. iii.]

can:[31] coincident in such sort, as not to be liable to be excited upon occasions and in degrees, impossible to be gratified consistently with the constitution of things, or the Divine appointments. So that *habits* of resignation may, upon this account, be requisite for all creatures: habits, I say; which signify what is formed by use. However, in general it is obvious that both self-love and particular affections in human creatures, considered only as passive feelings, distort and rend the mind; and therefore stand in need of discipline. Now denial of those particular affections, in a course of active virtue and obedience to God's will, has a tendency to moderate them; and seems also to have a tendency to habituate the mind, to be easy and satisfied with that degree of happiness which is allotted us, *i.e.* to moderate self-love.[32] But the proper discipline for resignation is affliction. For a right behaviour under that trial; recollecting ourselves so as to consider it in the view, in which Religion teaches us to consider it, as from the hand of God; receiving it as what He appoints, or thinks proper to permit, in His world and under His government; this will habituate the mind to a dutiful submission. And such submission, together with the active principle of obedience, make up the temper and character in us, which answers to His sovereignty; and which absolutely belongs to the condition of our being, as dependent creatures. Nor can it be said, that this is only breaking the mind to a submission to mere power; for mere power may be accidental, and precarious, and usurped: but it is forming within ourselves the temper of resignation to His rightful authority, Who is, by nature, supreme over all.[33]

hence habits of resignation requisite.

These may be cultivated by discipline of the passions,

but best by affliction.

[21.] Upon the whole: such a character, and such qualifications, are necessary for a mature state of life in the present world, as nature alone does in no wise bestow; but has put it upon us, in great part, to acquire, in our progress from one stage of life to another, from childhood to mature age; put it upon us to acquire them, by giving us capacities of doing it, and

Summary.

§§ 2, 3.

§ 4.

[31] § 13 above.

[32] [That self-love needs discipline, he explains more fully in Serm. xi. § 9.]

[33] ["It may, perhaps, be farther worth observing that, while the general union of utility with virtue answers a plain moral purpose, the occasional apparent interruptions of that connexion answer a moral purpose also, *compensatory* of a possible mischievous tendency of that connexion" (FitzGerald). Angus adds that *My yoke is easy* illustrates the first truth, *Take up the Cross*, the second.]

by placing us, in the beginning of life, in a condition fit for it. And this is a general analogy to our condition in the present world, as in a state of moral discipline for another. It is in vain then to object against the credibility of the present life's being intended for this purpose, that all the trouble and the danger, unavoidably accompanying such discipline, might have been saved us, by our being made at once the creatures and the characters, *which we were to be.* For we experience, that *what we were to be*, was to be the effect of *what we would do*: and that the general conduct of Nature is, not to save us trouble or danger, but to make us capable of going through them, and to put it upon us to do so. Acquirements of our own, experience and habits, are the *natural* supply to our deficiencies, and security against our dangers: since it is as plainly natural to set ourselves to acquire the qualifications, as the external things, which we stand in need of. In particular, it is as plainly a general law of Nature, that we should, with regard to our temporal interest, form and cultivate practical principles within us, by attention, use, and discipline, as anything whatever is a natural law; chiefly in the beginning of life, but also throughout the whole course of it. And the alternative is left to our choice: either to improve ourselves, and better our condition; or, in default of such improvement, to remain deficient and wretched. It is therefore perfectly credible, from the analogy of Nature, that the same may be our case, with respect to the happiness of a future state, and the qualifications necessary for it.

General principle.

The analogy drawn out.

[22.] There is a third thing, which may seem implied in the present world's being a state of probation;[34] that it is a theatre of action, for the manifestation of persons' characters, with respect to a future one: not to be sure to an all-knowing Being, but to His creation or part of it. This may, perhaps, be only a consequence of our being in a state of probation in the other senses. However, it is not impossible, that men's shewing and making manifest what is in their heart, what their real character is, may have respect to a future life, in ways and manners which we are not acquainted with: particularly

The present state of probation exhibits men's characters to each other,

[34] [It would seem that the other two implications of a state of probation which he has in his mind are (1) that, as explained in chap. iv., it implies trial, difficulties and danger; and (2) that, as explained in chap. v., it is intended for our moral discipline and improvement.]

it may be a means, for the Author of Nature does not appear to do any thing without means, of their being disposed of suitably to their characters; and of its being known to the creation, by way of example, that they are thus disposed of. But not to enter upon any conjectural account of this; one may just mention, that the manifestation of persons' characters contributes very much, in various ways, to the carrying on a great part of that general course of Nature, respecting mankind, which comes under our observation at present.[35] I shall only add, that probation, in both these senses, as well as in that treated of in the foregoing chapter, is implied in moral government; since by persons' behaviour under it, their characters cannot but be manifested, and, if they behave well, improved.

which helps on the moral government of the world.

NOTE D.

THE FUNCTION OF MOTIVE IN THE FORMATION OF HABITS.

In § 19 Butler deals with a psychological objection to his theory of moral discipline put forward by Shaftesbury in his *Inquiry* (Book I. Pt. III. § 3). "If there be a belief or conception of a Deity, Who is considered only as powerful over His creature, and enforcing obedience to His absolute will by particular rewards and punishments; and if on this account, through hope merely of reward, or fear of punishment, the creature be incited to do the good he hates, or restrained from doing the ill to which he is not otherwise in the least degree averse; there is in this case (as has been already shewn) no virtue or goodness whatsoever. The creature, notwithstanding his good conduct, is intrinsically of as little worth, as if he acted in his natural way, when under no dread or terror of any sort. . . . It may be considered withal, that in this religious sort of discipline, the principle of self-love, which is naturally so prevailing in us, being no way moderated or restrained, but rather improved and made stronger every day, by the exercise of the passions in a subject of more extended self-interest; there may be reason to apprehend lest the temper of this kind should extend itself in general through all the parts

[35] [FitzGerald adds the acute observation that our outward actions serve to manifest our real characters, not only to others, but also *to ourselves*, "showing us in a remarkable manner, sometimes that we are better, and often that we are worse than we could have suspected before the trial."]

of life . . . This, too, must be confessed; that if it be true piety, to love God for His own sake; the over-solicitous regard to private good expected from Him, must of necessity prove a diminution of piety. For whilst God is beloved only as the cause of private good, He is no otherwise beloved than as any other instrument or means of pleasure by any vicious creature." It is plain that the problem here proposed is intimately connected with that of the possibility of a disinterested love of God, which was so warmly debated between Fénélon and Bossuet (see further Butler's *Sermons*, Pref. § 43). Shaftesbury himself suggested the answer elsewhere. He pointed out that right action from inferior motives is a first stage of moral progress, and that in time these motives are replaced by others of true moral value. "Although this service of fear be allowed ever so low or base; yet religion still being a discipline and progress of the soul towards perfection, the motive of reward and punishment is primary and of the highest moment with us; till being capable of more sublime instruction, we are led from this servile state to the generous service of affection and love" (*The Moralists*, Part II. § 3).

Butler puts the answer in his own way. He urges that the habit of obedience to God will be formed by repeated acts of obedience, whatever the motive from which they proceed. "Doing what God commands, because He commands it, is obedience, though it proceeds from hope or fear. And a course of such obedience will form habits of it." This is, perhaps, not altogether consistent with his general doctrine of habits as laid down elsewhere. Thus he had said a few pages further back (ch. v. § 4, p. 79): "Habits of the mind are produced by the exertion of inward practical principles, *i.e.* by carrying them into act, or acting upon them; the principles of obedience, of veracity, justice, and charity. *Nor can those habits be formed by any external course of action, otherwise than as it proceeds from these principles*: because it is only these inward principles exerted, which are strictly acts of obedience, of veracity, of justice, and of charity."[1] And, again, in § 16 (p. 92), he said that materially virtuous actions may be an exercise of the principle of virtue, "and *when they are, they have a tendency to form and fix the habit of virtue*." It seems to me that Butler cannot be held to have expressed himself consistently throughout this chapter, but the view adopted in § 19 is probably the more true to experience. It is a consequence of the moral government of the world that conscience and self-love generally point in the same direction—*always*, if the

[1] Cp. also Part II. iii. 13, "Although a course of external acts, which without command would be immoral, make an immoral habit; yet a few detached commands have no such tendency."

view of self-love be enlarged so as to take in the future life (see further, § 20, and *Sermons*, iii. § 8). And it is confirmed by daily observation that, as Butler says in § 19, "he who begins a good life from any one of [these motives] and perseveres in it, as he is already in some degree, so he cannot fail of becoming more and more, of that character, which is correspondent to the constitution of nature as moral."[2]

An interesting literary parallel to Butler's words may be traced in Philo's treatise *de Abrahamo*. He raises the same difficulty which Butler here discusses, and resolves it in the same way: τὰ μὲν πρῶτα τῶν ἄθλων κείσεται τοῖς ἐμὲ θεραπεύουσι δι' ἐμὲ αὐτὸν, τὰ δὲ δεύτερα τοῖς δι' αὐτοὺς τυχεῖν ἀγαθῶν ἐλπίζουσιν ἢ τιμωριῶν ἀπαλλαγὴν εὑρεῖν προσδοκῶσι· καὶ γὰρ εἰ ἔμμισθος ἡ τῶνδε θεραπεία καὶ μὴ ἀδέκαστος, ἀλλ' οὐδὲν ἧττον ἐντὸς εἱλεῖται θείων περιβόλων καὶ οὐκ ἔξω πλάζεται . . . οὐ γὰρ ἀγνοῶ, ὅτι πρὸς τῷ χείρους μὴ γίγνεσθαι καὶ βελτίους ἔσονται τῷ συνεχεῖ τῆς θεραπείας εἰλικρινῆ καὶ καθαρὰν εὐσέβειαν ἀσκήσαντες. Εἰ γὰρ καὶ μάλιστα οἱ τρόποι διαφέρουσιν, ἀφ' ὧν ποιοῦνται τὰς πρὸς ἀρέσκειαν ὁρμάς, οὐκ αἰτιατέον, ὅτι σκοπὸς εἷς καὶ τέλος ἓν ἐστιν αὐτοῖς, τὸ θεραπεύειν ἐμέ (*de Abr.* § 25). That is, "The most valuable prizes shall be offered to those who worship Me for My own sake: the second best to those who hope by their own efforts to be able to attain to good, or to find a means of escape from punishments. For even if the service of these latter is mercenary and not unbought, yet it nevertheless revolves within the divine circumference, and does not stray beyond it. . . . For I am not ignorant that in addition to these men not becoming worse, they will become better, arriving at a sincere and pure piety by the continual discipline of service. For even if the dispositions, from which they make their first endeavours to please Me, differ widely, still they must not be blamed, because they have only one aim and purpose, the serving of Me."[3]

Butler's final observation that a man who diligently acts thus from the lower motive "cannot fail of obtaining that happiness" which is to be the future reward of righteousness, is in curious contrast with the rigid expressions of the 18th Article of the Church of England, where an anathema is pronounced on those "that presume to say, That every man shall be saved by the Law or Sect which he professeth, so that he be diligent to frame his life according to that Law and the light of Nature." However, the Article is patient of a more liberal interpretation than its words might suggest.

[2] Cp. also Part II. viii. 8 note.

[3] Cp. the language of Coleridge in his *Aids to Reflection*: "Art thou under the tyranny of sin? . . . O, how idle the dispute, whether the listening to the dictates of prudence from prudential and self-interested motives be virtue or merit, when the *not* listening is guilt, misery, madness, and despair!" (*Prudential Aphorisms*, IV.).

CHAPTER VI.

Of the Opinion of Necessity, considered as influencing Practice.[1]

If the doctrine of necessity be consistent with Natural Government, it may be also with Moral Government.

[1.] THROUGHOUT the foregoing treatise it appears, that the condition of mankind, considered as inhabitants of this world only, and under the government of God which we experience, is greatly analogous to our condition, as designed for another world, or under that further government, which Religion teaches us. If therefore any assert, as a fatalist must, that the opinion of universal necessity is reconcilable with the former; there immediately arises a question in the way of analogy, whether he must not also own it to be reconcilable with the latter, *i.e.* with the system of Religion itself, and the proof of it. The reader then will observe, that the question now before us is not absolute, Whether the opinion of fate be reconcilable with Religion; but hypothetical, Whether, upon supposition of its being reconcilable with the constitution of Nature, it be not reconcilable with Religion also: or, what pretence a fatalist, not other persons, but a fatalist, has to conclude from his opinion, that there can be no such thing as Religion. And as the

[1] [This chapter is a digression, introduced in view of the controversy as to necessity and free will, which was active in Butler's lifetime. With Collins' attempt to shew that man was a "necessary agent," and with Clarke's *Reply*, he was doubtless familiar; as also with Clarke's answer to Leibnitz, whose principle of the *Sufficient Reason* seemed to leave no place for human freedom. Berkeley shews (*Alciphron*, vii. 19) that the question was debated in his day, as indeed we might learn from § 10 of the present chapter: "The opinion of necessity seems to be the very basis, upon which infidelity grounds itself." Butler does not combat any refined theories of determinism, such as that advocated by some modern writers, whose thesis is that "the will is always determined by the strongest motive." But he had in view a doctrine of fate which eliminated responsibility from human life; and he was anxious to shew that, as such a doctrine is not practically applicable to the affairs of the present world, there is no reason to believe that it may be legitimately applied to those of the next.]

puzzle and obscurity, which must unavoidably arise from arguing upon so absurd a supposition as that of universal necessity, will, I fear, easily be seen; it will, I hope, as easily be excused.

[2.] But since it has been all along taken for granted, as a thing proved, that there is an intelligent Author of Nature, or natural Governor of the world; and since an objection may be made against the proof of this, from the opinion of universal necessity, as it may be supposed, that such necessity will itself account for the origin and preservation of all things: it is requisite, that this objection be distinctly answered; or that it be shewn, that a fatality, supposed consistent with what we certainly experience, does not destroy the proof of an intelligent Author and Governor of Nature; before we proceed to consider, whether it destroys the proof of a moral Governor of it, or of our being in a state of Religion.

The doctrine does not destroy the proofs of God's Natural Government, for,

[3.] Now, when it is said by a fatalist, that the whole constitution of Nature, and the actions of men, that everything, and every mode and circumstance of everything, is necessary, and could not possibly have been otherwise; it is to be observed, that this necessity does not exclude deliberation, choice, preference, and acting from certain principles, and to certain ends: because all this is matter of undoubted experience, acknowledged by all, and what every man may, every moment, be conscious of. And from hence it follows, that necessity, alone and of itself, is in no sort an account of the constitution of Nature, and how things came *to be* and *to continue* as they are; but only an account of this *circumstance* relating to their origin and continuance, that they could not have been otherwise than they are and have been. The assertion, that everything is by necessity of Nature, is not an answer to the question; Whether the world came into being as it is, by an intelligent Agent forming it thus, or not: but to quite another question; Whether it came into being as it is, in that way and manner which we call *necessarily*, or in that way and manner which we call *freely*. For suppose further, that one who was a fatalist, and one who kept to his natural sense of things, and believed himself a free agent, were disputing together, and vindicating their respective opinions; and they should happen to instance in a house: they would agree that it was built by an architect.

to say that everything is by necessity does not exclude choice and design, which are matters of experience,

but only describes the *mode* of its coming into existence,

which may be (*a*) by a *free*, or (*b*) by a necessary agent.

Their difference concerning necessity and freedom would occasion no difference of judgment concerning this; but only concerning another matter; whether the architect built it necessarily or freely. Suppose then they should proceed to inquire concerning the constitution of Nature: in a lax way of speaking, one of them might say, it was by necessity; and the other, by freedom: but if they had any meaning to their words, as the latter must mean a free agent, so the former must at length be reduced to mean an agent, whether he would say one or more, acting by necessity: for abstract notions can do nothing. Indeed we ascribe to God a necessary existence, uncaused by any agent. For we find within ourselves the idea of infinity, *i.e.* immensity and eternity, impossible, even in imagination, to be removed out of being. We seem to discern intuitively, that there must, and cannot but be, somewhat, external to ourselves, answering this idea, or the archetype of it. And from hence (for *this abstract*, as much as any other, implies a *concrete*) we conclude, that there is, and cannot but be, an infinite and immense eternal Being existing, prior to all design contributing to His existence, and exclusive of it.[2] And from the scantiness of language, a manner of speaking has been introduced; that necessity is the foundation, the reason, the account of the existence of

A priori proof of God's necessary existence.

[2] [The interesting correspondence between Butler and Clarke printed at the end of Vol. I. shews that Butler had at first reading been inclined to question Clarke's *a priori* argument for the existence of a Supreme Being based on the nature of space, but that he accepted it in the end as satisfactory. Clarke's argument was originally stated by himself in the following terms: "Infinite Space is nothing else but abstract Immensity or Infinity; even as infinite Duration is abstract Eternity. And it would be just as proper to say that Eternity is the essence of the Supreme Cause; as to say that Immensity is so. Indeed they seem both to be but *modes* of an essence or substance incomprehensible to us" (*A Demonstration of the Being and Attributes of God*, p. 40, ed. 1738). Or, again: "When we are endeavouring to suppose that there is no Being in the Universe that exists necessarily; we always find in our minds some ideas, as of Infinity and Eternity, which to remove, that is to suppose that there is no Being, no Substance in the Universe, to which these Attributes or Modes of Existence are necessarily inherent, is a contradiction in the very terms. For modes and attributes exist only by the existence of the Substance to which they belong. Now he that can suppose Eternity and Immensity (and consequently the Substance by whose existence these modes or attributes exist) removed out of the Universe; may, if he please, as easily remove the relation of equality between twice two and four" (*loc. cit.* p. 16). This argument is, in its main outlines, reproduced by Butler in the passage before us (§ 3). It was, as Clarke points out in a reference in his *Answer* to Butler's Fifth Letter, suggested by a passage from Newton's *Principia*, which he quotes.

God. But it is not alleged, nor can it be at all intended, that *everything* exists as it does, by this kind of necessity; a necessity antecedent in Nature to design: it cannot, I say, be meant that everything exists as it does, by this kind of necessity, upon several accounts; and particularly because it is admitted, that design, in the actions of men, contributes to many alterations in Nature. For if any deny this, I shall not pretend to reason with them.

But created Nature does not exist by this kind of necessity, for man's designs can alter it.

[4.] From these things it follows; first, That when a fatalist asserts, that everything is *by necessity*, he must mean, *by an agent acting necessarily*; he must I say mean this, for I am very sensible he would not choose to mean it: and secondly, That the necessity, by which such an agent is supposed to act, does not exclude intelligence and design. So that, were the system of fatality admitted, it would just as much account for the formation of the world, as for the structure of an house, and no more. Necessity as much requires and supposes a necessary agent, as freedom requires and supposes a free agent, to be the former of the world. And the appearances of *design* and of *final causes* in the constitution of Nature as really prove this acting agent to be an *intelligent designer*, or to act from choice; upon the scheme of necessity, supposed possible, as upon that of freedom.

Hence necessity (1) supposes a necessary agent and

(2) does not exclude design.

Therefore the Design Argument still holds good.

It will probably occur to the reader that, as stated by Butler, the argument lacks solidity. To base the existence of God on the principle that "every abstract implies a concrete" is to build on sand, for the principle is obviously untrue in its plainest sense. Where is the concrete corresponding to a centaur? Or to a unicorn? But it is hardly conceivable that this difficulty was not present to Butler's mind, and I suppose him to have contemplated the argument in the far more plausible form in which it is put by Clarke, though without formal approval, in another passage: "The bare having the Idea of the proposition, *There is a self-existent Being*, proves indeed the thing not to be impossible (for of an impossible proposition there can be no Idea); but that it actually Is, cannot be proved from the Idea, unless the certainty of the actual existence of a necessarily existing Being follows from the possibility of the existence of such a Being. Which that it does *in this particular case*, many learned men have indeed thought" (*loc. cit.* p. 21). Clarke prefers his own line of argument, but nevertheless he has here touched the real point, and indicated at the same time the *crux* in all *a priori* proofs of the Existence of God. Certainly the argument from the idea to the reality, from the abstract to the concrete, is not valid as a rule; but it may be urged that there is something peculiar in the Idea of God which makes the transition legitimate in that particular case, and in that alone. And it was this that Hegel urged against Kant's criticism of the Ontological Argument for the Existence of the Supreme Being, viz. that in the case of this one unique Idea, the μετάβασις εἰς ἄλλο γένος, which is involved in the passage from the *thought* of God to the *being* of God, is valid.]

necessity be speculatively true, it is practically false.

necessity were speculatively true; yet, with regard to practice, it is as if it were false, so far as our experience reaches; that is, to the whole of our present life. For, the constitution of the present world, and the condition in which we are actually placed, is, as if we were free.[6] And it may perhaps justly be concluded, that since the whole process of action, through every step of it, suspense, deliberation, inclining one way, determining, and at last doing as we determine, is as if we were free, therefore we are so. But the thing here insisted upon is, that under the present natural government of the world, we find we are treated and dealt with, as if we were free, prior to all consideration whether we are or not. Were this opinion therefore of necessity admitted to be ever so true; yet such is in fact our condition and the natural course of things, that whenever we apply it to life and practice, this application of it always misleads us, and cannot but mislead us, in a most dreadful manner, with regard to our present interest. And how can people think themselves so very secure then, that the same application of the same opinion may not mislead them also, in some analogous manner, with respect to a future, a more general, and more important interest? For, Religion being a practical subject; and the analogy of Nature shewing us, that we have not faculties to apply this opinion, were it a true one, to practical subjects; whenever we do apply it to the subject of Religion, and thence conclude, that we are free from its obligations, it is plain this conclusion cannot be depended upon. There will still remain just reason to think, whatever appearances are, that we deceive ourselves; in somewhat of a like manner, as when people fancy they can draw contradictory conclusions from the idea of infinity.

Practical proof of Freedom.

But Religion is a practical subject.

Therefore the doctrine of necessity is not applicable to it.

Thus the evidences of

[7.] From these things together, the attentive reader will see

[6] [Butler's practical proof of human freedom is, in substance, that advanced by Clarke (*Remarks on Collins' Inquiry*, p. 24) and by Berkeley (*Alciphron*, vii. 20). We act *as if* we were free agents, and so we must suppose ourselves to be free. This line of thought is not to be confused with the facile observation with which Dr. Johnson escaped the difficulty. "Sir," he said, "we *know* our will to be free, and there's an end on't" (*Life*, ch. xx.). Butler's argument is, indeed, remarkably akin to that by which Kant afterwards defended human freedom from the practical point of view: "Even though the speculative proof should not be made out, yet a being that cannot act except with the idea of freedom is bound by the same laws that would oblige a being who was actually free" (*Fundamental Principles of the Metaphysic of Morals*, p. 80, ed. Rosenkranz).]

Religion remain untouched by doctrine of necessity.

it follows, that if upon supposition of freedom the evidence of Religion be conclusive, it remains so, upon supposition of necessity, because the notion of necessity is not applicable to practical subjects: *i.e.* with respect to them, is as if it were not true. Nor does this contain any reflection upon reason: but only upon what is unreasonable. For to pretend to act upon reason, in opposition to practical principles, which the Author of our Nature gave us to act upon; and to pretend to apply our reason to subjects, with regard to which, our own short views, and even our experience, will shew us, it cannot be depended upon; and such, at best, the subject of necessity must be; this is vanity, conceit, and unreasonableness.

Necessity consistent with a *character* in man, and therefore with a character in God.

[8.] But this is not all. For we find within ourselves a will, and are conscious of a character. Now if this, in us, be reconcilable with fate, it is reconcilable with it, in the Author of Nature.[7] And besides, natural government and final causes imply a character and a will in the Governor and Designer;[8] a will concerning the creatures whom He governs. The Author of Nature then being certainly of some character or other, notwithstanding necessity; it is evident this necessity is as reconcilable with the particular character of benevolence, veracity, and justice in Him, which attributes are the foundation of Religion, as with any other character: since we find this necessity no more hinders *men* from being benevolent, than cruel; true, than faithless; just, than unjust; or if the fatalist pleases, what we call unjust. For it is said indeed, that what, upon supposition of freedom, would be just punishment; upon supposition of necessity, becomes manifestly unjust: because it is punishment inflicted for doing that which persons could not avoid doing. As if the necessity, which is supposed to destroy the injustice of murder, for instance, would not also destroy the injustice of punishing it.[9] However, as little to the purpose as this objection is in itself, it is very much

Natural Government (which is untouched by necessity) implies a Divine character.

No reason why this should not be a moral character.

(Universal necessity does not make punishment unjust.)

[7] [Cp. Part I. concl. § 1, where this is restated.]

[8] By *will* and *character* is meant that, which, in speaking of men, we should express, not only by these words, but also by the words *temper*, *taste*, *dispositions*, *practical principles: that whole frame of mind, from whence we act in one manner rather than another*. [Cp. *Dissert.* "On Virtue," § 2 *sub init.*]

[9] [The retort is as old as Zeno: *δοῦλον ἐπὶ κλοπῇ, φασιν, ἐμαστίγου· τοῦ δ' εἰπόντος, Εἵμαρτό μοι κλέψαι· καὶ δαρῆναι, ἔφη* (Diog. Laert. VII. i. 23): *i.e.* "They say that he was once scourging a slave for thieving; and when the slave said, 'It was fated that I should steal,' he answered, 'Yes, and that you should be beaten.'" Butler repeats the remark, Part II. viii. 8.]

objection to Proof iii., because it rests on *facts* of our moral nature,

this general proof of religion. None against the proposition reasoned upon, that we have such a moral faculty and discernment; because this is a mere matter of fact, a thing of experience, that human kind is thus constituted: none against the conclusion; because it is immediate and wholly from this fact. For the conclusion, that God will finally reward the righteous and punish the wicked, is not here drawn, from its appearing to us fit[17] that *He should*; but from its appearing, that He has told us, *He will.* And this He hath certainly told us, in the promise and threatening, which it hath been observed the notion of a command implies, and the sense of good and ill desert which He has given us, more distinctly expresses. And this reasoning from fact is confirmed, and in some degree even verified, by other facts; by the natural tendencies of virtue and of vice;[18] and by this, that God, in the natural course of His providence, punishes vicious actions as mischievous to society; and also vicious actions as such in the strictest sense.[19] So that the general proof of Religion is unanswerably real, even upon the wild supposition which we are arguing upon.

confirmed by the facts of God's moral government.

(iv) External evidence, viz.:

[13.] It must likewise be observed further, that natural Religion hath, besides this, an external evidence; which the doctrine of necessity, if it could be true, would not affect. For suppose a person, by the observations and reasoning above, or by any other, convinced of the truth of Religion; that there is a God, Who made the world, Who is the moral Governor and Judge of mankind, and will upon the whole deal with every one according to his works: I say, suppose

[17] However, I am far from intending to deny that the will of God is determined, by what is fit, by the right and reason of the case; though one chooses to decline matters of such abstract speculation, and to speak with caution when one does speak of them. But if it be intelligible to say, that *it is fit and reasonable for every one to consult his own happiness*, then *fitness of action, or the right and reason of the case*, is an intelligible manner of speaking. And it seems as inconceivable to suppose God to approve one course of action, or one end, preferably to another, which yet His acting at all from design implies that He does, without supposing somewhat prior in that end, to be the ground of the preference; as to suppose Him to discern an abstract proposition to be true, without supposing somewhat prior in it, to be the ground of the discernment. It doth not therefore appear, that moral right is any more relative to perception, than abstract truth is; or that it is any more improper, to speak of the fitness and rightness of actions and ends, as founded in the nature of things, than to speak of abstract truth, as thus founded. [See Note E at end of chapter.]

[18] Part I. iii. 17, 18.

[19] Part I. iii. 8.

a person convinced of this by reason; but to know nothing at all of antiquity, or the present state of mankind: it would be natural for such an one to be inquisitive, what was the history of this system of doctrine; at what time, and in what manner, it came first into the world; and whether it were believed by any considerable part of it. And were he upon inquiry to find, that a particular person, in a late age, first of all proposed it, as a deduction of reason, and that mankind were before wholly ignorant of it; then, though its evidence from reason would remain, there would be no additional probability of its truth, from the account of its discovery. (some such religious system has been professed) But instead of this being the fact of the case, on the contrary, he would find, what could not but afford him a very strong confirmation of its truth: First, That somewhat of this system, with more or fewer additions and alterations, hath been professed in all ages and countries, of which we have any certain information relating to this matter. ((*a*) in all ages and countries,) Secondly, That it is certain historical fact, so far as we can trace things up, that this whole system of belief, that there is one God, the Creator and moral Governor of the world, and that mankind is in a state of Religion, was received in the first ages. ((*b*) even in the *first* ages;) And Thirdly, That as there is no hint or intimation in history, that this system was first reasoned out; so there is express historical or traditional evidence, as ancient as history, that it was taught first by revelation. ((*c*) express evidence that it was then revealed.) Now these things must be allowed to be of great weight. (*a*) The first of them, general consent, shews this system to be conformable to the common sense of mankind. (*b*) The second, namely, that Religion was believed in the first ages of the world, especially as it does not appear that there were then any superstitious or false additions to it, cannot but be a further confirmation of its truth. For it is a proof of this alternative: (α) either that it came into the world by revelation; (β) or that it is natural, obvious, and forces itself upon the mind. The former of these is the conclusion of learned men. And whoever will consider, how unapt for speculation rude and uncultivated minds are, will, perhaps from hence alone, be strongly inclined to believe it the truth. And as it is shewn in the second part[20] of this treatise, that there is nothing of such peculiar presumption against a revelation in the beginning of the world, as there

[20] Part II. ii. §§ 6-10.

is supposed to be against subsequent ones: a sceptic could not, I think, give any account, which would appear more probable even to himself, of the early pretences to revelation; than by supposing some real original one, from whence they (c) were copied. And the third thing above mentioned, that there is express historical or traditional evidence as ancient as history, of the system of Religion being taught mankind by revelation; this must be admitted as some degree of real proof, that it was so taught. For why should not the most ancient tradition be admitted, as some additional proof of a fact, against which there is no presumption? And this proof is mentioned here, because it has its weight to shew, that Religion came into the world by revelation, prior to all consideration of the proper authority of any book supposed to contain it; and even prior to all consideration, whether the revelation itself be uncorruptly handed down, and related, or mixed and darkened with fables. Thus the historical account, which we have, of the origin of Religion, taken in all circumstances, is a real confirmation of its truth, no way affected by the opinion of necessity. And the *external* evidence, even of natural Religion, is by no means inconsiderable.

Nothing of this affected by necessity.

Caution: Conscience may be at fault quite as much as Intellect.

[14.] But it is carefully to be observed, and ought to be recollected after all proofs of virtue and religion, which are only general; that as speculative reason may be neglected, prejudiced, and deceived, so also may our moral understanding be impaired and perverted,[21] and the dictates of it not impartially attended to. This indeed proves nothing against the reality of our speculative or practical faculties of perception; against their being intended by Nature, to inform us in the theory of things, and instruct us how we are to behave, and what we are to expect in consequence of our behaviour. Yet our liableness, in the degree we are liable, to prejudice and perversion, is a most serious admonition to us to be upon our guard, with respect to what is of such consequence, as our determinations concerning virtue and religion; and particularly not to take custom, and fashion, and slight notions of honour, or imaginations of present ease, use, and convenience to mankind, for the only moral rule.[22]

These considerations a

[15.] The foregoing observations, drawn from the nature of the thing, and the history of Religion, amount, when taken

[21] [See Serm. x. § 6.]

[22] *Dissertation* II.

together, to a real practical proof of it, not to be confuted: such a proof as, considering the infinite importance of the thing, I apprehend, would be admitted fully sufficient, in reason, to influence the actions of men, who act upon thought and reflection; if it were admitted that there is no proof of the contrary. But it may be said: "There are many probabilities, which cannot indeed be confuted, *i.e.* shewn to be no probabilities, and yet may be overbalanced by greater probabilities on the other side; much more by demonstration. And there is no occasion to object against particular arguments alleged for an opinion, when the opinion itself may be clearly shewn to be false, without meddling with such arguments at all, but leaving them just as they are.[23] Now the method of government by rewards and punishments, and especially rewarding and punishing good and ill desert as such respectively, must go upon supposition, that we are free and not necessary agents. And it is incredible, that the Author of Nature should govern us upon a supposition as true, which He knows to be false: and therefore absurd to think, He will reward or punish us for our actions hereafter; especially that He will do it under the notion, that they are of good or ill desert." Here then the matter is brought to a point. And the answer to all this is full, and not to be evaded: that the whole constitution and course of things, the whole analogy of Providence, shews beyond possibility of doubt, that the conclusion from this reasoning is false; wherever the fallacy lies. The doctrine of freedom indeed clearly shews where: in supposing ourselves necessary, when in truth we are free agents. But upon the supposition of necessity, the fallacy lies in taking for granted, that it is incredible necessary agents should be rewarded and punished. But that, somehow or other, the conclusion now mentioned is false, is most certain. For it is fact, that God does govern even brute creatures by the method of rewards and punishments, in the natural course of things. And men are rewarded and punished for their actions, punished for actions mischievous to society as being so, punished for vicious actions as such; by the natural instrumentality of each other, under the present conduct of Providence. Nay even the affection of gratitude, and the passion of resentment, and the rewards

real practical proof.

Objection: Probabilities cannot outweigh the certainty that we are not free agents, and that therefore we shall not be rewarded or punished hereafter by God.

Answer: If we were necessary agents (which we are not), the analogy of the present world would prove that necessary agents may be rewarded and punished.

[23] Pp. 1, 9.

and punishments following from them, which in general are to be considered as natural, *i.e.* from the Author of Nature; these rewards and punishments, being naturally[24] annexed to actions considered as implying good intention and good desert, ill intention and ill desert; these natural rewards and punishments, I say, are as much a contradiction to the conclusion above, and shew its falsehood, as a more exact and complete rewarding and punishing of good and ill desert as such. So that if it be incredible, that necessary agents should be thus rewarded and punished; then, men are not necessary but free; since it is matter of fact, that they are thus rewarded and punished. But if, on the contrary, which is the supposition we have been arguing upon, it be insisted, that men are necessary agents; then, there is nothing incredible in the further supposition of necessary agents being thus rewarded and punished: since we ourselves are thus dealt with.

Thus, the doctrine of necessity does not destroy the proof of God's moral government; and, as a practical doctrine, is false.

[16.] From the whole therefore it must follow, that a necessity supposed possible, and reconcilable with the constitution of things, does in no sort prove that the Author of Nature will not, nor destroy the proof that He will, finally and upon the whole, in His eternal government, render His creatures happy or miserable, by some means or other, as they behave well or ill. Or, to express this conclusion in words conformable to the title of the chapter, the analogy of Nature shews us, that the opinion of necessity, considered as practical, is false. And if necessity, upon the supposition above mentioned, doth not destroy the proof of natural Religion, it evidently makes no alteration in the proof of revealed.

It is destructive of Religion,

(*a*) practically by encouraging the vicious,

(*b*) speculatively because it contradicts the constitution of experience.

[17.] From these things likewise we may learn, in what sense to understand that general assertion, that the opinion of necessity is essentially destructive of all religion. First, in a practical sense; that by this notion, atheistical men pretend to satisfy and encourage themselves in vice, and justify to others their disregard to all religion. And secondly, in the strictest sense; that it is a contradiction to the whole constitution of Nature, and to what we may every moment experience in ourselves, and so overturns every thing. But by no means is this assertion to be understood, as if necessity,

[24] Serm. viii. [§§ 13, 14].

supposing it could possibly be reconciled with the constitution of things and with what we experience, were not also reconcilable with Religion: for upon this supposition, it demonstrably is so.

NOTE E.

IMMUTABLE MORALITY.

Butler's note on § 12 of the preceding chapter contains in brief space a discussion of a subtle question at one time much debated by the schoolmen. It was urged on the one hand by the Nominalists that the ultimate standard of morality was the arbitrary Will of God. *Good* was that which was commanded by God, evil that which He discountenanced. A *reductio ad absurdum* of such a doctrine was furnished by the thesis of the famous English Nominalist, William of Ockham, that "If God had commanded His creatures to hate Himself, the hatred of God would have been praiseworthy." The prevailing view in the Church, however, was that of Aquinas, viz. that while God always wills what is just, nothing is just solely because He wills it. He held that the ideas of right and wrong are eternally and immutably resident in the Divine Intellect. And the English philosophers whom Butler followed, for the most part, had taken the same line. The title of Cudworth's *Eternal and Immutable Morality* explains itself. "There is," said Clarke, "such a thing as Fitness and Unfitness, eternally, necessarily, and unchangeably in the Nature and Reason of things" (*On the Attributes*, Prop. xii.). And, again, "Originally and in reality, 'tis as *natural* and (morally speaking) *necessary*, that the will should be determined in every action by the reason of the thing, and the right of the case; as 'tis *natural* and (absolutely speaking) *necessary* that the understanding should submit to a demonstrated truth" (*Evidences*, Prop. i. § 3).

Even Shaftesbury declared that "whoever thinks there is a God and pretends formally to believe that He is just and good, must suppose that there is independently such a thing as Justice and Injustice, Truth and Falsehood, Right and Wrong; according to which he pronounces that God is just, righteous, and true. If the mere Will, Decree, or Law of God be said absolutely to constitute Right and Wrong, then are these latter words of no significancy at all. For thus if each part of a contradiction were affirmed for truth by the Supreme Power, they would consequently become true" (*Inquiry*, Book I. iii. § 2).

Butler unhesitatingly adopts this view. He assures us elsewhere that he believes in "the moral fitness and unfitness of actions, prior to all will whatever" (Part II. viii. 11); he uses the phrase "immutable morality" (Part II. iii. 13); and speaks of "the eternal rule of right" (Part II. v. 6). So, too, in the *Dissertation on Virtue* (§ 5) he applies the epithets "incongruous, unsuitable, disproportionate, unfit, to actions which our moral faculty determines to be vicious"; as in the *Sermons* (xiv. § 13) he had already spoken of "the conformity of the Divine Will to the Law of Truth in which the moral attributes of God consist."

The point is here only alluded to by Butler in passing; but it is of the highest importance when viewed in relation to his doctrine of conscience and of virtue.

CHAPTER VII.

Of the Government of God, considered as a Scheme or Constitution, imperfectly comprehended.[1]

[1.] THOUGH it be, as it cannot but be, acknowledged, that the analogy of Nature gives a strong credibility to the general doctrine of Religion, and to the several particular things contained in it, considered as so many matters of fact; and likewise that it shews this credibility not to be destroyed by any notions of necessity: yet still, objections may be insisted upon, against the wisdom, equity, and goodness of the Divine government implied in the notion of Religion, and against the method by which this government is conducted; to which objections analogy can be no direct answer. For the credibility, or the certain truth, of a matter of fact, does not immediately prove anything concerning the wisdom or goodness of it: and analogy can do no more immediately or directly, than shew such and such things to be true or credible, considered only as matters of fact. But still, if, upon supposition of a moral constitution of Nature and a moral government over it, analogy suggests and makes it credible, that this government must be a scheme, system, or constitution of government, as distinguished from a number of single unconnected acts of distributive justice and goodness; and likewise, that

Analogy an answer to objections against the *credibility* of Divine government;

no *direct* answer to objections against its wisdom and goodness;

yet an *indirect* answer by suggesting that the Divine government is a scheme imperfectly comprehended

[1] [The general idea of this chapter had been already put forth by Butler in his sermon "On the Ignorance of Man" (No. XV. at the Rolls). In nothing is he more conspicuously superior to his contemporaries than in his sense of the immeasurable greatness of God and the littleness of man. Though the word had not then been invented, Butler recognised the truth which lies at the heart of *Agnosticism*, and, unlike the majority of writers of his day, he is ever ready to confess that our knowledge, though real and trustworthy so far as it goes, is only "in part." This chapter should be compared all through with the parallel chap. iv. in Part II.]

it must be a scheme, so imperfectly comprehended, and of such a sort in other respects, as to afford a direct general answer to all objections against the justice and goodness of it: then analogy is, remotely, of great service in answering those objections; both by suggesting the answer, and shewing it to be a credible one.

The answer is twofold.

[2.] Now this, upon inquiry, will be found to be the case. I. For, first, Upon supposition that God exercises a moral government over the world, the analogy of His natural government suggests and makes it credible, that His moral government must be a scheme, quite beyond our comprehension: and this affords a general answer to all objections against the justice and goodness of it. II. And, secondly, A more distinct observation of some particular things contained in God's scheme of natural government, the like things being supposed, by analogy, to be contained in His moral government, will further shew, how little weight is to be laid upon these objections.

I. The analogy of God's natural government suggests that (*a*) His moral government is a scheme which implies innumerable relations

[3.] I. Upon supposition that God exercises a moral government over the world, the analogy of His natural government suggests and makes it credible, that His moral government must be a scheme, quite beyond our comprehension; and this affords a general answer to all objections against the justice and goodness of it. It is most obvious, analogy renders it highly credible, that, upon supposition of a moral government, it must be a scheme: for the world, and the whole natural government of it, appears to be so: to be a scheme, system, or constitution, whose parts correspond to each other, and to a whole; as really as any work of art, or as any particular model of a civil constitution and government. In this great scheme of the natural world, individuals have various peculiar relations to other individuals of their own species. And whole species are, we find, variously related to other species, upon this earth. Nor do we know, how much further these kinds of relations may extend. And, as there is not any action or natural event, which we are acquainted with, so single and unconnected, as not to have a respect to some other actions and events: so possibly each of them, when it has not an immediate, may yet have a remote, natural relation to other actions and events, much beyond the compass of this present world.[2] There seems

(earthly relations which may go beyond earth),

[2] [Cp. Part II. viii. 8.]

indeed nothing, from whence we can so much as make a conjecture, whether all creatures, actions, and events, throughout the whole of Nature, have relations to each other. But, as it is obvious, that all events have future unknown consequences; so if we trace any, as far as we can go, into what is connected with it, we shall find, that if such event were not connected with somewhat further in Nature unknown to us, somewhat both past and present, such event could not possibly have been at all. Nor can we give the whole account of any one thing whatever; of all its causes, ends, and necessary adjuncts; those adjuncts, I mean, without which it could not have been. By this most astonishing connexion, these reciprocal correspondencies and mutual relations, everything which we see in the course of Nature is actually brought about. And things seemingly the most insignificant imaginable are perpetually observed to be necessary conditions to other things of the greatest importance: so that any one thing whatever may, for ought we know to the contrary, be a necessary condition to any other. The natural world then, and natural government of it, being such an incomprehensible scheme; so incomprehensible, that a man must, really in the literal sense, know nothing at all, who is not sensible of his ignorance in it; this immediately suggests, and strongly shews the credibility, that the moral world and government of it may be so too. Indeed the natural and moral constitution and government of the world are so connected, as to make up together but one scheme: and it is highly probable, that the first is formed and carried on merely in subserviency to the latter; as the vegetable world is for the animal, and organized bodies for minds. But the thing intended here is, without inquiring how far the administration of the natural world is subordinate to that of the moral, only to observe the credibility, that one should be analogous or similar to the other: that therefore every act of Divine justice and goodness may be supposed to look much beyond itself, and its immediate object; may have some reference to other parts of God's moral administration, and to a general moral plan; and that every circumstance of this His moral government may be adjusted beforehand with a view to the whole of it. Thus for example: the determined length of time, and the degrees and ways, in which virtue is to remain in a state of warfare and

and their consequences.

(*b*) This scheme is incomprehensible.

Whether natural government is or is not subservient to moral government, the two are analogous.

Example.

(1) Under natural government, ends are brought about by the use of means, often seemingly undesirable.

[6.] First, As in the scheme of the natural world, no ends appear to be accomplished without means; so we find that means very undesirable, often conduce to bring about ends in such a measure desirable, as greatly to overbalance the disagreeableness of the means. And in cases where such means are conducive to such ends, it is not reason, but experience, which shews us, that they are thus conducive. Experience also shews many means to be conducive and necessary to accomplish ends, which means, before experience, we should have thought, would have had even a contrary tendency. Now from these observations relating to the natural scheme of the world, the moral being supposed analogous to it, arises a great credibility, that the putting our misery in each other's power to the degree it is, and making men liable to vice to the degree we are; and in general, that those things which are objected against the moral scheme of Providence, may be, upon the whole, friendly and assistant to virtue, and productive of an overbalance of happiness: *i.e.* the things objected against may be means, by which an overbalance of good will, in the end, be found produced. And from the same observations, it appears to be no presumption against this, that we do not, if indeed we do not, see those means to have any such tendency; or that they seem to us to have a contrary one. Thus those things, which we call irregularities, may not be so at all: because they may be means of accomplishing wise and good ends more considerable. And it may be added, as above,[5] that they may also be the only means, by which these wise and good ends are capable of being accomplished.

So virtue may be promoted by

(*a*) our power over each other's happiness, (*b*) our liability to err.

Nevertheless, although happiness and virtue may be promoted by

(*a*) the *permission*,

[7.] After these observations it may be proper to add, in order to obviate an absurd and wicked conclusion[6] from any of them, that though the constitution of our nature, from whence we are capable of vice and misery, may, as it undoubtedly does, contribute to the perfection and happiness of the world; and though the actual permission of evil may

[5] P. 123.

[6] [Butler, no doubt, had in his mind writers of the school of Mandeville, whose famous thesis that "private vices are public benefits" had excited a great deal of angry controversy a few years before. FitzGerald quotes a remarkable passage from a later writer, Jonathan Edwards, who attempted to give a religious colouring to the doctrine that there is nothing evil, in respect of the whole, but only in respect of partial views of it. Cp. *Rom.* iii. 8.]

be beneficial to it: (*i.e.* it would have been more mischievous, not that a wicked person had himself abstained from his own wickedness, but that any one had forcibly prevented it, than that it was permitted:)[7] yet notwithstanding, it might have been much better for the world, if this very evil had never been done. Nay it is most clearly conceivable, that the very commission of wickedness may be beneficial to the world, and yet, that it would be infinitely more beneficial for men to refrain from it. For thus, in the wise and good constitution of the natural world, there are disorders which bring their own cures; diseases, which are themselves remedies. Many a man would have died, had it not been for the gout or a fever; yet it would be thought madness to assert, that sickness is a better or more perfect state than health; though the like, with regard to the moral world, has been asserted. But,

and even, by (β) the *commission* of evil, it does not follow that evil is better than good.

Illustration.

[8.] Secondly, The natural government of the world is carried on by general laws. For this there may be wise and good reasons: the wisest and best, for ought we know to the contrary. And that there are such reasons, is suggested to our thoughts by the analogy of Nature: by our being made to experience good ends to be accomplished, as indeed all the good which we enjoy is accomplished, by this means, that the laws, by which the world is governed, are general. For we have scarce any kind of enjoyments, but what we are, in some way or other, instrumental in procuring ourselves,[8] by acting in a manner which we foresee likely to procure them: now this foresight could not be at all, were not the government of the world carried on by general laws.[9] And though, for ought we know to the contrary, every single case may be, at length, found to have been provided for even by these: yet to prevent all irregularities, or remedy them as they arise, by the wisest and best general laws, may be impossible in the nature of things; as we see it is absolutely impossible in civil government.[10] But then we are ready to think, that, the constitution of Nature remaining as it is, and the course of things being

(2) Natural government is by general laws.

For this there may be good reason, *e.g.* the rewarding of foresight.

Yet it may be impossible that general laws should cover all particular cases.

[7] [This principle may be illustrated by the well-known saying of Archbishop Magee of York, that "England *free* was preferable to England *sober*," if the sobriety was to be enforced by Acts of Parliament. See Life, ii. p. 44, *sqq.*]

[8] [See Part I. ii. 2 above.]

[9] [Cp. Berkeley, who said of the establishment of the Laws of Nature, that "this gives us a sort of foresight which enables us to regulate our actions for the benefit of life" (*Principles*, § 31).]

[10] [See Part I. iii. 15, and the editor's note thereon.]

judgment of our own mind, unless perverted, which we cannot violate without being self-condemned. And they would be certain too, from considerations of interest. For though it were doubtful, what will be the future consequences of virtue and vice; yet it is, however, credible, that they may have those consequences, which Religion teaches us they will: and this credibility is a certain[16] obligation in point of prudence, to abstain from all wickedness, and to live in the conscientious practice of all that is good. But,

(β) from prudence.

(*c*) The analogical argument applied above to God's moral government as imperfectly comprehended,

[12.] Thirdly, The answers above given to the objections against religion cannot equally be made use of to invalidate the proof of it. For, upon supposition that God exercises a moral government over the world, analogy does most strongly lead us to conclude, that this moral government must be a scheme, or constitution, beyond our comprehension. And a thousand particular analogies shew us, that parts of such a scheme, from their relation to other parts, may conduce to accomplish ends, which we should have thought they had no tendency at all to accomplish: nay ends, which, before experience, we should have thought such parts were contradictory to, and had a tendency to prevent. And therefore all these analogies shew, that the way of arguing made use of in objecting against Religion is delusive: because they shew it is not at all incredible, that, could we comprehend the whole, we should find the permission of the disorders objected against to be consistent with justice and goodness; and even to be instances of them. Now this is not applicable to the proof of Religion, as it is to the objections against it;[17] and therefore cannot invalidate that proof, as it does these objections.

cannot be turned against the proof of it.

(*d*) This answer to objections is not based on ignorance *simpliciter*, but on the fact that our ignorance makes us incompetent judges.

[13.] Lastly, From the observation now made, it is easy to see, that the answers above given to the objections against Providence, though, in a general way of speaking, they may be said to be taken from our ignorance; yet are by no means taken merely from that, but from somewhat which analogy shews us concerning it.[18] For analogy shews us positively, that our ignorance in the possibilities of things, and the various relations in Nature, renders us incompetent judges, and leads us to false conclusions, in cases similar to this, in which we pre-

[16] P. 3; and Part II. vi. 3. [See Note A at end of Introduction.]

[17] Serm. XV. § 6 ff. [See also above, Introd. § 12.]

[18] [Cp. Part II. Concl. § 2 below.]

tend to judge and to object. So that the things above insisted upon are not mere suppositions of unknown impossibilities and relations: but they are suggested to our thoughts, and even forced upon the observation of serious men, and rendered credible too, by the analogy of Nature. And therefore, to take these things into the account, is to judge by experience, and what we do know: and it is not judging so, to take no notice of them.

CONCLUSION.

The present world part of a larger whole,

[1.] THE observations of the last chapter lead us to consider this little scene of human life, in which we are so busily engaged, as having a reference, of some sort or other, to a much larger plan of things. Whether we are, any way, related to the more distant parts of the boundless universe, into which we are brought, is altogether uncertain. But it is evident, that the course of things, which comes within our view, is connected with somewhat, past, present, and future, beyond it.[1] So that we are placed, as one may speak, in the middle of a scheme, not a fixed but a progressive one, every way incomprehensible: incomprehensible, in a manner equally, with respect to what has been, what now is, and what shall be hereafter. And this scheme cannot but contain in it somewhat as wonderful, and as much beyond our thought and conception,[2] as anything in that of Religion. For, will any man in his senses say, that it is less difficult to conceive, how the world came to be and to continue as it is, without, than with, an intelligent Author and Governor of it? or, admitting an intelligent Governor of it, that there is some other rule of government more natural, and of easier conception, than that which we call moral? Indeed, without an intelligent Author and Governor of Nature, no account at all can be given, how this universe, or the part of it particularly in which we are concerned, came to be, and the course of it to be carried on, as it is: nor any, of its general end and design, without a moral Governor of it. That there is an intelligent Author of Nature, and natural Governor of the world, is a principle gone upon in the foregoing treatise; as proved, and generally known and confessed to be proved.

and therefore beyond our comprehension.

An Intelligent and Moral Governor a rational postulate.

[1] Part I. vii. 3. [Cp. Serm. xv. § 15, note.]

[2] See Part II. ii. 4.

And the very notion of an intelligent Author of Nature, proved by particular final causes, implies a will and a character.[3] Now, as our whole nature, the nature which He has given us, leads us to conclude His will and character to be moral, just, and good: so we can scarce in imagination conceive, what it can be otherwise. However, in consequence of this His will and character, whatever it be, He formed the universe as it is, and carries on the course of it as He does, rather than in any other manner; and has assigned to us, and to all living creatures, a part and a lot in it. Irrational creatures act this their part, and enjoy and undergo the pleasures and the pains allotted them, without any reflection. But one would think it impossible, that creatures endued with reason could avoid reflecting sometimes upon all this; reflecting, if not from whence we came, yet, at least, whither we are going; and what the mysterious scheme, in the midst of which we find ourselves, will, at length, come out and produce: a scheme in which it is certain we are highly interested, and in which we may be interested even beyond conception. For many things prove it palpably absurd to conclude, that we shall cease to be, at death. Particular analogies do most sensibly shew us, that there is nothing to be thought strange, in our being to exist in another state of life. And that we are now living beings, affords a strong probability that we shall *continue* so; unless there be some positive ground, and there is none from reason or analogy, to think death will destroy us. Were a persuasion of this kind ever so well grounded, there would, surely, be little reason to take pleasure in it. But indeed it can have no other ground, than some such imagination, as that of our gross bodies being ourselves; which is contrary to experience. Experience too most clearly shews us the folly of concluding, from the body and the living agent affecting each other mutually, that the dissolution of the former is the destruction of the latter. And there are remarkable instances of their not affecting each other, which lead us to a contrary conclusion. The supposition then, which in all reason we are to go upon, is, that our living nature will *continue* after death. And it is infinitely unreasonable to form an institution of

This implies a Divine character of goodness.

So wondrous a scheme demands attention.

Summary. Chap. i.

§ 2. § 3. § 4. § 5. § 8. § 18. § 24.

[3] Part I. vi. 8.

Chap. ii. life, or to act upon any other supposition. Now all expecta-
§ 1. tion of immortality, whether more or less certain, opens an
unbounded prospect to our hopes and our fears: since we
see the constitution of Nature is such, as to admit of misery,
as well as to be productive of happiness, and experience
ourselves to partake of both in some degree; and since we
cannot but know, what higher degrees of both we are capable
§ 2. of. And there is no presumption against believing further,
that our future interest depends upon our present behaviour:
§ 10. for we see our present interest doth; and that the happiness
and misery, which are naturally annexed to our actions, very
frequently do not follow, till long after the actions are done,
Chap. iii. to which they are respectively annexed. So that were specu-
lation to leave us uncertain, whether it were likely, that the
Author of Nature, in giving happiness and misery to His
creatures, hath regard to their actions or not: yet, since we
find by experience that He hath such regard, the whole sense
of things which He has given us, plainly leads us, at once and
§ 6 without any elaborate inquiries, to think, that it may, indeed
must, be to good actions chiefly that He hath annexed happi-
ness, and to bad actions misery; or that He will, upon the
whole, reward those who do well, and punish those who do
evil. To confirm this from the constitution of the world, it
§ 7. has been observed, that some sort of moral government is
necessarily implied in that natural government of God, which
we experience ourselves under: that good and bad actions,
§ 8. at present, are naturally rewarded and punished, not only
as beneficial and mischievous to society, but also as virtuous
§ 10. and vicious: and that there is, in the very nature of the thing,
§ 17. a tendency to their being rewarded and punished in a much
§ 20. higher degree than they are at present. And though this
higher degree of distributive justice, which Nature thus points
out and leads towards, is prevented for a time from taking
place; it is by obstacles, which the state of this world un-
happily throws in its way, and which therefore are in their
nature temporary. Now, as these things in the natural
conduct of Providence are observable on the side of virtue;
§ 22. so there is nothing to be set against them on the side of
vice. A moral scheme of government then is visibly estab-
lished, and, in some degree, carried into execution: and this,
together with the essential tendencies of virtue and vice duly

considered, naturally raise in us an apprehension, that it will § 27.
be carried on further towards perfection in a future state, and that every one shall there receive according to his deserts. And if this be so, then our future and general interest, under Chap. iv.
the moral government of God, is appointed to depend upon § 1.
our behaviour; notwithstanding the difficulty, which this may occasion, of securing it, and the danger of losing it: just in § 2.
the same manner as our temporal interest, under His natural government, is appointed to depend upon our behaviour; notwithstanding the like difficulty and danger. For, from our original constitution, and that of the world which we inhabit, we are naturally trusted with ourselves; with our own conduct and our own interest. And from the same § 7.
constitution of Nature, especially joined with that course of things which is owing to men, we have temptations to be unfaithful in this trust; to forfeit this interest, to neglect it and run ourselves into misery and ruin. From these temp- § 8.
tations arise the difficulties of behaving so as to secure our temporal interest, and the hazard of behaving so as to miscarry in it. There is therefore nothing incredible in supposing § 9.
there may be the like difficulty and hazard with regard to that chief and final good, which Religion lays before us. Indeed the whole account, how it came to pass that we were Chap. v.
placed in such a condition as this, must be beyond our § 1.
comprehension. But it is in part accounted for by what Religion teaches us, that the character of virtue and piety § 2.
must be a necessary qualification for a future state of security and happiness, under the moral government of God; in like manner, as some certain qualifications or other are necessary for every particular condition of life, under His natural government: and that the present state was intended to be a school § 3.
of discipline, for improving in ourselves that character. Now this intention of Nature is rendered highly credible by observing; that we are plainly made for improvement of all § 4.
kinds: that it is a general appointment of Providence, that we cultivate practical principles, and form within ourselves habits of action, in order to become fit for what we were wholly unfit for before: that in particular, childhood and § 7.
youth is naturally appointed to be a state of discipline for mature age: and that the present world is peculiarly fitted § 16.
for a state of moral discipline. And, whereas objections are Chap. vi.

urged against the whole notion of moral government and a probation state, from the opinion of necessity: it has been shewn, that God has given us the evidence, as it were, of experience, that all objections against Religion, on this head, are vain and delusive. He has also, in His natural government, suggested an answer to all our shortsighted objections, against the equity and goodness of His moral government; and in general He has exemplified to us the latter by the former.

Chap. vii.

These facts demand attention.

[2.] These things, which, it is to be remembered, are matters of fact, ought, in all common sense, to awaken mankind; to induce them to consider in earnest their condition, and what they have to do. It is absurd, absurd to the degree of being ridiculous, if the subject were not of so serious a kind, for men to think themselves secure in a vicious life; or even in that immoral thoughtlessness, which far the greatest part of them are fallen into. And the credibility of Religion, arising from experience and facts here considered, is fully sufficient, in reason, to engage them to live in the general practice of all virtue and piety; under the serious apprehension, though it should be mixed with some doubt,[4] of a righteous administration established in Nature, and a future judgment in consequence of it: especially when we consider, how very questionable it is, whether anything at all can be gained by vice;[5] how unquestionably little, as well as precarious, the pleasures and profits of it are at the best; and how soon they must be parted with at the longest. For, in the deliberations of reason, concerning what we are to pursue and what to avoid, as temptations to anything from mere passion are supposed out of the case: so inducements to vice, from cool expectations of pleasure and interest so small and uncertain and short, are really so insignificant, as, in the view of reason, to be almost nothing in themselves; and in comparison with the importance of Religion, they quite disappear and are lost. Mere passion indeed may be alleged, though not as a reason, yet as an excuse, for a vicious course of life. And how sorry an excuse it is, will be manifest by observing, that we are placed in a condition, in which we are unavoidably inured to govern our passions, by being necessitated to govern them:

Vice not secure.

The credibility of God's moral government makes virtue the prudent part,

and is sufficient to control passion,

especially as nature requires such control of us.

[4] Part II. ch. vi.

[5] Part I. iii. 5.

and to lay ourselves under the same kind of restraints, and as great ones too, from temporal regards, as virtue and piety, in the ordinary course of things, require. The plea of ungovernable passion then, on the side of vice, is the poorest of all things; for it is no reason, and but a poor excuse. But the proper motives to Religion are the proper proofs of it, from our moral nature, from the presages of conscience, and our natural apprehension of God under the character of a righteous Governor and Judge; a nature and conscience and apprehension given us by Him; and from the confirmation of the dictates of reason, by "life and immortality brought to light by the Gospel; and the wrath of God revealed from Heaven against all ungodliness and unrighteousness of men." [6]

The proper motives to Religion.

[6] [2 *Tim.* i. 10; *Rom.* i. 18.]

THE ANALOGY OF RELIGION

TO THE

CONSTITUTION AND COURSE OF NATURE.

PART II.

OF REVEALED RELIGION.

CHAPTER I.

Of the Importance of Christianity.

[1.] SOME persons, upon pretence of the sufficiency of the light of Nature, avowedly reject all revelation, as, in its very notion, incredible, and what must be fictitious.[1] And indeed it is certain, no revelation would have been given, had the light of Nature been sufficient in such a sense, as to render one not wanting and useless. But no man, in seriousness and simplicity of mind, can possibly think it so, who considers the state of Religion in the heathen world before revelation, and a
its present state in those places which have borrowed no light b
from it: particularly the doubtfulness of some of the greatest c
men, concerning things of the utmost importance, as well as the natural inattention and ignorance of mankind in general. d

Some reject revelation as incredible in itself. But, if possible, it is not superfluous.

[1] [The writers whom Butler had in view are generally known as the English Deists. Lord Herbert of Cherbury (1581-1648) may be counted the founder of the school; but its two most influential members were John Toland (1670-1722), the title of whose work, *Christianity not mysterious*, sufficiently explains itself, and Matthew Tindal (1656-1733). It is against the work of the last-named writer, *Christianity as old as the Creation* (1730), that Butler seems especially to have directed his *Analogy*. Tindal maintained that the light of natural reason was a sufficient guide to man, and that the light of revelation was but an *ignis fatuus*, whose leading was hard to discern and always to

II. as a revelation.

to promote natural piety and virtue: and secondly, as containing an account of a dispensation of things not discoverable by reason, in consequence of which, several distinct precepts are enjoined us.[6] For though natural Religion is the foundation and principal part of Christianity, it is not in any sense the whole of it.

I. It is a republication of the truths of Natural Religion,

[5.] I. Christianity is a republication of natural Religion. It instructs mankind in the moral system of the world: that it is the work of an infinitely perfect Being, and under His government; that virtue is His law; and that He will finally judge mankind in righteousness, and render to all according to their works, in a future state. And, which is very material, it teaches natural Religion in its genuine simplicity; free from those superstitions, with which it was totally corrupted, and under which it was in a manner lost.

in their (1) *simplicity*;

(2) an *authoritative* republication, for it has the authority of miracle and prophecy,

[6.] Revelation is further, an authoritative publication of natural Religion, and so affords the evidence of testimony for the truth of it. Indeed the miracles and prophecies recorded in Scripture, were intended to prove a particular dispensation of Providence, the redemption of the world by the Messiah: but this does not hinder, but that they may also prove God's general providence over the world, as our moral Governor and Judge. And they evidently do prove
α it; because this character of the Author of Nature, is necessarily connected with and implied in that particular
β revealed dispensation of things: it is likewise continually taught expressly, and insisted upon, by those persons who wrought the miracles and delivered the prophecies. So that indeed natural Religion seems as much proved by the Scripture revelation, as it would have been, had the design of revelation been nothing else than to prove it.

which give additional credibility to any teaching.

[7.] But it may possibly be disputed, how far miracles can prove natural Religion; and notable objections may be urged against this proof of it, considered as a matter of speculation: but considered as a practical thing, there can be none.[7] For

[6] [Cp. Part II. vii. 29.]

[7] [Two questions as to the evidential value of miracle seem necessary to distinguish. (1) How far, as a matter of *logic*, does the power of working miracles in itself establish the claim of the miracle worker that his teaching is Divine? To this the answer must be that miracles, regarded merely as τέρατα, as wonderful tokens of power, do *not* establish the goodness or truthfulness of the agent who works them. They might, for example, be of Satanic origin (cp. *2 Thess.* ii. 9). What is superhuman is not *necessarily* Divine.

suppose a person to teach natural Religion to a nation, who had lived in total ignorance or forgetfulness of it; and to declare He was commissioned by God so to do: suppose Him, in proof of His commission, to foretell things future, which no human foresight would have guessed at; to divide the sea with a word; feed great multitudes with bread from heaven; cure all manner of diseases; and raise the dead, even Himself, to life: would not this give additional credibility to His teaching, a credibility beyond what that of a common man would have; and be an authoritative publication of the law of Nature, *i.e.* a new proof of it? It would be a practical one, of the strongest kind, perhaps, which human creatures are capable of having given them. The Law of Moses then, and the Gospel of Christ, are authoritative publications of the religion of Nature; they afford a proof of God's general providence, as moral Governor of the world, as well as of His particular dispensations of providence towards sinful creatures, revealed in the Law and the Gospel. As they are the only evidence of the latter, so they are an additional evidence of the former.

Hence both Law and Gospel are authoritative republications of Natural Religion.

[8.] To shew this further, let us suppose a man of the greatest and most improved capacity, who had never heard of revelation, convinced upon the whole, notwithstanding the disorders of the world, that it was under the direction and moral government of an infinitely perfect Being; but ready to question, whether he were not got beyond the reach of his faculties: suppose him brought, by this suspicion, into great danger of being carried away by the universal bad example of

The value of revelation, in this regard, shewn by an example.

Thus Matthew Arnold asked what possible evidence of authority as a teacher would be shewn by a man's turning a pen into a pen-wiper before our eyes. And truly the answer is, None whatever! We must remember the principle, *miracula sine doctrina nihil valent*. We must examine the context of the miracle. If the doctrine which it accompanies commend itself to the conscience as good, then, and only then, the miracle seals it as Divine. But Butler declines to enter into any such fine drawn speculation. The difficulty indeed does not present itself in the case of Christianity, whose doctrines are admittedly *good* and morally beneficial. And Butler rather asks, (2) How far, as a matter of *fact*, did the power of working miracle which Christ exhibited confirm the doctrines which He taught? And to this the answer of Nicodemus, "We know that Thou art a teacher come from God, for no man can do these signs that Thou doest except God be with him" (*St. John* iii. 2), is an answer which will always be accepted as valid by the majority of mankind. So Pearson writes (without any qualification) of the spectators of the miracles of Moses, "They which saw in his hand God's omnipotency, could not suspect in his tongue God's veracity" (*On the Creed*, Art. I, § 12). Butler returns to the subject again, Part II. vii. 10. See further, Hastings' *Bible Dictionary*, s.v. 'Miracle' (iii. 2, 3).]

Objections: (*a*) abuses of Christianity; (*b*) its slight influence on conduct.

[12.] The objections against all this, from the perversion of Christianity, and from the supposition of its having had but little good influence, however innocently they may be proposed, yet cannot be insisted upon as conclusive, upon any principles, but such as lead to downright Atheism: because the manifestation of the law of Nature by reason, which, upon all principles of Theism, must have been from God, has been perverted and rendered ineffectual in the same manner. It may indeed, I think, truly be said, that the good effects of Christianity have not been small; nor its supposed ill effects, any effects at all of it, properly speaking. Perhaps too the things themselves done have been aggravated; and if not, Christianity hath been often only a pretence; and the same evils in the main would have been done upon some other pretence. However, great and shocking as the corruptions and abuses of it have really been, they cannot be insisted upon as arguments against it, upon principles of Theism. For one cannot proceed one step in reasoning upon natural Religion, any more than upon Christianity, without laying it down as a first principle, that the dispensations of Providence are not to be judged of by their perversions, but by their genuine tendencies: not by what they do actually seem to effect, but by what they would effect if mankind did their part; that part which is justly put and left upon them. It is altogether as much the language of one as of the other; "He that is unjust, let him be unjust still: and he that is holy, let him be holy still."[11] The light of reason does not, any more than that of revelation, force men to submit to its authority; both admonish them of what they ought to do and avoid, together with the consequences of each; and after this, leave them at full liberty to act just as they please, till the appointed time of judgment. Every moment's experience shews, that this is God's general rule of government.

Answer to (*b*): The good effects have not been small.

Answer to (*a*): (α) the abuses exaggerated; (β) not due to Christianity;

(γ) we must not judge a system from its perversions, but from its tendencies.

Neither Reason nor Revelation force man's obedience.

[13.] To return then: Christianity being a promulgation of the law of Nature; being moreover an authoritative promulgation of it; with new light, and other circumstances of peculiar advantage, adapted to the wants of mankind; these things fully shew its importance. And it is to be observed further, that as the nature of the case requires, so all Christians

(5) It is the very scheme of the Gospel that each

[11] *Rev.* xxii. 11.

are commanded to contribute, by their profession of Christianity, to preserve it in the world, and render it such a promulgation and enforcement of Religion. For it is the very scheme of the Gospel, that each Christian should, in his degree, contribute towards continuing and carrying it on: all by uniting in the public profession and external practice of Christianity; some by instructing, by having the oversight and taking care of this religious community, the Church of God. Now this further shews the importance of Christianity; and, which is what I chiefly intend, its importance in a practical sense: or the high obligations we are under, to take it into our most serious consideration; and the danger there must necessarily be, not only in treating it despitefully, which I am not now speaking of, but in disregarding and neglecting it. For this is neglecting to do what is expressly enjoined us, for continuing those benefits to the world, and transmitting them down to future times. And all this holds, even though the only thing to be considered in Christianity, were its subserviency to natural Religion. But,

Christian should propagate its moral teaching.

[14.] II. Christianity is to be considered in a further view; as containing an account of a dispensation of things, not at all discoverable by reason, in consequence of which several distinct precepts are enjoined us. Christianity is not only an external institution of natural Religion, and a new promulgation of God's general providence, as righteous Governor and Judge of the world; but it contains also a revelation of a particular dispensation of Providence, carrying on by His Son and Spirit, for the recovery and salvation of mankind, who are represented in Scripture to be in a state of ruin. And in consequence of this revelation being made, we are commanded to be baptized, not only "in the name of the Father," but also, "of the Son, and of the Holy Ghost:"[12] and other obligations of duty, unknown before, to the Son and the Holy Ghost, are revealed. Now the importance of these duties may be judged of, by observing that they arise, not from positive command merely, but also from the offices, which appear, from Scripture, to belong to those Divine persons in the Gospel dispensation; or from the relations, which, we are there informed, they stand in to us. By reason

II. It is a revelation of new truths.

[12] [*St. Matt.* xxviii. 19.]

together positive and moral duties, the Scripture always puts the stress of Religion upon the latter, and never upon the former: which, though no sort of allowance to neglect the former, when they do not interfere with the latter, yet is a plain intimation, that when they do, the latter are to be preferred. And further, as mankind are for placing the stress of their Religion anywhere, rather than upon virtue; lest both the reason of the thing, and the general spirit of Christianity, appearing in the intimation now mentioned, should be ineffectual against this prevalent folly: our Lord Himself, from Whose command alone the obligation of positive institutions arises, has taken occasion to make the comparison between them and moral precepts; when the Pharisees censured Him, for "eating with publicans and sinners";[18] and also when they censured His disciples, for "plucking the ears of corn on the Sabbath-day."[19] Upon this comparison, He has determined expressly, and in form, which shall have the preference when they interfere. And by delivering His authoritative determination in a proverbial manner of expression, He has made it general: "I will have mercy, and not sacrifice."[20] The propriety of the word *proverbial* is not the thing insisted upon: though I think the manner of speaking is to be called so. But that the manner of speaking very remarkably renders the determination general, is surely indisputable. For, had it, in the latter case, been said only, that God preferred mercy

(γ) the words of Christ.

This was a general statement.

a to the rigid observance of the Sabbath; even then, by parity of reason, most justly might we have argued, that He preferred mercy likewise, to the observance of other ritual institutions; and in general, moral duties, to positive ones. And thus the determination would have been general; though its being so were inferred and not expressed. But as the passage really

b stands in the Gospel, it is much stronger. For the sense and the very literal words of our Lord's answer are as applicable to any other instance of a comparison, between positive and moral duties, as to this upon which they were spoken. And if, in case of competition, mercy is to be preferred to positive institutions, it will scarce be thought, that justice is to give place to them. It is remarkable too, that, as the words are a quotation from the Old Testament, they are introduced, on

18 [*St. Mark* ii. 16.]
19 [*St. Luke* vi. 1.]
20 *St. Matt.* ix. 13 and xii. 7.

both the forementioned occasions, with a declaration, that the Pharisees did not understand the meaning of them. This, c I say, is very remarkable. For, since it is scarce possible, for the most ignorant person, not to understand the literal α sense of the passage, in the Prophet;[21] and since understanding the literal sense would not have prevented their β "condemning the guiltless;"[22] it can hardly be doubted, that the thing which our Lord really intended in that declaration was, that the Pharisees had not learnt from it, as they might, wherein the *general* spirit of Religion consists: that it consists in moral piety and virtue, as distinguished from forms, and ritual observances. However, it is certain we may learn this from His Divine application of the passage, in the Gospel.

Yet we must not forget that positive precepts of God carry a moral obligation.

[27.] But, as it is one of the peculiar weaknesses of human nature, when, upon a comparison of two things, one is found to be of greater importance than the other, to consider this other as of scarce any importance at all: it is highly necessary that we remind ourselves, how great presumption it is, to make light of any institutions of Divine appointment; that our obligations to obey all God's commands whatever are absolute and indispensable; and that commands merely positive, admitted to be from Him, lay us under a moral obligation to obey them: an obligation moral in the strictest and most proper sense.

We must expect to find *new* truths in revelation.

[28.] To these things I cannot forbear adding, that the account now given of Christianity most strongly shews and enforces upon us the obligation of searching the Scriptures, in order to see, what the scheme of revelation really is; instead of determining beforehand, from reason, what the scheme of it must be.[23] Indeed if in revelation there be found any

[21] *Hosea* vi. 6.

[22] See *St. Matt.* xii. 7.

[23] See chap. iii. [§§ 1, 13. This is an observation of the highest importance. No study of Scripture can be profitable which is undertaken without the expectation that we shall receive from it more than we bring to it. "What is the meaning of a Revelation," asked Lessing, "which reveals *nothing*?" If Scripture be the record of a revelation, we rightly expect that it shall teach us some things which we could not discover without its aid. The "determining beforehand" what "the scheme" of revelation must be is a fruitful source of theological controversy, but such *a priori* methods are of little service to the seeker after truth.

One presupposition, however, we are entitled to make, viz. that no alleged dictum of revelation can outweigh the plain and unmistakable laws of reason or of conscience. We cannot believe a contradiction, no matter what we wish, for reason will not permit us. And again, we cannot allow the elementary dictates

passages, the seeming meaning of which is contrary to natural Religion; we may most certainly conclude, such seeming meaning not to be the real one. But it is not any degree of a presumption against an interpretation of Scripture, that such interpretation contains a doctrine, which the light of Nature cannot discover;[24] or a precept, which the law of Nature does not oblige to.

of conscience to be overruled by any precept, whether found in Scripture or elsewhere, without poisoning the springs of our moral life. Man's conscience is as much the gift of God as Holy Scripture itself. It needs correction and education; it may be depraved. And so we are not to assume all at once, in case of a conflict between the individual conscience and the apparent teaching of Scripture, that conscience is right and Scripture wrong. But, all necessary pains having been taken before forming our judgment, it remains true that "Reason can, and it ought, to judge, not only of the meaning, but also of the morality of revelation" (chap. iii. § 13)].

[24] Part II. ii. 3, 4.

CHAPTER II.

Of the supposed Presumption against a Revelation, considered as miraculous.

Is there a presumption against revelation in general?

[1.] HAVING shewn the importance of the Christian revelation, and the obligations which we are under seriously to attend to it, upon supposition of its truth, or its credibility: the next thing in order, is to consider the supposed presumptions against revelation in general; which shall be the subject of this chapter: and the objections against the Christian in particular; which shall be the subject of some following ones.[1] For it seems the most natural method, to remove the prejudices against Christianity, before we proceed to the consideration of the positive evidence for it, and the objections against that evidence.[2]

Is more evidence needed for miracles than for ordinary events?

[2.] It is, I think, commonly supposed, that there is some peculiar presumption, from the analogy of Nature, against the Christian scheme of things; at least against miracles; so as that stronger evidence is necessary to prove the truth and reality of them, than would be sufficient to convince us of other events, or matters of fact. Indeed the consideration of this supposed presumption cannot but be thought very insignificant, by many persons. Yet, as it belongs to the subject of this treatise; so it may tend to open the mind, and remove some prejudices: however needless the consideration of it be, upon its own account.

I. No presumption, from analogy, against the general Christian scheme;

[3.] I. I find no appearance of a presumption, from the analogy of Nature, against the general scheme of Christianity, that God created and invisibly governs the world by Jesus Christ; and by Him also will hereafter judge it in righteousness, *i.e.* render to every one according to his works; and

[1] Chaps. iii., iv., v., vi. [2] Chap. vii.

that good men are under the secret influence of His Spirit. Whether these things are, or are not, to be called miraculous, is, perhaps, only a question about words; or however, is of no moment in the case. If the analogy of Nature raises any presumption against this general scheme of Christianity,
(1) it must be, either because it is not discoverable by reason
(2) or experience; or else, because it is unlike that course of Nature, which is. But analogy raises no presumption against the truth of this scheme, upon either of these accounts.

for (1) although undiscoverable by reason or experience, we only know a small part of a vast whole;

[4.] First, There is no presumption, from analogy, against the truth of it, upon account of its not being discoverable by reason or experience. For suppose one who never heard of revelation, of the most improved understanding, and acquainted with our whole system of natural philosophy and natural religion: such an one could not but be sensible, that it was but a very small part of the natural and moral system of the universe, which he was acquainted with. He could not but be sensible, that there must be innumerable things, in the dispensations of Providence past, in the invisible government over the world at present carrying on, and in what is to come; of which he was wholly ignorant,[3] and which could not be discovered without revelation. Whether the scheme of Nature be, in the strictest sense, infinite or not; it is evidently vast, even beyond all possible imagination.[4] And doubtless that part of it, which is opened to our view, is but as a point, in comparison of the whole plan of Providence, reaching throughout eternity past and future; in comparison of what is even now going on in the remote parts of the boundless universe; nay in comparison of the whole scheme of this world. And therefore, that things lie beyond the natural reach of our faculties, is no sort of presumption against the truth and reality of them: because it is certain, there are innumerable things, in the constitution and government of the universe, which are thus beyond the natural reach of our faculties.

(2) even if it be unlike the known course of nature,

(*a*) the unknown may not

Secondly, Analogy raises no presumption against any of the things contained in this general doctrine of Scripture now mentioned, upon account of their being unlike the known course of Nature. For there is no presumption at all from analogy, that the *whole* course of things, or Divine

[3] Part I. vii. 3.

[4] [Cp. Part I. i. 23.]

government, naturally unknown to us, and *everything* in it, is like to anything in that which is known;[5] and therefore no peculiar presumption against anything in the former, upon account of its being unlike to anything in the latter. And in the constitution and natural government of the world, as well as in the moral government of it, we see things, in a great degree, unlike one another: and therefore ought not to wonder at such unlikeness between things visible and invisible. However, the scheme of Christianity is by no means entirely unlike the scheme of Nature; as will appear in the following part of this treatise.

everywhere resemble the known;

(*b*) we observe unlikeness sometimes in nature;

(*c*) the alleged unlikeness is not complete.

[5.] The notion of a miracle, considered as a proof of a Divine mission, has been stated with great exactness by divines; and is, I think, sufficiently understood by every one. There are also invisible miracles, the Incarnation of Christ, for instance, which, being secret, cannot be alleged as a proof of such a mission; but require themselves to be proved by visible miracles. Revelation itself too is miraculous; and miracles are the proof of it; and the supposed presumption against these shall presently be considered. All which I have been observing here is, that, whether we choose to call everything in the dispensations of Providence, not discoverable without revelation, nor like the known course of things, miraculous; and whether the general Christian dispensation now mentioned is to be called so, or not; the foregoing observations seem certainly to shew, that there is no presumption against it from the analogy of Nature.

Thus no presumption lies against the general Christian scheme, whether we call it miraculous or no.

[6.] II. There is no presumption, from analogy, against some operations, which we should now call miraculous; particularly

II. No presumption against a

[5] [That is to say, it is only safe to apply the argument from analogy *negatively*—to answer objections. It is not legitimate for an objector to say, "Unless you can shew me a natural analogue for this doctrine of religion, I will not accept it." We have no right to assume that natural law holds everywhere in the spiritual world. Indeed, the very ground of the Christian hope is that in certain cases such natural law (*natural*, that is, in the sense of being the law which obtains in this world of space and time in which we find ourselves) does *not* hold in the spiritual region beyond. "Thou fool," says St. Paul, "that which thou sowest is *not* that body which shall be. . . . If there is a *natural* body there is also a *spiritual* body" (*1 Cor.* xv. 36, 44). The true value of the argument from analogy is to answer objections. The sceptic says, "This spiritual principle is incredible." An unanswerable rejoinder is furnished by shewing that just such a principle obtains and is recognised by him in the field of experience. And these are the limits within which the argument is confined by Butler. (Cp. Introd. § 6.)]

primitive revelation, for

(i) *miracle* is relative to a *course* of nature.

none against a revelation at the beginning of the world: nothing of such presumption against it, as is supposed to be implied or expressed in the word *miraculous*. For a miracle, in its very notion, is relative to a course of Nature; and implies somewhat different from it, considered as being so. Now,
a either there was no course of Nature at the time which we
b are speaking of; or if there were, we are not acquainted what the course of Nature is, upon the first peopling of worlds. And therefore the question, whether mankind had a revelation made to them at that time, is to be considered, not as a question concerning a miracle, but as a common question of fact. And we have the like reason, be it more or less, to admit the report of tradition, concerning this question, and concerning common matters of fact of the same antiquity; for instance, what part of the earth was first peopled.

(ii) Revelation may well have followed Creation, which is an admitted fact.

[7.] Or thus: When mankind was first placed in this state, there was a power exerted, totally different from the present course of Nature. Now, whether this power, thus wholly different from the present course of Nature, for we cannot properly apply to it the word *miraculous*; whether this power stopped immediately after it had made man, or went on, and exerted itself further in giving him a revelation, is a question of the same kind, as whether an ordinary power exerted itself in such a particular degree and manner, or not.

(iii) The further miracle no additional difficulty.

[8.] Or suppose the power exerted in the formation of the world be considered as miraculous, or rather, be called by that name; the case will not be different: since it must be acknowledged, that such a power was exerted. For supposing it acknowledged, that our Saviour spent some years in a course of working miracles: there is no more presumption, worth mentioning, against His having exerted this miraculous power, in a certain degree greater, than in a certain degree less; in one or two more instances, than in one or two fewer; in this, than in another manner.[6]

[9.] It is evident then, that there can be no peculiar pre-

[6] [There is no aid to faith in the mere reduction in number of the Gospel miracles. Matthew Arnold compared this modern artifice to the plea that, while it is extravagant to suppose Cinderella's fairy godmother to have actually changed the pumpkin into a coach and six, we may believe that she did change it into a one-horse cab (*God and the Bible*, p. 23). The illustration is flippant, but it precisely illustrates the point which Butler here desires to bring out.]

sumption, from the analogy of Nature, against supposing a revelation, when man was first placed upon the earth.

[10.] Add, that there does not appear the least intimation in history or tradition, that Religion was first reasoned out: but the whole of history and tradition makes for the other side, that it came into the world by revelation. Indeed the state of Religion in the first ages, of which we have any account, seems to suppose and imply, that this was the original of it amongst mankind. And these reflections together, without taking in the peculiar authority of Scripture, amount to real and a very material degree of evidence, that there was a revelation at the beginning of the world. Now this, as it is a confirmation of natural Religion, and therefore mentioned in the former part of this treatise:[7] so likewise it has a tendency to remove any prejudices against a subsequent revelation.

(iv) Tradition declares that Religion was revealed at the first.

[11.] III. But still it may be objected, that there is some peculiar presumption, from analogy, against miracles; particularly against revelation, after the settlement and during the continuance of a course of Nature.

III. No presumption from analogy against miracles in historic times, for

[12.] Now with regard to this supposed presumption, it is to be observed in general, that before we can have ground for raising what can, with any propriety, be called an *argument* from analogy, for or against revelation considered as somewhat miraculous, we must be acquainted with a similar or parallel case. But the history of some other world, seemingly in like circumstances with our own, is no more than a parallel case: and therefore nothing short of this can be so. Yet, could we come at a presumptive proof, for or against a revelation, from being informed, whether such world had one, or not; such a proof, being drawn from one single instance only, must be infinitely precarious. More particularly: First of all; There is a very strong presumption against common speculative truths, and against the most ordinary facts, before the proof of them; which yet is overcome by almost any proof. There is a presumption of millions to one, against the story of Cæsar, or of any other man. For suppose a number of common facts so and so circumstanced, of which one had no kind of proof, should happen to come into one's thoughts; every one would,

(*a*) we have no parallel case of a second fallen world;

(*b*) in particular, (i) there is a presumption against all alleged facts before testimony, none after testimony.

[7] Part I. vi. 13.

without any possible doubt, conclude them to be false. And the like may be said of a single common fact. And from hence it appears, that the question of importance, as to the matter before us, is, concerning the degree of the peculiar presumption supposed against miracles; not whether there be any peculiar presumption at all against them. For, if there be the presumption of millions to one, against the most common facts; what can a small presumption, additional to this, amount to, though it be peculiar? It cannot be estimated, and is as nothing. The only material question is, whether there be any such presumption against miracles, as to render them in any sort incredible.[8] Secondly, If we leave out the consideration of Religion, we are in such total darkness, upon what causes, occasions, reasons, or circumstances, the present course of Nature depends; that there does not appear any improbability for or against supposing, that five or six thousand years may have given scope for causes, occasions, reasons, or circumstances, from whence miraculous interpositions may have arisen. And from this, joined with the foregoing observation, it will follow, that there must be a presumption, beyond all comparison, greater, against the *particular* common facts just now instanced in, than against miracles *in general*; before any evidence of either. But, thirdly, Take in the consideration of Religion, or the moral system of the world, and then we see distinct particular reasons for miracles: to afford mankind instruction additional to that of Nature, and to attest the truth of it. And this gives a real credibility to the supposition, that it might be part of the original plan of things, that there should be miraculous interpositions. Then, lastly, Miracles must not be compared to common natural events; or to events which, though uncommon, are similar to what we daily experience: but to the extraordinary phenomena of Nature. And then the comparison will be between the presumption against miracles, and the presumption against such uncommon appearances, suppose, as comets, and against there being any such powers in Nature as magnetism and electricity, so contrary to the properties of other bodies not endued with these powers. And before any one can determine, whether there be any peculiar presumption

(ii) Reasons for miraculous intervention may have arisen in 5000 years.

(iii) Man's need of supernatural guidance is such a reason.

(iv) Miracles comparable to *extraordinary* events, against which some presumption always lies.

[8] [See Note F on "The Improbability of Miracle" at the end of the chapter.]

against miracles, more than against other extraordinary things; he must consider, what, upon first hearing would be the presumption against the last-mentioned appearances and powers, to a person acquainted only with the daily, monthly, and annual course of Nature respecting this earth, and with those common powers of matter which we every day see.

[13.] Upon all this I conclude; that there certainly is no such presumption against miracles, as to render them in any wise incredible: that on the contrary, our being able to discern reasons for them, gives a positive credibility to the history of them, in cases where those reasons hold: and that it is by no means certain, that there is any peculiar presumption at all, from analogy, even in the lowest degree, against miracles, as distinguished from other extraordinary phenomena: though it is not worth while to perplex the reader with inquiries into the abstract nature of evidence, in order to determine a question, which, without such inquiries, we see[9] is of no importance.

Thus (*a*) Miracles not incredible.

(*b*) In some cases, *a priori* probable.

(*c*) In no case is there a peculiar presumption against them.

NOTE F.

THE IMPROBABILITY OF MIRACLE.

It must be admitted that the reasoning adopted by Butler on this head (§ 12) is not altogether satisfactory. J. S. Mill pointed out very clearly in his *Logic* (vol. ii. p. 173) the confusion of which our author here is guilty. Butler has not distinguished between two different kinds of improbability, which may be called respectively improbability *before* the fact and improbability *after* the fact. The antecedent presumption against any series of occurrences (*e.g.* the story of Julius Cæsar) taking place, which it comes into my head to *imagine* taking place, is immense; but if a credible witness asserts that it *has* taken place, that improbability becomes as nothing. This is the improbability before the fact. In short, that any ordinary event should take place is improbable *before* testimony has been given, but not a whit improbable *after* testimony. But the case of miracles is quite different; the presumption against a miracle is not merely a presumption against a specific event, but against that *kind* of

[9] § 12.

event taking place. And this presumption remains, and must be allowed for, even after testimony has been given. Butler really compares the improbability of miracles (which *remains* after testimony to their occurrence has been given) with the improbability of the truth of a random guess (which *vanishes* after estimony to its accuracy has been brought forward), and this is to compare two things not fairly comparable at all.

The truth is that more and higher evidence is required to substantiate a miracle than is required to substantiate ordinary matters of fact. As the course of nature is generally uniform, there is *some* special improbability attaching to the allegation that an event of the miraculous order has been witnessed. To overcome this special improbability, it is needful (1) to adduce some seemingly adequate reason why the Creator should deviate from that observed course of action which (save in the specific case of alleged miracles) prior experience proves to have been His rule; and (2) that we should have stronger and more unimpeachable direct evidence than that which is required for an ordinary event. (See further, Hastings' *Bible Dictionary*, s.v. 'Miracle,' ii. § 5.)

FitzGerald justly points out that the comparison (later on in § 12) of miracles to the extraordinary phenomena of nature, such as those of electricity and magnetism, etc., is also inadequate. For in the case of these forces, given the same physical antecedents, the same physical consequents will always follow; and the truth of this can be verified by experiment. But it is of the very essence (seemingly) of miracles, as effects produced by the direct intervention of the spiritual in the physical order, that they do *not* thus repeat themselves.

CHAPTER III.

Of our Incapacity of judging, what were to be expected in a Revelation; and the Credibility, from Analogy, that it must contain Things appearing liable to Objections.

[1.] Besides the objections against the evidence for Christianity, many are alleged against the scheme of it; against the whole manner in which it is put and left with the world; as well as against several particular relations in Scripture: objections drawn from the deficiencies of revelation; from things in it appearing to men *foolishness*;[1] from its containing matters of offence, which have led, and it must have been foreseen would lead, into strange enthusiasm and superstition, and be made to serve the purposes of tyranny and wickedness; from its not being universal; and, which is a thing of the same kind, from its evidence not being so convincing and satisfactory as it might have been: for this last is sometimes turned into a positive argument against its truth.[2] It would be tedious, indeed impossible, to enumerate the several particulars comprehended under the objections here referred to; they being so various, according to the different fancies of men. There are persons, who think it a strong objection against the authority of Scripture, that it is not composed by rules of art, agreed upon by critics, for polite and correct writing. And the scorn is inexpressible, with which some of the prophetic parts of Scripture are treated: partly through the rashness of interpreters; but very much also, on account of the hieroglyphical and figurative language, in which they are left us. Some of the principal things of this sort shall be particularly considered in the following chapters. But my design at present is to observe in general, with respect to this whole way of arguing,

Objections:
(i) The mode of the revelation of Christianity,
(ii) its omissions,
(iii) its stumbling' blocks,
(iv) its lack of universal acceptance,

[1] *1 Cor.* i. 28.

[2] See chap. vi.

i.e. objections to the *scheme*, as distinct from objections to the *evidence*, of Christianity are frivolous.

that, upon supposition of a revelation, it is highly credible beforehand, we should be incompetent judges of it to a great degree: and that it would contain many things appearing to us liable to great objections; in case we judge of it otherwise, than by the analogy of Nature. And therefore, though objections against the evidence of Christianity are most seriously to be considered; yet objections against Christianity itself are, in a great measure, frivolous: almost all objections against it, excepting those which are alleged against the particular proofs of its coming from God. I express myself with caution, lest I should be mistaken to vilify reason; which is indeed the only faculty we have wherewith to judge concerning anything, even revelation itself: or be misunderstood to assert, that a supposed revelation cannot be proved false, from internal characters. For, it may contain clear immoralities or contradictions; and either of these would prove it false.[3] Nor will I take upon me to affirm, that nothing else can possibly render any supposed revelation incredible. Yet still the observation above is, I think, true beyond doubt; that objections against Christianity, as distinguished from objections against its evidence, are frivolous. To make out this, is the general design of the present chapter. And with regard to the whole of it, I cannot but particularly wish, that the proofs might be attended to; rather than the assertions cavilled at, upon account of any unacceptable consequences, whether real or supposed, which may be drawn from them. For, after all, that which is true, must be admitted, though it should shew us the shortness of our faculties; and that we are in no wise judges of many things, of which we are apt to think ourselves very competent ones. Nor will this be any objection with reasonable men, at least upon second thought it will not be any objection with such, against the justness of the following observations.

Although reason must judge of its coherence and its morality,

we are incompetent to judge *a priori* of its scheme.

Our incompetence to judge *a priori* of God's natural government

[2.] As God governs the world, and instructs His creatures, according to certain laws or rules, in the known course of Nature, known by reason together with experience: so the Scripture informs us of a scheme of Divine providence, additional to this. It relates, that God has, by revelation, instructed men in things concerning His government, which

[3] [See Part II. i. 28 note above.]

they could not otherwise have known; and reminded them of things, which they might otherwise know; and attested the truth of the whole by miracles. Now if the natural and the revealed dispensation of things are both from God, if they coincide with each other, and together make up one scheme of Providence; our being incompetent judges of one, must render it credible, that we may be incompetent judges also of the other. Since, upon experience, the acknowledged constitution and course of Nature is found to be greatly different from what, before experience, would have been expected; and such as, men fancy, there lie great objections against: this renders it beforehand highly credible, that they may find the revealed dispensation likewise, if they judge of it as they do of the constitution of Nature, very different from expectations formed beforehand; and liable, in appearance, to great objections: objections against the scheme itself, and against the degrees and manners of the miraculous interpositions, by which it was attested and carried on. Thus suppose a prince to govern his dominions in the wisest manner possible, by common known laws; and that upon some exigencies he should suspend these laws; and govern, in several instances, in a different manner: if one of his subjects were not a competent judge beforehand, by what common rules the government should or would be carried on; it could not be expected, that the same person would be a competent judge, in what exigencies, or in what manner, or to what degree, those laws commonly observed would be suspended or deviated from. If he were not a judge of the wisdom of the ordinary administration, there is no reason to think he would be a judge of the wisdom of the extraordinary. If he thought he had objections against the former; doubtless, it is highly supposable, he might think also, that he had objections against the latter. And thus, as we fall into infinite follies and mistakes, whenever we pretend, otherwise than from experience and analogy, to judge of the constitution and course of Nature; it is evidently supposable beforehand, that we should fall into as great, in pretending to judge, in like manner, concerning revelation. Nor is there any more ground to expect that this latter should appear to us clear of objections, than that the former should.

suggests, by analogy, that we are incompetent to judge *a priori* of His revealed dispensation.

Illustration.

Thus, we are as incompetent to judge *a priori* of the mode and measure of inspiration,

[3.] These observations, relating to the whole of Christianity, are applicable to inspiration in particular. As we are in no sort judges beforehand, by what laws or rules, in what degree, or by what means, it were to have been expected, that God would naturally instruct us; so upon supposition of His affording us light and instruction by revelation, additional to what He has afforded us by reason and experience, we are in no sort judges, by what methods, and in what proportion, it were to be expected, that this supernatural light and instruction would be afforded us. We know not beforehand, what degree or kind of natural information, it were to be expected God would afford men, each by his own reason and experience: nor how far He would enable and effectually dispose them to communicate it, whatever it should be, to each other; nor whether the evidence of it would be certain, highly probable, or doubtful; nor whether it would be given with equal clearness and conviction to all. Nor could we guess, upon any good ground I mean, whether natural knowledge, or even the faculty itself, by which we are capable of attaining it, reason, would be given us at once, or gradually. In like manner, we are wholly ignorant, what degree of new knowledge, it were to be expected, God would give mankind by revelation, upon supposition of His affording one: or how far, or in what way, He would interpose miraculously, to qualify them, to whom He should originally make the revelation, for communicating the knowledge given by it; and to secure their doing it to the age in which they should live; and to secure its being transmitted to posterity. We are equally ignorant, whether the evidence of it would be certain, or highly probable, or doubtful:[4] or whether all who should have any degree of instruction from it, and any degree of evidence of its truth, would have the same: or whether the scheme would be revealed at once, or unfolded gradually. Nay we are not in any sort able to judge, whether it were to have been expected, that the revelation should have been committed to writing; or left to be handed down, and consequently corrupted, by verbal tradition, and at length sunk under it, if mankind so pleased, and during such time as they are permitted, in the degree they evidently are, to act as they will.

as of the degree of natural knowledge which we may reach.

So also, as to the degree of evidence for the truth of inspiration.

[4] See chap. vi.

[4.] But it may be said, "that a revelation in some of the above-mentioned circumstances, one, for instance, which was not committed to writing, and thus secured against danger of corruption, would not have answered its purpose." I ask, what purpose? It would not have answered all the purposes, which it has now answered, and in the same degree: but it would have answered others, or the same in different degrees. And which of these were the purposes of God, and best fell in with His general government, we could not at all have determined beforehand.

Objection: "At any rate a revelation must be *written*."

Answer: "Why?"

[5.] Now since it has been shewn, that we have no principles of reason, upon which to judge beforehand, how it were to be expected revelation should have been left, or what was most suitable to the Divine plan of government, in any of the forementioned respects; it must be quite frivolous to object afterwards as to any of them, against its being left in one way, rather than another: for this would be to object against things, upon account of their being different from expectations, which have been shewn to be without reason. And thus we see, that the only question concerning the truth of Christianity is, whether it be a real revelation; not whether it be attended with every circumstance which we should have looked for: and concerning the authority of Scripture, whether it be what it claims to be; not whether it be a book of such sort, and so promulged, as weak men are apt to fancy a book containing a Divine revelation should. And therefore, neither obscurity, nor seeming inaccuracy of style, nor various readings, nor early disputes about the authors of particular parts; nor any other things of the like kind, though they had been much more considerable in degree than they are, could overthrow the authority of the Scripture: unless the Prophets, Apostles, or our Lord, had promised, that the book containing the Divine revelation should be secure from those things. Nor indeed can any objections overthrow such a kind of revelation as the Christian claims to be, since there are no objections against the morality of it,[5] but such as can shew, that there is no proof of miracles wrought originally in attestation of it; no appearance of any thing miraculous in its obtaining in the world; nor any of prophecy, that is, of events foretold, which human

We cannot object to any apparent characteristics of the Christian revelation,

unless it has been promised that such shall not be present.

(Objections which would be fatal to the Christian revelation.)

[5] § 13 below.

sagacity could not foresee. If it can be shewn, that the proof alleged for all these is absolutely none at all, then is revelation overturned. But were it allowed, that the proof of any one or all of them is lower than is allowed; yet, whilst any proof of them remains, revelation will stand upon much the same foot it does at present, as to all the purposes of life and practice, and ought to have the like influence upon our behaviour.

E.g. we cannot assume that the meaning of Scripture always lies on the surface.

[6.] From the foregoing observations too, it will follow, and those who will thoroughly examine into revelation will find it worth remarking; that there are several ways of arguing, which, though just with regard to other writings, are not applicable to Scripture: at least not to the prophetic parts of it. We cannot argue, for instance, that this cannot be the sense or intent of such a passage of Scripture; for, if it had, it would have been expressed more plainly, or have been represented under a more apt figure or hieroglyphic: yet we may justly argue thus, with respect to common books. And the reason of this difference is very evident; that in Scripture we are not competent judges, as we are in common books, how plainly it were to have been expected,[6] what is the true sense should have been expressed, or under how apt an image figured. The only question is, what appearance there is, that this is the sense; and scarce at all, how much more determinately or accurately it might have been expressed or figured.

Internal improbabilities weaken proof: but what *are* improbabilities here?

[7.] "But is it not self-evident, that internal improbabilities of all kinds weaken external probable proof?" Doubtless. But to what practical purpose can this be alleged here, when it has been proved before,[7] that real internal improbabilities, which rise even to moral certainty, are overcome by the most ordinary testimony; and when it now has been made appear, that we scarce know what are improbabilities, as to the matter we are here considering; as it will further appear from what follows.

[8.] For though from the observations above made it is manifest, that we are not in any sort competent judges, what supernatural instruction were to have been expected; and though it is self-evident, that the objections of an incompetent

[6] [See Part II. i. 28 above. There is a wise saying which deserves a wider currency than it has received: Begin by treating Scripture like any other book, and you will end by finding it *unlike* every other.]

[7] Part II. ii. 12.

judgment must be frivolous; yet it may be proper to go one step further, and observe; that if men will be regardless of these things, and pretend to judge of the Scripture by preconceived expectations; the analogy of Nature shews beforehand, not only that it is highly credible they may, but also probable that they will, imagine they have strong objections against it, however really unexceptionable: for so, prior to experience, they would think they had, against the circumstances, and degrees, and the whole manner of that instruction which is afforded by the ordinary course of Nature. Were the instruction which God affords to brute creatures by instincts and mere propensions, and to mankind by these together with reason, matter of probable proof, and not of certain observation; it would be rejected as incredible, in many instances of it, only upon account of the means by which this instruction is given, the seeming disproportions, the limitations, necessary conditions, and circumstances of it. For instance: would it not have been thought highly improbable, that men should have been so much more capable of discovering, even to certainty, the general laws of matter, and the magnitudes, paths, and revolutions of the heavenly bodies; than the occasions and cures of distempers, and many other things, in which human life seems so much more nearly concerned, than in astronomy? How capricious and irregular a way of information, would it be said, is that of *invention*, by means of which Nature instructs us in matters of science, and in many things, upon which the affairs of the world greatly depend: that a man should, by this faculty, be made acquainted with a thing in an instant, when perhaps he is thinking of somewhat else, which he has in vain been searching after, it may be, for years. So likewise the imperfections attending the only method, by which Nature enables and directs us to communicate our thoughts to each other, are innumerable. Language is, in its very nature, inadequate, ambiguous, liable to infinite abuse, even from negligence; and so liable to it from design, that every man can deceive and betray by it.[8] And, to mention but one instance more; that brutes, without reason, should act in many respects, with a sagacity and foresight vastly greater than what men have in those respects, would be thought impossible. Yet it is

Seeming *a priori* improbability of the conditions of *natural* knowledge;

e.g. (*a*) we know more about astronomy than about medicine,

(*b*) the tricks of the inventive faculty,

(*c*) the imperfections

and abuses of words,

(*d*) the frequent superiority of instinct to reason.

[8] [This had been elaborately treated by Locke (*Essay* III. ix. and x.).]

Hence, it is credible that the conditions of *supernatural* knowledge should be *a priori* improbable.

certain they do act with such superior foresight: whether it be their own indeed, is another question.[9] From these things, it is highly credible beforehand, that upon supposition God should afford men some additional instruction by revelation, it would be with circumstances, in manners, degrees, and respects, which we should be apt to fancy we had great objections against the credibility of. Nor are the objections against the Scripture, nor against Christianity in general, at all more or greater, than the analogy of Nature would beforehand—not perhaps give ground to expect; for this analogy may not be sufficient, in some cases, to ground an expectation upon; but no more nor greater, than analogy would shew it, beforehand, to be supposable and credible, that there might seem to lie against revelation.

E.g. the miraculous gifts of the Spirit may be abused

[9.] By applying these general observations to a particular objection, it will be more distinctly seen, how they are applicable to others of the like kind: and indeed to almost all objections against Christianity, as distinguished from objections against its evidence. It appears from Scripture, that, as it was not unusual in the apostolic age, for persons, upon their conversion to Christianity, to be endued with miraculous gifts; so, some of those persons exercised these gifts in a strangely irregular and disorderly manner; and this is made an objection against their being really miraculous. Now the foregoing observations quite remove this objection, how considerable soever it may appear at first sight. For, consider a person endued with any of these gifts; for instance, that of tongues: it is to be supposed, that he had the same power over this miraculous gift, as he would have had over it, had it been the effect of habit, of study and use, as it ordinarily is; or the same power over it, as he had over any other natural endowment. Consequently, he would use it in the same manner he did any other; either regularly, and upon proper occasions only, or irregularly, and upon improper ones: according to his sense of decency, and his character of prudence.[10] Where then is the objection? Why, if this miraculous

like any natural gift;

[9] [Butler probably means by this qualifying clause that the instinct of animals may be the unconscious reflex of the Intelligence which is the source of all natural life. Berkeley hinted at this doctrine in *Siris*: "It is this gives instincts, teaches the spider her web, and the bee her honey" (§ 277; cp. § 257). See Part I. iii. 18 above.]

[10] [Cp. *1 Cor.* xiv. 32.]

power was indeed given to the world to propagate Christianity, and attest the truth of it, we might, it seems, have expected, that other sort of persons should have been chosen to be invested with it; or that these should, at the same time, have been endued with prudence; or that they should have been continually restrained and directed in the exercise of it: *i.e.* that God should have miraculously interposed, if at all, in a different manner, or higher degree. But, from the observations made above, it is undeniably evident, that we are not judges in what degrees and manners it were to have been expected He should miraculously interpose; upon supposition of His doing it in some degree and manner. Nor, in the natural course of Providence, are superior gifts of memory, eloquence, knowledge, and other talents of great influence, conferred only on persons of prudence and decency, or such as are disposed to make the properest use of them. Nor is the instruction and admonition naturally afforded us for the conduct of life, particularly in our education, commonly given in a manner the most suited to recommend it; but often with circumstances apt to prejudice us against such instruction.

although we might expect, in both cases, that superior gifts would be reserved for those who use them well.

[10.] One might go on to add, that there is a great resemblance between the light of Nature and of revelation, in several other respects. Practical Christianity, or that faith and behaviour which renders a man a Christian, is a plain and obvious thing: like the common rules of conduct, with respect to our ordinary temporal affairs. The more distinct and particular knowledge of those things, the study of which the Apostle calls *going on unto perfection*,[11] and of the prophetic parts of revelation, like many parts of natural and even civil knowledge, may require very exact thought, and careful consideration. The hindrances too, of natural, and of supernatural light and knowledge, have been of the same kind. And as it is owned the whole scheme of Scripture is not yet understood; so, if it ever comes to be understood, before the *restitution of all things*,[12] and without miraculous interpositions; it must be in the same way as natural knowledge is come at: by the continuance and progress of learning and of liberty; and by particular persons attending to, com-

Further analogies between light of nature and of revelation,

(*a*) practical rules easy,

(*b*) theoretical subtleties difficult,

(*c*) the hindrances similar,

(*d*) knowledge advances in both cases by similar means,

[11] *Heb.* vi. 1.

[12] *Acts* iii. 21.

paring and pursuing, intimations scattered up and down it, which are overlooked and disregarded by the generality of the world.[13] For this is the way, in which all improvements are made; by thoughtful men's tracing on obscure hints, as it were, dropped us by Nature accidentally, or which seem to come into our minds by chance. Nor is it at all incredible, that a book, which has been so long in the possession of mankind, should contain many truths as yet undiscovered. For, all the same phenomena, and the same faculties of investigation, from which such great discoveries in natural knowledge have been made in the present and last age, were equally in the possession of mankind, several thousand years before. And possibly it might be intended, that events, as they come to pass, should open and ascertain the meaning of several parts of Scripture.

(*e*) discoveries still possible.

Objection i.: Natural knowledge unimportant. Answer: (*a*) Nature's general instruction *is* important. (*b*) So are some branches of natural knowledge. (*c*) This does not affect the analogy.

[11.] It may be objected, that this analogy fails in a material respect: for that natural knowledge is of little or no consequence. But I have been speaking of the general instruction which Nature does or does not afford us. And besides, some parts of natural knowledge, in the more common restrained sense of the words, are of the greatest consequence to the ease and convenience of life. But suppose the analogy did, as it does not, fail in this respect; yet it might be abundantly supplied, from the whole constitution and course of Nature: which shews, that God does not dispense His gifts according to our notions of the advantage and consequence they would be of to us. And this in general, with His method of dispensing knowledge in particular, would together make out an analogy full to the point before us.

Objection ii.: How could revelation, the remedy for sin, be long delayed and confined to a few?

[12.] But it may be objected still further and more generally; "The Scripture represents the world as in a state of ruin, and Christianity as an expedient to recover it, to help in these respects where Nature fails: in particular, to supply the deficiencies of natural light. Is it credible then, that so many ages should have been let pass, before a matter of such a sort, of so great and so general importance, was made

[13] [These pregnant sentences contain Butler's opinion on the doctrine of *development*. He distinctly recognises the possibility of progress, and of a better understanding by the Church of the terms of her charter, as the ages pass; but he does not contemplate any positive additions to the essentials of the faith "once for all delivered to the saints." Cp. Part II. iv. 2.]

known to mankind; and then that it should be made known to so small a part of them? Is it conceivable, that this supply should be so very deficient, should have the like obscurity and doubtfulness, be liable to the like perversions, in short, lie open to all the like objections, as the light of Nature itself?"[14] Without determining how far this in fact is so, I answer; it is by no means incredible, that it might be so, if the light of Nature and of revelation be from the same hand. Men are naturally liable to diseases: for which God, in His good providence, has provided natural remedies.[15] But remedies existing in Nature have been unknown to mankind for many ages: are known but to few now; probably many valuable ones are not known yet. Great has been and is the obscurity and difficulty, in the nature and application of them. Circumstances seem often to make them very improper, where they are absolutely necessary. It is after long labour and study, and many unsuccessful endeavours, that they are brought to be as useful as they are; after high contempt and absolute rejection of the most useful we have; and after disputes and doubts, which have seemed to be endless. The best remedies too, when unskilfully, much more if dishonestly applied, may produce new diseases; and with the rightest application the success of them is often doubtful. In many cases they are not at all effectual: where they are, it is often very slowly: and the application of them, and the necessary regimen accompanying it, is, not uncommonly, so disagreeable, that some will not submit to them; and satisfy themselves with the excuse, that, if they would, it is not certain whether it would be successful. And many persons, who labour under diseases, for which there are known natural remedies, are not so happy as to be always, if ever, in the way of them. In a word, the remedies which Nature has provided for diseases are neither certain, perfect, nor universal. And indeed the same principles of arguing, which would lead us to conclude, that they must be so, would lead us likewise to conclude, that there could be no occasion for them; *i.e.* that there could be no diseases at all. And therefore our experience that there are diseases shews, that it is credible beforehand, upon supposition Nature has provided

Answer:

(*a*) The remedies for disease are neither

(α) certain,

(β) perfect,

nor

(γ) universal;

(*b*) such *a priori* argument would prove that there could be neither sin nor disease.

[14] Chap. vi.

[15] See chap. v.

remedies for them, that these remedies may be, as by experience we find they are, not certain, nor perfect, nor universal; because it shews, that the principles upon which we should expect the contrary are fallacious.

This is not to belittle reason, which ought to judge,

[13.] And now, what is the just consequence from all these things? Not that reason is no judge of what is offered to us as being of Divine revelation. For this would be to infer, that we are unable to judge of anything, because we are unable to judge of all things. Reason can, and it ought to judge, not only of the meaning, but also of the morality and the evidence of revelation.[16] First, It is the province of reason to judge of the morality of the Scripture; *i.e.* not whether it contains things different from what we should have expected from a wise, just, and good Being; for objections from hence have been now obviated: but whether it contains things plainly contradictory to wisdom, justice, or goodness; to what the light of Nature teaches us of God. And I know nothing of this sort objected against Scripture, excepting such objections as are formed upon suppositions, which would equally conclude, that the constitution of Nature is contradictory to wisdom, justice, or goodness; which most certainly it is not. Indeed there are some particular precepts in Scripture, given to particular persons, requiring actions, which would be immoral and vicious, were it not for such precepts.[17] But it is easy to see, that all these are of such a kind, as that the precept changes the whole nature of the case and of the action; and both constitutes and shews that not to be unjust or immoral, which, prior to the precept, must have appeared and really have been so: which may well be, since none of these precepts are contrary to immutable morality.[18] If it were commanded, to cultivate the principles and act from the spirit of treachery, ingratitude,

(1) of the meaning, (2) of the morality of revelation.

Particular precepts seemingly immoral, justified because

(*a*) they are God's commands,

[16] [See above Part II. i. 28, with the editor's note at that place.]

[17] [Such were, for example, the command to Abraham to sacrifice Isaac (*Gen.* xxii. 1 ff.), and the command to Israel to exterminate the Canaanites (*Deut.* vii. 1 ff.). Butler likens them to the command of the State to the public executioner to take away the life of a criminal; in both cases the act has the sanction of the highest possible authority, and is no way parallel to a similar act performed *without* such sanction.]

[18] [This thesis is developed by Mansel in his *Bampton Lectures* (vii. and viii.); see especially p. 138 (ed. 4): "We are not justified in regarding the occasional suspension of human duties, by the same authority which enacted them, as a violation of the immutable principles of morality itself." But however congruous to Mansel's theological system

cruelty; the command would not alter the nature of the case or of the action, in any of these instances. But it is quite otherwise in precepts, which require only the doing an external action: for instance, taking away the property or life of any. For men have no right to either life or property, but what arises solely from the grant of God: when this grant is revoked, they cease to have any right at all in either: and when this revocation is made known, as surely it is possible it may be, it must cease to be unjust to deprive them of either. And though a course of external acts, which without command would be immoral, must make an immoral habit; yet a few detached commands have no such natural tendency.[19] I thought proper to say thus much of the few Scripture precepts, which require, not vicious actions, but actions which would have been vicious had it not been for such precepts; because they are sometimes weakly urged as immoral, and great weight is laid upon objections drawn from them. But to me there seems no difficulty at all in these precepts, but what arises from their being offences: *i.e.* from their being liable to be perverted, as indeed they are, by wicked designing men, to serve the most horrid purposes; and, perhaps, to mislead the weak and enthusiastic. And objections from this head are not objections against revelation; but against the whole notion of religion, as a trial; and against the general constitution of Nature. Secondly, Reason is able to judge, and must, of the evidence

and (*b*) they do not form an immoral habit.

this view may seem, it is hardly consistent with Butler's general doctrine of the identity of good and evil for man and for God (see Part I. vi. 12 note). Butler's argument here (which may have been borrowed from Waterland) is somewhat unsatisfactory. The difficulty he touches is treated in a masterly fashion in Mozley's *Ruling Ideas in Early Ages.*]

[19] [It is doubtful if this is consistent with Butler's general theory of the formation of habits. Nevertheless it is true that, as a matter of fact, the command to Abraham to sacrifice Isaac did *not* lead to the practice of human sacrifice; and again that the command to exterminate the Canaanites did *not* breed the habit of cruelty in conquest. "We have decisive proof, that it was with reluctance, and almost by compulsion that the Jews executed the sentence of Divine justice on the condemned nations; because it is certain that, as soon as the terror of immediate punishment on themselves was in any degree withdrawn, they neglected to execute the Divine command, they spared the remaining Canaanites . . . and in process of time began to regard them with affection" (Graves *On the Pentateuch*, ii. 77). It should be remembered also that "the same Divine authority which granted the chosen nation the land of Canaan . . . positively restrained them . . . from attacking the neighbouring nations" (*l.c.* p. 98). See further, Note D at the end of Part I. ch. v.]

(3) Reason ought to judge of the evidence of revelation.

The latter class of objections, viz. against the evidence of Christianity, alone serious.

of revelation, and of the objections urged against that evidence: which shall be the subject of a following chapter.[20]

[14.] But the consequence of the foregoing observations is, that the question upon which the truth of Christianity depends is scarce at all, what objections there are against its scheme, since there are none against the morality of it; but *what objections there are against its evidence;* or, *what proof there remains of it, after due allowances made for the objections against that proof:* because it has been shewn, that the *objections against Christianity, as distinguished from objections against its evidence, are frivolous.* For surely very little weight, if any at all, is to be laid upon a way of arguing and objecting, which, when applied to the general constitution of Nature, experience shews not to be conclusive: and such, I think, is the whole way of objecting treated of throughout this chapter. It is resolvable into principles, and goes upon suppositions, which mislead us to think, that the Author of Nature would not act, as we experience He does; or would act in such and such cases, as we experience He does not in like cases. But the unreasonableness of this way of objecting will appear yet more evidently from hence, that the chief things thus objected against are justified, as shall be further shewn,[21] by distinct, particular, and full analogies, in the constitution and course of Nature.

The consistency and morality of the Christian scheme proves it not the product of enthusiasm or policy.

[15.] But it is to be remembered, that, as frivolous as objections of the foregoing sort against revelation are, yet, when a supposed revelation is more consistent with itself, and has a more general and uniform tendency to promote virtue, than, all circumstances considered, could have been expected from enthusiasm and political views; this is a presumptive proof of its not proceeding from them, and so of its truth: because we are competent judges, what might have been expected from enthusiasm and political views.

[20] Chap. vii.

[21] Chap. iv. latter part, [§ 6] and v. vi.

CHAPTER IV.

Of Christianity, considered as a Scheme or Constitution, imperfectly comprehended.

Objections to the morality of the Christian dispensation are like those urged against the constitution of Nature, and are answered in the same way.

[1.] It hath been now shewn,[1] that the analogy of Nature renders it highly credible beforehand, that supposing a revelation to be made, it must contain many things very different from what we should have expected, and such as appear open to great objections: and that this observation, in good measure, takes off the force of those objections, or rather precludes them. But it may be alleged, that this is a very partial answer to such objections, or a very unsatisfactory way of obviating them: because it doth not shew at all, that the things objected against can be wise, just, and good; much less that it is credible they are so. It will therefore be proper to shew this distinctly; by applying to these objections against the wisdom, justice, and goodness of Christianity, the answer above[2] given to the like objections against the constitution of Nature: before we consider the particular analogies in the latter, to the particular things objected against in the former. Now that which affords a sufficient answer to objections against the wisdom, justice, and goodness of the constitution of Nature, is its being a constitution, a system, or scheme, imperfectly comprehended; a scheme in which means are made use of to accomplish ends; and which is carried on by general laws. For from these things it has been proved, not only to be possible, but also to be credible, that those things which are objected against may be consistent with wisdom, justice, and goodness; nay, may be instances of them: and even that the constitution and government of

[1] In the foregoing chapter.

[2] Part I. ch. vii. to which this all along refers.

Nature may be perfect in the highest possible degree. If Christianity then be a scheme, and of the like kind; it is evident, the like objections against it must admit of the like answer. And,

I. Christianity is a scheme beyond our comprehension,

[2.] I. Christianity is a scheme, quite beyond our comprehension. The moral government of God is exercised, by gradually conducting things so in the course of His providence, that every one, at length and upon the whole, shall receive according to his deserts; and neither fraud nor violence, but truth and right, shall finally prevail.

a particular dispensation tending to the completion of God's moral government

Christianity is a particular scheme under this general plan of Providence, and a part of it, conducive to its completion, with regard to mankind: consisting itself also of various parts, and a mysterious economy, which has been carrying on from the time the world came into its present wretched state, and is still carrying on, for its recovery, by a Divine person,

through the reign of Christ;

the Messiah; Who is to "gather together in one the children of God that are scattered abroad,"[3] and establish "an everlasting kingdom, wherein dwelleth righteousness."[4] And

involving (*a*) preparation for His Advent.

in order to it; after various manifestations of things, relating to this great and general scheme of Providence, through a succession of many ages: (for "the Spirit of Christ which was in the prophets, testified beforehand His sufferings, and the glory that should follow: unto whom it was revealed, that not unto themselves, but unto us they did minister the things which are now reported unto us by them that have preached the Gospel; which things the angels desire to look into:"[5])—after various dispensations, looking forward, and preparatory, to this final salvation; *in the fulness of time*, when infinite wisdom thought fit; "He, being in the form of God,—made Himself of no reputation, and took upon Him the form of a servant, and was made in the likeness of men; and being found in fashion as a man, He humbled Himself, and became obedient to death, even the death of the cross: wherefore God also hath highly exalted Him and given Him a name, which is above every name: that at the name of Jesus every knee should bow, of things in heaven, and things in the earth, and things under the earth: and that every tongue should confess, that Jesus Christ is

[3] *St. John* xi. 52.
[4] *2 Pet.* iii. 13.
[5] *1 Pet.* i. 11, 12.

Lord, to the glory of God the Father."[6] Parts likewise of this economy are the miraculous mission of the Holy Ghost, and His ordinary assistances given to good men: the invisible government, which Christ at present exercises over His Church: that which He Himself refers to in these words; "In My Father's house are many mansions—I go to prepare a place for you":[7] and His future return to *judge the world in righteousness*, and completely re-establish the kingdom of God. "For the Father judgeth no man; but hath committed all judgment unto the Son: that all men should honour the Son, even as they honour the Father."[8] "All power is given unto Him in heaven and in earth."[9] "And He must reign, till He hath put all enemies under His feet. Then cometh the end, when He shall have delivered up the kingdom to God, even the Father; when He shall have put down all rule, and all authority and power. And when all things shall be subdued unto Him, then shall the Son also Himself be subject unto Him that put all things under Him, that God may be all in all."[10] Now little, surely, need be said to shew, that this system, or scheme of things, is but imperfectly comprehended by us. The Scripture expressly asserts it to be so.[11] And indeed one cannot read a passage relating to this "great mystery of godliness,"[12] but what immediately runs up into something which shews us our ignorance in it; as everything in Nature shews us our ignorance in the constitution of Nature.[13] And whoever will seriously consider that part of the Christian scheme, which is revealed in Scripture, will find so much more unrevealed,[14] as will convince him, that, to all the purposes of judging and objecting, we know as little of it, as of the constitution of Nature. Our ignorance, therefore, is as much an answer to our objections against the perfection of one, as against the perfection of the other.[15]

(*b*) The mission of the Spirit.

(*c*) The present kingship of Christ.

(*d*) His future judgment.

This scheme is imperfectly comprehended.
(i) Scripture says so.

(ii) The known runs up into the unknown.

(iii) Much yet unrevealed.

[6] *Phil.* ii. 6-11.
[7] *St. John* xiv. 2.
[8] *St. John* v. 22, 23.
[9] *St. Matt.* xxviii. 18.
[10] *1 Cor.* xv. 25-28.
[11] [I suppose that Butler alludes to *1 Tim.* iii. 16, which he quotes in the next line. But, if so, he has mistaken the meaning of the Greek word *μυστήριον*, which does not necessarily carry with it the idea of *mysteriousness*, in the modern sense of incomprehensibility; it simply means a *secret*, and τὸ τῆς εὐσεβείας *μυστήριον*, *the secret of piety*, is, according to St. Paul, the Person of Christ Himself. Cp., however, *1 Cor.* xiii. 9.]
[12] *1 Tim.* iii. 16.
[13] [Cp. the saying, 'omnia exeunt in mysterium'; and see Part I. i. 23.]
[14] [Cp. Part II. iii. 10, note.]
[15] Part I. vii. 3, etc.

II. In the Christian dispensation means are used to accomplish ends.

[3.] II. It is obvious too, that in the Christian dispensation, as much as in the natural scheme of things, means are made use of to accomplish ends. And the observation of this furnishes us with the same answer, to objections against the perfection of Christianity, as to objections of the like kind, against the constitution of Nature. It shews the credibility, that the things objected against, how *foolish*[16] soever they appear to men, may be the very best means of accomplishing the very best ends. And their appearing *foolishness* is no presumption against this, in a scheme so greatly beyond our comprehension.[17]

III. It is credible that it is carried on by general laws.

[4.] III. The credibility, that the Christian dispensation may have been, all along, carried on by general laws,[18] no less than the course of Nature, may require to be more distinctly made out. Consider then, upon what ground it is we say, that the whole common course of Nature is carried on according to general foreordained laws. We know indeed several of the general laws of matter: and a great part of the natural behaviour of living agents is reducible to general laws. But we know in a manner nothing, by what laws, storms and tempests, earthquakes, famine, pestilence, become the instruments of destruction to mankind. And the laws, by which persons born into the world at such a time and place are of such capacities, geniuses, tempers; the laws, by which thoughts come into our mind, in a multitude of cases; and by which innumerable things happen, of the greatest influence upon the affairs and state of the world; these laws are so wholly unknown to us, that we call the events, which come to pass by them, accidental: though all reasonable men know certainly, that there cannot, in reality, be any such thing as chance; and conclude, that the things which have this appearance are the result of general laws, and may be reduced into them. It is then but an exceeding little way, and in but a very few respects, that we can trace up the natural course of things before us, to general laws. And it is only from analogy, that we conclude the whole of it to be capable of being reduced into them: only from our seeing, that part is so. It is from our finding, that the course of Nature, in some respects and so far, goes on by general laws, that we conclude this of the rest.

Our ignorance of many natural laws does not prevent us from believing nature to be governed by law.

16 *1 Cor.* i. [18].
17 Part I. vii. 3, etc.
18 Part I. vii. 8.

And if that be a just ground for such a conclusion, it is a just ground also, if not to conclude, yet to apprehend, to render it supposable and credible, which is sufficient for answering objections, that God's miraculous interpositions may have been all along, in like manner, by *general* laws of wisdom.[19] Thus, that miraculous powers should be exerted, at such times, upon such occasions in such degrees and manners, and with regard to such persons, rather than others; that the affairs of the world, being permitted to go on in their natural course so far, should, just at such a point, have a new direction given them by miraculous interpositions; that these interpositions should be exactly in such degrees and respects only; all this may have been by general laws. These laws are unknown indeed to us: but no more unknown, than the laws from whence it is, that some die as soon as they are born, and others live to extreme old age; that one man is so superior to another in understanding; with innumerable more things, which, as was before observed, we cannot reduce to any laws or rules at all, though it is taken for granted, they are as much reducible to general ones, as gravitation. Now, if the revealed dispensations of Providence, and miraculous interpositions be by general laws, as well as God's ordinary government in the course of Nature, made known by reason and experience; there is no more reason to expect, that every exigence, as it arises, should be provided for by these general laws or miraculous interpositions, than that every exigence in Nature should, by the general laws, of Nature: yet there might be wise and good reasons, that miraculous interpositions should be by general laws; and that these laws should not be broken in upon, or deviated from, by other miracles.

So *miracles*, no less than *accidents*, may be instances of unknown law, as regards the time of their occurrence.

Thus we cannot expect miracles to be provided for every exigence.

[5.] Upon the whole then: the appearance of deficiencies and irregularities in Nature is owing to its being a scheme but in part made known, and of such a certain particular kind in other respects. Now we see no more reason why the frame and course of Nature should be such a scheme, than why Christianity should. And that the former is such a scheme,

Hence *a priori* probability of seeming deficiencies and irregularities in Christianity as in nature.

[19] [Observe that Butler's suggestion is not that miracles, viewed as physical phenomena, may with wider knowledge be interpreted as the operations of physical law. This suggestion has often been made in our own time; but Butler's words only have reference to the *principles* which may be supposed to determine the Divine Will to interpose miraculously in human affairs.]

renders it credible, that the latter, upon supposition of its truth, may be so too. And as it is manifest, that Christianity is a scheme revealed but in part, and a scheme in which means are made use of to accomplish ends, like to that of Nature: so the credibility, that it may have been all along carried on by general laws, no less than the course of Nature, has been distinctly proved. And from all this it is beforehand credible that there might, I think probable that there would, be the like appearance of deficiencies and irregularities in Christianity, as in Nature: *i.e.* that Christianity would be liable to the like objections, as the frame of Nature. And these objections are answered by these observations concerning Christianity; as the like objections against the frame of Nature are answered by the like observations concerning the frame of Nature.

[6.] THE objections against Christianity, considered as a matter of fact,[20] having, in general, been obviated in the preceding chapter; and the same, considered as made against the wisdom and goodness of it, having been obviated in this: the next thing, according to the method proposed, is to shew, that the principal objections, in particular, against Christianity, may be answered, by particular and full analogies in Nature. And as one of them is made against the whole scheme of it together, as just now described, I choose to consider it here, rather than in a distinct chapter by itself. The thing objected against this scheme of the Gospel is, "that it seems to suppose God was reduced to the necessity of a long series of intricate means, in order to accomplish His ends, the recovery and salvation of the world: in like sort as men, for want of understanding or power, not being able to come at their ends directly, are forced to go round-about ways, and make use of many perplexed contrivances to arrive at them."[21] Now every-

Objection: To use intricate means to accomplish ends indicates a lack of power in God.

[20] Part I. vii. 1, etc.

[21] [Butler's argument that, as the Governor of Nature employs means to accomplish ends, there is no antecedent difficulty of belief that the Author of the Gospel may do the same, would be met by some writers with the retort that the objection lies against the omnipotence and wisdom of the God of Nature quite as much as against the omnipotence and wisdom of the God of Christianity. "It is not too much to say," wrote J. S. Mill, "that every indication of Design in the Kosmos is so much evidence against the Omnipotence of the Designer. For what is meant by Design? Contrivance: the adaptation of means to an end. But the necessity for contrivance—the need of employing means—is a consequence of the limitation of power. Who would have recourse to means if to attain his end his

thing which we see shews the folly of this, considered as an objection against the truth of Christianity. For, according to our manner of conception, God makes use of variety of means, what we often think tedious ones, in the natural course of providence, for the accomplishment of all His ends. Indeed it is certain there is somewhat in this matter quite beyond our comprehension: but the mystery is as great in Nature as in Christianity. We know what we ourselves aim at, as final ends: and what courses we take, merely as means conducing to those ends. But we are greatly ignorant how far things are considered by the Author of Nature, under the single notion of means and ends; so as that it may be said, this is merely an end, and that merely means, in His regard. And whether there be not some peculiar absurdity in our very manner of conception, concerning this matter, somewhat contradictory arising from our extremely imperfect views of things, it is impossible to say. However, thus much is manifest, that the whole natural world

Answer: (1) In nature tedious means often used.

(2) We cannot certainly distinguish means from ends, in the Divine purposes.

mere word was sufficient? The very idea of means implies that the means have an efficacy which the direct action of the being who employs them has not. Otherwise they are not means, but an incumbrance" (*Essays on Religion*, p. 177). It will be remembered that Butler has already answered this by anticipation in Part I. vii. 8, where he shews the manifest superiority, in the interests of human moral progress, of government by law to government by repeated interpositions. And Mill, in a subsequent paragraph of his *Essay*, is driven to take up the curious position that the use of means, inasmuch as it negatives the direct action of will, betokens of itself a limitation of power. An Omnipotent Being, he urges, would not have to choose between *this* way of acting and *that*. Both alternative courses could be reconciled by Omnipotence. This view is worth examining, not only for its bearing on Butler's argument before us, but because it illustrates a frequent misunderstanding of the adjective *omnipotent* as applied to God. No instructed thinker supposes that Omnipotence involves the power of making good, evil, and evil, good—of making the same statement true and false at the same time—of reconciling logical contradictions. In attributing to God, Reason, Mind, Thought, and in asserting that our finite minds are made in His image, we imply that the fundamental laws which govern human thought are of universal range because they are also the laws of Divine thought. Logicians call these laws the Laws of Identity, Contradiction, and Excluded Middle. The last of these demands that in speaking of God as acting in a certain way we shall regard all other ways as absolutely excluded. Thus the belief that the world is governed by intelligent purpose and law, though exclusive of the possibility of its being governed by an unconnected series of Divine acts of will, does not derogate from the *omnipotence*—in any intelligible meaning of the word—of the Author of Nature. To sway the world-forces by direct volition would, we do not doubt, be alike easy to Him Who chooses to employ means; but the mere fact of employing means cannot be said—because it excludes the other mode of working—to imply on that account limits to His power. This had all been seen by Clarke (*On the Attributes*, p. 102).]

Indeed the whole natural order is a gradual adjustment of means to ends.

and government of it is a scheme or system; not a fixed, but a progressive one: a scheme, in which the operation of various means takes up a great length of time, before the ends they tend to can be attained. The change of seasons, the ripening of the fruits of the earth, the very history of a flower, is an instance of this: and so is human life. Thus vegetable bodies, and those of animals, though possibly formed at once, yet grow up by degrees to a mature state. And thus rational agents, who animate these latter bodies, are naturally directed to form each his own manners and character, by the gradual gaining of knowledge and experience, and by a long course of action. Our existence is not only successive, as it must be of necessity; but one state of our life and being is appointed by God, to be a preparation for another; and that to be the means of attaining to another succeeding one: infancy to childhood; childhood to youth; youth to mature age. Men are impatient, and for precipitating things: but the Author of Nature appears deliberate throughout His operations; accomplishing His natural ends by slow successive steps. And there is a plan of things beforehand laid out, which, from the nature of it, requires various systems of means, as well as length of time, in order to the carrying on its several parts into execution. Thus, in the daily course of natural providence, God operates in the very same manner, as in the dispensation of Christianity: making one thing subservient to another; this, to somewhat further; and so on, through a progressive series of means, which extend, both backward and forward, beyond our utmost view. Of this manner of operation, every thing we see in the course of Nature is as much an instance, as any part of the Christian dispensation.

God moves slowly.

CHAPTER V.

Of the particular System of Christianity; the Appointment of a Mediator, and the Redemption of the World by Him.

[1.] THERE is not, I think, anything relating to Christianity, which has been more objected against, than the mediation of Christ, in some or other of its parts. Yet, upon thorough consideration, there seems nothing less justly liable to it. For,

The mediation of Christ.

[2.] I. The whole analogy of Nature removes all imagined presumption against a general notion of "a Mediator between God and man."[1] For we find all living creatures are brought into the world, and their life in infancy is preserved, by the instrumentality of others: and every satisfaction of it, some way or other, is bestowed by the like means. So that the visible government, which God exercises over the world, is by the instrumentality and mediation of others. And how far His invisible government be or be not so, it is impossible to determine at all by reason. And the supposition, that part of it is so, appears, to say the least, altogether as credible, as the contrary. There is then no sort of objection, from the light of Nature, against the general notion of a mediator between God and man, considered as a doctrine of Christianity, or as an appointment in this dispensation: since we find by experience, that God does appoint mediators, to be the instruments of good and evil to us; the instruments of His justice and His mercy. And the objection here referred to is urged, not against mediation in that high, eminent, and peculiar sense, in which Christ is our mediator; but absolutely against the whole notion itself of a mediator at all.

I. Analogy of Nature removes all presumption against the general notion of a Mediator.

[3.] II. As we must suppose, that the world is under the proper moral government of God, or in a state of religion,

II. God's moral government teaches

[1] *1 Tim.* ii. 5.

that misery shall follow vice.

before we can enter into consideration of the revealed doctrine, concerning the redemption of it by Christ; so that supposition is here to be distinctly taken notice of. Now the Divine moral government which religion teaches us, implies, that the consequence of vice shall be misery, in some future state, by the righteous judgment of God. That such consequent punishment shall take effect by His appointment, is necessarily implied. But, as it is not in any sort to be supposed, that we are made acquainted with all the ends or reasons, for which it is fit future punishments should be inflicted, or why God has appointed such and such consequent misery should follow vice; and as we are altogether in the dark, how or in what manner it shall follow, by what immediate occasions, or by the instrumentality of what means; there is no absurdity in supposing it may follow in a way analogous to that, in which many miseries follow such and such courses of action at present; poverty, sickness, infamy, untimely death by diseases, death from the hands of civil justice. There is no absurdity in supposing future punishment may follow wickedness of course, as we speak, or in the way of natural consequence from God's original constitution of the world;[2] from the nature He has given us, and from the condition in which He places us; or in a like manner, as a person rashly trifling upon a precipice, in the way of natural consequence, falls down; in the way of natural consequence, breaks his limbs, suppose, in the way of natural consequence of this, without help perishes.

This may be by natural consequence.

(Even so, such retribution would be (α) God's work, and (β) it is so described in Scripture.)

[4.] Some good men may perhaps be offended with hearing it spoken of as a supposable thing, that the future punishments of wickedness may be in the way of natural consequence: as if this were taking the execution of justice out of the hands of God, and giving it to Nature. But they should remember, that when things come to pass according to the course of Nature, this does not hinder them from being His doing, Who is the God of Nature: and that the Scripture ascribes those punishments to Divine justice, which are known to be natural; and which must be called so, when distinguished from such as are miraculous. But after all, this supposition, or rather this way of speaking, is here made use of only by way of

[2] [Cp. Part I. ii. 4.]

illustration of the subject before us. For since it must be admitted, that the future punishment of wickedness is not a matter of arbitrary appointment, but of reason, equity, and justice; it comes, for ought I see, to the same thing, whether it is supposed to be inflicted in a way analogous to that, in which the temporal punishments of vice and folly are inflicted, or in any other way. And though there were a difference, it is allowable, in the present case, to make this supposition, plainly not an incredible one; that future punishment may follow wickedness in the way of natural consequence, or according to some general laws of government already established in the universe.

[5.] III. Upon this supposition, or even without it, we may observe somewhat, much to the present purpose, in the constitution of Nature or appointments of Providence: the provision which is made, that all the bad natural consequences of men's actions should not always actually follow; or that such bad consequences, as, according to the settled course of things, would inevitably have followed, if not prevented, should, in certain degrees, be prevented. We are apt presumptuously to imagine, that the world might have been so constituted, as that there would not have been any such thing as misery or evil. On the contrary we find the Author of Nature permits it: but then He has provided reliefs, and in many cases perfect remedies for it, after some pains and difficulties; reliefs and remedies even for that evil, which is the fruit of our own misconduct; and which, in the course of Nature, would have continued, and ended in our destruction, but for such remedies. And this is an instance both of severity and of indulgence, in the constitution of Nature. Thus all the bad consequences, now mentioned, of a man's trifling upon a precipice, might be prevented. And though all were not, yet some of them might, by proper interposition, if not rejected: by another's coming to the rash man's relief, with his own laying hold on that relief, in such sort as the case required. Persons may do a great deal themselves towards preventing the bad consequences of their follies:[3] and more may be done by themselves, together with the assistance of others their fellow-creatures; which assistance

III. The bad consequences of imprudence do not *always* ensue;

they are sometimes prevented,

(α) by men's own efforts,

(β) by the help of their fellows.

[3] [Cp. Part I. ii. 2.]

Nature requires and prompts us to. This is the general constitution of the world. Now suppose it had been so constituted, that after such actions were done, as were foreseen naturally to draw after them misery to the doer, it should have been no more in human power to have prevented that naturally consequent misery, in any instance, than it is, in all; no one can say, whether such a more severe constitution of things might not yet have been really good. But, that, on the contrary, provision is made by Nature, that we may and do, to so great degree, prevent the bad natural effects of our follies; this may be called mercy or compassion[4] in the original constitution of the world: compassion, as distinguished from goodness in general. And, the whole known constitution and course of things affording us instances of such compassion, it would be according to the analogy of Nature, to hope, that, however ruinous the natural consequences of vice might be, from the general laws of God's government over the universe; yet provision might be made, possibly might have been originally made, for preventing those ruinous consequences from inevitably following: at least from following universally, and in all cases.

This compassion of Nature suggests that the bad consequences of vice may not be inevitable.

[6.] Many, I am sensible, will wonder at finding this made a question, or spoken of as in any degree doubtful. The generality of mankind are so far from having that awful sense of things, which the present state of vice and misery and darkness seems to make but reasonable, that they have scarce any apprehension or thought at all about this matter, any way: and some serious persons may have spoken unadvisedly concerning it. But let us observe, what we experience to be, and what, from the very constitution of Nature, cannot but be, the consequences of irregular and disorderly behaviour; even of such rashness, wilfulness, neglects, as we scarce call vicious. Now it is natural to apprehend, that the bad consequences of irregularity will be greater, in proportion as the irregularity is so. And there is no comparison between these irregularities, and the greater instances of vice, or a dissolute profligate disregard to all religion; if there be anything at all in religion. For consider what it is for creatures, moral agents, presumptuously to introduce that confusion and misery into

Vice a far worse disorder than imprudence, with worse consequences;

[4] [Another illustration of "nature's compassion" is given in the *Sermons*, vi. § 5. See also Part II. Concl., § 2 below.]

the kingdom of God, which mankind have in fact introduced; to blaspheme the Sovereign Lord of all; to contemn His authority; to be injurious, to the degree they are, to their fellow-creatures, the creatures of God. Add that the effects of vice in the present world are often extreme misery, irretrievable ruin, and even death: and upon putting all this together, it will appear, that as no one can say, in what degree fatal the unprevented consequences of vice may be, according to the general rule of Divine government; so it is by no means intuitively certain, how far these consequences could possibly, in the nature of the thing, be prevented, consistently with the eternal rule of right,[5] or with what is, in fact, the moral constitution of Nature. However, there would be large ground to hope, that the universal government was not so severely strict, but that there was room for pardon, or for having those penal consequences prevented. Yet,

of which we could not know *a priori* if they could be prevented.

[7.] IV. There seems no probability, that anything we could do would alone and of itself prevent them: prevent their following, or being inflicted. But one would think, at least, it were impossible that the contrary should be thought certain. For we are not acquainted with the whole of the case. We are not informed of all the reasons, which render it fit that future punishments should be inflicted: and therefore cannot know, whether anything we could do would make such an alteration, as to render it fit that they should be remitted. We do not know what the whole natural or appointed consequences of vice are; nor in what way they would follow, if not prevented: and therefore can in no sort say, whether we could do anything which would be sufficient to prevent them. Our ignorance being thus manifest, let us recollect the analogy of Nature or Providence. For, though this may be but a slight ground to raise a positive opinion upon in this matter; yet it is sufficient to answer a mere arbitrary assertion, without any kind of evidence, urged by way of objection against a doctrine, the proof of which is not reason, but revelation. Consider then: people ruin their fortunes by extravagance; they bring diseases upon themselves by excess; they incur the penalties of civil laws; and surely civil government is natural; will sorrow for these follies past,

IV. Our own efforts insufficient to prevent them; because we do not know

(*a*) all the reasons for punishment;

(*b*) all the consequences of vice.

Analogy shews that

sorrow and amendment are inadequate

[5] [Cp. Part I. vi. 12, note.]

to remedy imprudence,

and behaving well for the future, alone and of itself prevent the natural consequences of them? On the contrary, men's natural abilities of helping themselves are often impaired: or if not, yet they are forced to be beholden to the assistance of others, upon several accounts, and in different ways: assistance which they would have had no occasion for, had it not been for their misconduct; but which, in the disadvantageous condition they have reduced themselves to, is absolutely necessary to their recovery, and retrieving their affairs. Now since this is our case, considering ourselves merely as inhabitants of this world, and as having a temporal interest here, under the natural government of God, which however has a great deal moral in it;[6] why is it not supposable that this may be our case also, in our more important capacity, as under His perfect moral government, and having a more general and future interest depending? If we have misbehaved in this higher capacity, and rendered ourselves obnoxious to the future punishment, which God has annexed to vice: it is plainly credible, that behaving well for the time to come may be—not useless, God forbid—but wholly insufficient, alone and of itself, to prevent that punishment; or to put us in the condition, which we should have been in, had we preserved our innocence.

and the mediation of others is necessary for recovery of position.

That repentance alone is not efficacious to avert the penalties of vice, shown by (*a*) the analogy of Nature;

[8.] And though we ought to reason with all reverence, whenever we reason concerning the Divine conduct: yet it may be added, that it is clearly contrary to all our notions of government, as well as to what is, in fact, the general constitution of Nature, to suppose, that doing well for the future should, in all cases, prevent all the judicial bad consequences of having done evil, or all the punishment annexed to disobedience. And we have manifestly nothing from whence to determine, in what degree, and in what cases, reformation would prevent this punishment, even supposing that it would in some. And though the efficacy of repentance itself alone, to prevent what mankind had rendered themselves obnoxious to, and recover what they had forfeited, is now insisted upon, in opposition to Christianity, yet, by the general prevalence of propitiatory sacrifices over the heathen world, this notion, of repentance alone being sufficient to

(*b*) our general notions of government;

(*c*) the consent of mankind.

[6] [Cp. Part I. iii. 7.]

expiate guilt, appears to be contrary to the general sense of mankind.[7]

Thus our own efforts are insufficient to avert the penalties of sin.

[9.] Upon the whole then; had the laws, the general laws of God's government been permitted to operate, without any interposition in our behalf, the future punishment, for ought we know to the contrary, or have any reason to think, must inevitably have followed, notwithstanding anything we could have done to prevent it. Now,

V. Revelation confirms our belief in (a) sin's inevitable penalty; (b) the world's sinfulness; (c) the inefficacy of repentance, and suggests (d) the possibility of compassionate intervention.

[10.] V. In this darkness, or this light of Nature, call it which you please, revelation comes in; confirms every doubting fear, which could enter into the heart of man, concerning the future unprevented consequence of wickedness; supposes the world to be in a state of ruin; (a supposition which seems the very ground of the Christian dispensation,[8] and which, if not provable by reason, yet is in no wise contrary to it;) teaches us too, that the rules of Divine government are such, as not to admit of pardon immediately and directly upon repentance, or by the sole efficacy of it: but then teaches at the same time, what Nature might justly have hoped, that the moral government of the universe was not so rigid, but that there was room for an interposition, to avert the fatal consequences of vice; which therefore, by this means, does admit of pardon. Revelation teaches us, that the unknown laws of God's more general government, no less than the particular laws by which we experience He governs us at present, are compassionate,[9] as well as good in the more general notion of goodness: and that He hath mercifully provided, that there should be an interposition to prevent the destruction of human kind; whatever that destruction unprevented would have been. "God so loved the world, that He gave His only begotten Son, that whosoever believeth," not, to be sure, in a speculative, but in a practical sense, "that whosoever believeth in Him, should not perish:"[10] gave His Son in the same way of goodness to the world, as

[7] [Clarke had made this observation in his *Evidences*, p. 349, "We find the custom of sacrificing to have prevailed universally over the heathen world in all ages; which, how unreasonable soever an expectation it was, to think that the blood of beasts could truly expiate sin, yet thus much it plainly and undeniably shows, that it has been the common apprehension of man in all ages, that God would not be appeased nor pardon sin without some punishment or satisfaction."]

[8] [Cp. Part I. iv. 8 and the editor's note at that place.]

[9] § 5 above.

[10] *St. John* iii. 16.

He affords particular persons the friendly assistance of their fellow-creatures; when, without it, their temporal ruin would be the certain consequence of their follies: in the same way of goodness, I say; though in a transcendent and infinitely higher degree. And the Son of God *loved us and gave Himself for us*, with a love, which He Himself compares to that of human friendship: though, in this case, all comparisons must fall infinitely short of the thing intended to be illustrated by them. He interposed in such a manner as was necessary and effectual to prevent that execution of justice upon sinners, which God had appointed should otherwise have been executed upon them: or in such a manner, as to prevent that punishment from actually following, which, according to the general laws of Divine government, must have followed the sins of the world, had it not been for such interposition.[11]

Mankind is here assumed to be in a fallen state;

[11.] If anything here said should appear, upon first thought, inconsistent with Divine goodness; a second, I am persuaded, will entirely remove that appearance. For were we to suppose the constitution of things to be such, as that the whole creation must have perished, had it not been for somewhat, which God had appointed should be, in order to prevent that ruin: even this supposition would not be inconsistent, in any degree, with the most absolutely perfect

[11] It cannot, I suppose, be imagined, even by the most cursory reader, that it is, in any sort, affirmed or implied in anything said in this chapter, that none can have the benefit of the general redemption, but such as have the advantage of being made acquainted with it in the present life. But it may be needful to mention, that several questions, which have been brought into the subject before us, and determined, are not in the least entered into here: questions which have been, I fear, rashly determined, and perhaps with equal rashness contrary ways. For instance, whether God could have saved the world by other means than the death of Christ, consistently with the general laws of His government. And had not Christ come into the world, what would have been the future condition of the better sort of men; those just persons over the face of the earth, for whom, Manasses in his prayer asserts, repentance was not appointed. The meaning of the first of these questions is greatly ambiguous: and neither of them can properly be answered, without going upon that infinitely absurd supposition, that we know the whole of the case. And perhaps the very inquiry, *What would have followed, if God had not done as He has*, may have in it some very great impropriety; and ought not to be carried on any further than is necessary to help our partial and inadequate conceptions of things. [The words of the 'Prayer of Manasses, King of Judah, when he was holden captive in Babylon' are: "Thou, therefore, O Lord that art the God of the just, hast not appointed repentance to the just, to Abraham and Isaac and Jacob, which have not sinned against Thee; but Thou hast appointed repentance to me that am a sinner" (v. 4).]

goodness. But still it may be thought, that this whole manner of treating the subject before us supposes mankind to be naturally in a very strange state. And truly so it does. But it is not Christianity, which has put us into this state. Whoever will consider the manifold miseries, and the extreme wickedness of the world; that the best have great wrongnesses within themselves, which they complain of, and endeavour to amend; but that the generality grow more profligate and corrupt with age; that heathen moralists thought the present state to be a state of punishment:[12] and, what might be added, that the earth our habitation has the appearances of being a ruin: whoever, I say, will consider all these, and some other obvious things, will think he has little reason to object against the Scripture account, that mankind is in a state of degradation;[13] against this being the fact: how difficult soever he may think it to account for, or even to form a distinct conception of the occasions and circumstances of it. But that the crime of our first parents was the occasion of our being placed in a more disadvantageous condition, is a thing throughout and particularly analogous to what we see in

but observation confirms this: α β γ δ ε

[12] [It is worth while to compare Newman's tremendous statement of the same fact of the world's fallen condition, as patent to observation. "To consider the world in its length and breadth, its various history, the many races of man, their starts, their fortunes, their mutual alienation, their conflicts; and then their ways, habits, governments, forms of worship; their enterprises, their aimless courses, their random achievements and acquirements, the impotent conclusion of long-standing facts, the tokens so faint and broken of a superintending design, the blind evolution of what turn out to be great powers or truths, the progress of things, as if from unreasoning elements, not towards final causes, the greatness and littleness of man, his far-reaching aims, his short duration, the curtain hung over his futurity, the disappointments of life, the defeat of good, the success of evil, physical pain, mental anguish, the prevalence and intensity of sin, the pervading idolatries, the corruptions, the dreary hopeless irreligion, that condition of the whole race, so fearfully yet exactly described in the Apostle's words 'having no hope and without God in the world'—all this is a vision to dizzy and appal; and inflicts upon the mind the sense of a profound mystery, which is absolutely beyond human solution. What shall be said to this heart-piercing, soul-bewildering fact? I can only answer that either there is no Creator, or this living society of men is in a true sense discarded from His presence" (*Apologia*, ch. v.).

Butler's third point that "the generality grow more profligate and corrupt with age" has been expounded with keen insight by Liddon in his sermon on Solomon (*Sermons on O. T. Subjects*, p. 161). The thesis would require many qualifications; but in certain directions its truth is patent to consciousness and to observation, *e.g.* in the gradual lowering of the ideals of youth, and in the less keen sense of indignation against vice, which are brought about by experience of the difficulties and temptations of life.]

[13] [See Part II. Concl., § 2 note.]

the daily course of natural Providence; as the recovery of the world by the interposition of Christ has been shewn to be so in general.

VI. Scriptural account of Christ's mediation.

[12.] VI. The particular manner in which Christ interposed in the redemption of the world, or His office as *Mediator*, in the largest sense, *between God and man*, is thus represented to us in the Scripture. "He is the light of the world";[14] the revealer of the will of God in the most eminent sense. He is a propitiatory sacrifice;[15] the "Lamb of God":[16] and, as He voluntarily offered Himself up, He is styled our High-Priest.[17] And, which seems of peculiar weight, He is described beforehand in the Old Testament, under the same characters of a priest, and an expiatory victim.[18] And whereas it is objected, that all this is merely by way of allusion to the sacrifices of the Mosaic Law, the Apostle on the contrary affirms, that the "Law was a shadow of good things to come, and not the very image of the things":[19] and that "the priests that offer gifts according to the Law——serve unto the example and shadow of heavenly things, as Moses was admonished of God, when he was about to make the tabernacle. For see, saith He, that thou make all things according to the pattern shewed to thee in the mount":[20] *i.e.* the Levitical priesthood was a shadow of the priesthood of Christ; in like manner as the tabernacle made by Moses was according to that shewed him in the mount. The priesthood of Christ, and the tabernacle in the mount, were the originals: of the former of which the Levitical priesthood was a type; and of the latter the tabernacle made by Moses was a copy. The doctrine of this Epistle then plainly is, that the legal sacrifices were allusions to the great and final atonement to be made by the blood of Christ; and not that this was an allusion to those. Nor can anything be more express or determinate, than the following passage. "It is not possible that the blood of bulls and of goats should take away sin. Wherefore when He cometh into the world, He saith, Sacrifice and offering," *i.e.* of bulls and of goats, "Thou wouldest not, but a body hast

He is (*a*) the Revealer of God; (*b*) a propitiatory sacrifice; (*c*) our High Priest.

Language of N.T. not merely allusive, but categorical.

[14] *St. John* i. and viii. 12.

[15] *Rom.* iii. 25 and v. 11; *1 Cor.* v. 7; *Eph.* v. 2; *1 John* ii. 2; *St. Matt.* xxvi. 28.

[16] *St. John* i. 29, 36, and throughout the *Book of Revelation.*

[17] Throughout the *Epistle to the Hebrews.*

[18] *Isa.* liii.; *Dan.* ix. 24; *Ps.* cx. 4.

[19] *Heb.* x. 1.

[20] *Heb.* viii. 4, 5.

Thou prepared me—Lo, I come to do Thy will, O God. By which will we are sanctified, through the offering of the body of Jesus Christ once for all."[21] And to add one passage more of the like kind: "Christ was once offered to bear the sins of many; and unto them that look for Him shall He appear the second time, without sin"; *i.e.* without bearing sin, as He did at His first coming, by being an offering for it; without having our iniquities again "laid upon Him," without being any more a sin offering:—"unto them that look for Him shall He appear the second time, without sin, unto salvation."[22] Nor do the inspired writers at all confine themselves to this manner of speaking concerning the satisfaction of Christ; but declare an efficacy in what He did and suffered for us, additional to and beyond mere instruction, example, and government, in great variety of expression: "That Jesus should die for that nation," the Jews: "and not for that nation only, but that also," plainly by the efficacy of His death, "He should gather together in one the children of God that were scattered abroad":[23] that "He suffered for sins, the just for the unjust":[24] that "He gave His life, Himself, a ransom":[25] that "we are bought, bought with a price":[26] that "He redeemed us with His blood; redeemed us from the curse of the law, being made a curse for us":[27] that He is our "advocate, intercessor," and "propitiation":[28] that "He was made perfect," or consummate, "through sufferings": and being thus "made perfect, He became the author of salvation":[29] that "God was in Christ reconciling the world to Himself; by the death of His Son, by the cross; not imputing their trespasses unto them":[30] and lastly, that "through death He destroyed him that had the power of death."[31] Christ then having thus "humbled Himself, and become obedient to death, even the death of the cross; God also hath highly exalted Him, and given Him a name, which is above every name: hath given all things into His hands: hath committed

The objective efficacy of Christ's Death.

[21] *Heb.* x. 4, 5, 7, 9, 10.
[22] *Heb.* ix. 28.
[23] *St. John* xi. 51, 52.
[24] *1 Pet.* iii. 18.
[25] *St. Matt.* xx. 28; *St. Mark* x. 45; *1 Tim.* ii. 6.
[26] *2 Pet.* ii. 1; *Rev.* xiv. 4; *1 Cor.* vi. 20.
[27] *1 Pet.* i. 19; *Rev.* v. 9; *Gal.* iii. 13.
[28] *Heb.* vii. 25; *1 John* ii. 1, 2.
[29] *Heb.* ii. 10 and v. 9.
[30] *2 Cor.* v. 19; *Rom.* v. 10; *Eph.* ii. 16.
[31] *Heb.* ii. 14. See also a remarkable passage in the *Book of Job* xxxiii. 24.

all judgment unto Him; that all men should honour the Son, even as they honour the Father."[32] For, "worthy is the Lamb that was slain, to receive power, and riches, and wisdom, and strength, and honour, and glory, and blessing. And every creature which is in heaven, and on the earth, heard I saying, Blessing, and honour, and glory, and power, be unto Him, that sitteth upon the throne, and unto the Lamb for ever and ever."[33]

Christ's Mediatorial office threefold.

[13.] These passages of Scripture seem to comprehend and express the chief parts of Christ's office, as Mediator between God and man, so far, I mean, as the nature of this His office is revealed; and it is usually treated of by divines under three heads.

(1) He is, eminently, the Prophet.

[14.] First, He was, by way of eminence, the Prophet: "that Prophet that should come into the world,"[34] to declare
a the Divine will. He published anew the law of Nature, which men had corrupted; and the very knowledge of which, to some degree, was lost among them. He taught mankind, taught us authoritatively, to "live soberly, righteously, and godly in this present world," in expectation of the future judgment of God. He confirmed the truth of this moral system of
b Nature, and gave us additional evidence of it; the evidence
c of testimony.[35] He distinctly revealed the manner, in which God would be worshipped, the efficacy of repentance, and the rewards and punishments of a future life. Thus He was a prophet in a sense in which no other ever was. To which is to be added, that He set us a perfect "example, that we should follow His steps."

(2) The King.

[15.] Secondly, He has a kingdom which is "not of this world." He founded a Church, to be to mankind a standing memorial of religion, and invitation to it; which He promised to be with always even to the end. He exercises an invisible government over it Himself, and by His Spirit: over that part of it, which is militant here on earth, a government of discipline, "for the perfecting of the saints, for the edifying His body: till we all come in the unity of the faith, and of the knowledge of the Son of God, unto a perfect man, unto the measure of the stature of the fulness of Christ."[36] Of

[32] *Phil.* ii. 8, 9; *St. John* iii. 35 and v. 22, 23.

[33] *Rev.* v. 12, 13.

[34] *St. John* vi. 14.

[35] Part II. i. 7, etc.

[36] *Eph.* iv. 12, 13.

this Church, all persons scattered over the world, who live in obedience to His laws, are members. For these He is "gone to prepare a place," and "will come again to receive them unto Himself, that where He is, there they may be also; and reign with Him for ever and ever:"[37] and likewise "to take vengeance on them that know not God, and obey not His Gospel."[38]

[16.] Against these parts of Christ's office I find no objections, but what are fully obviated in the beginning of this chapter.

[17.] Lastly, Christ offered Himself a propitiatory sacrifice, and made atonement for the sins of the world; which is mentioned last, in regard to what is objected against it. Sacrifices of expiation were commanded the Jews, and obtained amongst most other nations, from tradition, whose original probably was revelation. And they were continually repeated, both occasionally, and at the returns of stated times: and made up great part of the external religion of mankind. "But now once in the end of the world Christ appeared to put away sin by the sacrifice of Himself."[39] And this sacrifice was, in the highest degree and with the most extensive influence, of that efficacy for obtaining pardon of sin, which the heathens may be supposed to have thought their sacrifices to have been, and which the Jewish sacrifices really were in some degree, and with regard to some persons.

(3) The propitiatory sacrifice for sin.

[18.] How and in what particular way it had this efficacy, there are not wanting persons who have endeavoured to explain: but I do not find that the Scripture has explained it. We seem to be very much in the dark concerning the manner in which the ancients understood atonement to be made, *i.e.* pardon to be obtained by sacrifices. And if the Scripture has, as surely it has, left this matter of the satisfaction of Christ, mysterious, left somewhat in it unrevealed, all conjectures about it must be, if not evidently absurd, yet at least uncertain. Nor has any one reason to complain for want of further information, unless he can shew his claim to it.

The mode of its efficacy not revealed.

[19.] Some have endeavoured to explain the efficacy of what Christ has done and suffered for us, beyond what the Scripture has authorized: others, probably because they could not ex-

But it is revealed as *objectively* efficacious,

[37] *St. John* xiv. 2, 3; *Rev.* iii. 21 and xi. 15.

[38] *2 Thess.* i. 8.

[39] *Heb.* ix. 26.

plain it, have been for taking it away, and confining His office as Redeemer of the world to His instruction, example, and government of the church. Whereas the doctrine of the Gospel appears to be, not only that He taught the efficacy of repentance, but rendered it of the efficacy which it is, by what He did and suffered for us: that He obtained for us the benefit of having our repentance accepted unto eternal life: not only that He revealed to sinners, that they were in a capacity of salvation, and how they might obtain it; but moreover that He put them into this capacity of salvation, by what He did and suffered for them; put us into a capacity of escaping

though we know not how.

future punishment, and obtaining future happiness. And it is our wisdom thankfully to accept the benefit, by performing the conditions, upon which it is offered, on our part, without disputing how it was procured on His.[40] For,

VII. Our ignorance

[20.] VII. Since we neither know by what means punish-
a ment in a future state would have followed wickedness in this;
b nor in what manner it would have been inflicted, had it not
c been prevented; nor all the reasons why its infliction would
d have been needful; nor the particular nature of that state of
happiness, which Christ is gone to prepare for His disciples:
e and since we are ignorant how far anything which we could

unfits us to judge *a priori* of

do, would, alone and of itself, have been effectual to prevent that punishment, to which we were obnoxious, and recover that happiness, which we had forfeited; it is most evident we

(1) the necessity of a Mediator;

are not judges, antecedently to revelation, whether a mediator was or was not necessary, to obtain those ends: to prevent that future punishment, and bring mankind to the final happi-

(2) the nature of His office, supposed necessary.

ness of their nature. And for the very same reasons, upon supposition of the necessity of a mediator, we are no more judges, antecedently to revelation, of the whole nature of His office, or the several parts of which it consists; of what was fit and requisite to be assigned Him, in order to accomplish

Thus objections to the revealed particulars of Christ's Mediation are futile,

the ends of Divine providence in the appointment. And from hence it follows, that to object against the expediency or usefulness of particular things, revealed to have been done or suffered by Him, because we do not see how they were conducive to those ends, is highly absurd. Yet nothing is more

[40] [In this deeply significant paragraph Butler reiterates the great principle, so often forgotten by controversialists, that it is not *theories* about the Death of Christ that are our salvation, but the *Death* itself.]

common to be met with, than this absurdity. But if it be acknowledged beforehand, that we are not judges in the case, it is evident that no objection can, with any shadow of reason, be urged against any particular part of Christ's mediatorial office revealed in Scripture, till it can be shewn positively not to be requisite or conducive to the ends proposed to be accomplished; or that it is in itself unreasonable.

unless α or β

[21.] And there is one objection made against the satisfaction of Christ, which looks to be of this positive kind: that the doctrine of His being appointed to suffer for the sins of the world, represents God as being indifferent whether He punished the innocent or the guilty. Now from the foregoing observations we may see the extreme slightness of all such objections; and (though it is most certain all who make them do not see the consequence) that they conclude altogether as much against God's whole original constitution of Nature, and the whole daily course of Divine providence in the government of the world, *i.e.* against the whole scheme of Theism and the whole notion of Religion, as against Christianity. For the world is a constitution or system, whose parts have a mutual reference to each other: and there is a scheme of things gradually carrying on, called the course of Nature, to the carrying on of which God has appointed us, in various ways, to contribute. And when, in the daily course of natural providence, it is appointed that innocent people should suffer for the faults of the guilty, this is liable to the very same objection, as the instance we are now considering. The infinitely greater importance of that appointment of Christianity, which is objected against, does not hinder but it may be, as it plainly is, an appointment of the very same kind, with what the world affords us daily examples of. Nay, if there were any force at all in the objection, it would be stronger, in one respect, against natural providence, than against Christianity: because under the former we are in many cases commanded, and even necessitated whether we will or no, to suffer for the faults of others; whereas the sufferings of Christ were voluntary. The world's being under the righteous government of God does indeed imply, that finally and upon the whole every one shall receive according to his personal deserts: and the general doctrine of the whole Scripture is, that this shall be the completion of the Divine government. But during the progress, and, for

One positive objection: It contravenes justice to punish the innocent for the guilty.

Answer: (α) This would apply also to the daily course of Nature;

(β) in a stronger degree, for Christ's mediatorial sufferings were voluntary.

Each shall suffer for his own sin at last:

meantime, vicarious punishment for sin analogous to vicarious punishment for imprudence.

ought we know, even in order to the completion of this moral scheme, vicarious punishments[41] may be fit, and absolutely necessary. Men by their follies run themselves into extreme distress; into difficulties which would be absolutely fatal to them, were it not for the interposition and assistance of others. God commands by the law of Nature, that we afford them this assistance, in many cases where we cannot do it without very great pains, and labour, and sufferings to ourselves. And we see in what variety of ways one person's sufferings contribute to the relief of another: and how, or by what particular means, this comes to pass, or follows, from the constitution and laws of Nature, which come under our notice: and, being familiarized to it, men are not shocked with it. So that the reason of their insisting upon objections of the foregoing kind against the satisfaction of Christ is, either that they do not consider God's settled and uniform appointments as His appointments at all; or else they forget that vicarious punishment[41] is a providential appointment of every day's experience: and then, from their being unacquainted with the more general laws of Nature or Divine government over the world, and not seeing how the sufferings of Christ could contribute to the redemption of it, unless by arbitrary and tyrannical will; they conclude His sufferings could not contribute to it any other way.

(γ) The doctrine a strong deterrent from sin.

And yet, what has been often alleged in justification of this doctrine, even from the apparent natural tendency of this method of our redemption; its tendency to vindicate the authority of God's laws, and deter His creatures from sin; this has never yet been answered, and is, I think, plainly unanswerable: though I am far from thinking it an account of the whole of the case.

(δ) It is not incredible because we cannot see its necessity or expediency.

But without taking this into consideration, it abundantly appears, from the observations above made, that this objection is, not an objection against Christianity, but against the whole general constitution of Nature. And if it were to be considered as an objection against Christianity, or considering it as it is, an objection against the constitution of Nature; it amounts to no more in

[41] [Here, and here only, Butler uses the much controverted phrase, "vicarious *punishment*"; elsewhere he writes "vicarious *suffering*." It is plain that the substitution in the present paragraph of the latter for the former expression would not disturb the argument, and would remove from it a plausible ground of objection. Yet, cp. Part I. ii. 4 above; see further Bp. Barry's *Manifold Witness for Christ*, p. 148 ff.]

conclusion than this, that a Divine appointment cannot be necessary or expedient, because the objector does not discern it to be so: though he must own that the nature of the case is such, as renders him incapable of judging, whether it be so or not; or of seeing it to be necessary, though it were so.

This way of arguing absurd, because of our ignorance.

[22.] It is indeed a matter of great patience to reasonable men, to find people arguing in this manner: objecting against the credibility of such particular things revealed in Scripture, that they do not see the necessity or expediency of them. For though it is highly right, and the most pious exercise of our understanding, to enquire with due reverence into the ends and reasons of God's dispensations: yet when those reasons are concealed, to argue from our ignorance, that such dispensations cannot be from God, is infinitely absurd. The presumption of this kind of objections seems almost lost in the folly of them. And the folly of them is yet greater, when they are urged, as usually they are, against things in Christianity analogous or like to those natural dispensations of Providence, which are matter of experience. Let reason be kept to: and if any part of the Scripture account of the redemption of the world by Christ can be shewn to be really contrary to it, let the Scripture, in the name of God, be given up: but let not such poor creatures as we go on objecting against an infinite scheme, that we do not see the necessity or usefulness of all its parts, and call this reasoning; and, which still further heightens the absurdity in the present case, parts which we are not actively concerned in. For it may be worth mentioning,

Information about our own duty plain, though not about the mode of God's action

[23.] Lastly, That not only the reason of the thing, but the whole analogy of Nature, should teach us, not to expect to have the like information concerning the Divine conduct, as concerning our own duty.[42] God instructs us by experience, (for it is not reason, but experience which instructs us,) what good or bad consequences will follow from our acting in such and such manners: and by this He directs us, how we are to behave ourselves. But, though we are sufficiently instructed for the common purposes of life: yet it is but an almost infinitely small part of natural providence, which we are at all let into. The case is the same with regard to revelation. The doctrine of a mediator between God and man, against

either in nature, or in grace.

[42] [See Part II. viii. 8 below.]

which it is objected, that the expediency of some things in it is not understood, relates only to what was done on God's part in the appointment, and on the Mediator's in the execution of it. For what is required of us, in consequence of this gracious dispensation, is another subject, in which none can complain for want of information. The constitution of the world, and God's natural government over it, is all mystery, as much as the Christian dispensation. Yet under the first He has given men all things pertaining to life; and under the other, all things pertaining unto godliness. And it may be added, that there is nothing hard to be accounted for in any of the common precepts of Christianity: though if there were, surely a Divine command is abundantly sufficient to lay us under the strongest obligations to obedience. But the fact is, that the reasons of all the Christian precepts are evident. Positive institutions are manifestly necessary to keep up and propagate religion amongst mankind. And our duty to Christ, the internal and external worship of Him; this part of the religion of the Gospel, manifestly arises out of what He has done and suffered, His authority and dominion, and the relation which He is revealed to stand in to us.[43]

The Christian precepts must be obeyed, being both

(*a*) of positive,

(*b*) of moral, obligation.

[43] Part II. i. 14, etc.

CHAPTER VI.

Of the Want of Universality in Revelation: and of the supposed Deficiency in the Proof of it.

[1.] It has been thought by some persons,[1] that if the evidence of revelation appears doubtful, this itself turns into a positive argument against it: because it cannot be supposed that, if it were true, it would be left to subsist upon doubtful evidence. And the objection against revelation from its not being universal is often insisted upon as of great weight.

Arguments against Revelation, from (i) its doubtful evidence, (ii) its non-universality

[2.] Now the weakness of these opinions may be shewn by observing the suppositions on which they are founded: which are really such as these; that it cannot be thought God would have bestowed any favour at all upon us, unless in the degree, which, we think, He might, and which, we imagine, would be most to our particular advantage; and also that it cannot be thought He would bestow a favour upon any, unless He bestowed the same upon all: suppositions, which we find contradicted, not by a few instances in God's natural government of the world, but by the general analogy of Nature together.

assume: (a) ... (b) ... which are contrary to analogy of Nature.

[3.] Persons who speak of the evidence of religion as doubtful, and of this supposed doubtfulness as a positive argument against it, should be put upon considering, what that evidence indeed is, which they act upon with regard to

For (i) we act on scanty evidence in temporal matters,

[1] [For example, the argument against revelation from its want of universality had been put forward by one Charles Blount (1654-1693), whose book, *Oracles of Reason*, Clarke thought worthy of mention and refutation (*Evidences*, p. 318). Clarke's answer is exactly that followed by Butler in §§ 3, 6 of this chapter, viz. that "all men are not endued with the same faculties and capacities," and that it does not follow because a revelation is made that "it must equally be made to all men." FitzGerald observes (*Life of Butler*, p. xxxvii.) that J. Foster's *Reply to Tindal* also took the same line.]

α their temporal interests. For, it is not only extremely difficult,
but in many cases absolutely impossible, to balance pleasure
and pain, satisfaction and uneasiness, so as to be able to say
β on which side the overplus is.[2] There are the like difficulties
and impossibilities in making the due allowances for a change
of temper and taste, for satiety, disgust, ill health: any of
which render men incapable of enjoying, after they have
γ obtained what they most eagerly desired. Numberless too
are the accidents, besides that one of untimely death, which
may even probably disappoint the best concerted schemes:
and strong objections are often seen to lie against them, not
to be removed or answered, but which seem overbalanced
by reasons on the other side; so as that the certain difficulties
and dangers of the pursuit are, by every one, thought justly
disregarded, upon account of the appearing greater advantages
in case of success, though there be but little probability of it.
δ Lastly, every one observes our liableness, if we be not upon
our guard, to be deceived by the falsehood of men, and
the false appearance of things: and this danger must be greatly
increased, if there be a strong bias within, suppose from
indulged passion, to favour the deceit. Hence arises that
great uncertainty and doubtfulness of proof, wherein our
temporal interest really consists; what are the most probable
means of attaining it; and whether those means will eventually
ε be successful. And numberless instances there are, in the
daily course of life, in which all men think it reasonable to
engage in pursuits, though the probability is greatly against
succeeding: and to make such provision for themselves, as
it is supposable they may have occasion for, though the plain
acknowledged probability is, that they never shall.

and (ii) God's natural gifts are unequally distributed.

Then
those who think the objection against revelation, from its
light not being universal, to be of weight, should observe, that
the Author of Nature, in numberless instances, bestows that
upon some, which He does not upon others, who seem equally
to stand in need of it.[3] Indeed He appears to bestow all
His gifts with the most promiscuous variety among creatures
of the same species: health and strength, capacities of pru-

[2] [Cp. Part I. iii. 5 above.]

[3] [Cp. Descartes: "Quelque adroit et savant ouvrier que je me le répresente, je ne dois pas pour cela penser qu'il ait dû mettre dans chacun de ses ouvrages toutes les perfections qu'il peut mettre dans quelques-uns" (*Méditation* 4me).]

dence and of knowledge, means of improvement, riches, and all external advantages. And as there are not any two men found, of exactly like shape and features; so it is probable there are not any two, of an exactly like constitution, temper and situation, with regard to the goods and evils of life. Yet, notwithstanding these uncertainties and varieties, God does exercise a natural government over the world: and there is such a thing as a prudent and imprudent institution of life, with regard to our health and our affairs, under that His natural government.

[4.] As neither the Jewish nor Christian revelation have been universal; and as they have been afforded to a greater or less part of the world, at different times; so likewise at different times, both revelations have had different degrees of evidence. The Jews who lived during the succession of prophets, that is, from Moses till after the Captivity, had higher evidence of the truth of their religion, than those had, who lived in the interval between the last-mentioned period, and the coming of Christ. And the first Christians had higher evidence of the miracles wrought in attestation of Christianity, than what we have now. They had also a strong presumptive proof of the truth of it, perhaps of much greater force, in way of argument, than many think, of which we have very little remaining; I mean the presumptive proof of its truth, from the influence which it had upon the lives of the generality of its professors. And we, or future ages, may possibly have a proof of it, which they could not have, from the conformity between the prophetic history, and the state of the world and of Christianity. And further: if we were to suppose the evidence, which some have of religion, to amount to little more than seeing that it may be true; but that they remain in great doubts and uncertainties about both its evidence and its nature, and great perplexities concerning the rule of life: others to have a full conviction of the truth of religion, with a distinct knowledge of their duty; and others severally to have all the intermediate degrees of religious light and evidence, which lie between these two—if we put the case, that for the present, it was intended, revelation should be no more than a small light, in the midst of a world greatly overspread, notwithstanding it, with ignorance and darkness: that certain glimmerings of this light should extend, and be

At different periods, different degrees of evidence, for

(*a*) Judaism,

(*b*) Christianity.

α

β

Prophecy a stronger proof now than formerly.

Thus (i) the doubtfulness of the evidence for revelation

but grow up to be so, and grow up to be so more and more, gradually from childhood to mature age.

Possible reasons of this inequality.

[7.] What, in particular, is the account or reason of these things, we must be greatly in the dark, were it only that we (*a*) know so very little even of our own case. Our present state may possibly be the consequence of somewhat past, which we are wholly ignorant of: as it has a reference to somewhat to come, of which we know scarce any more than is necessary (*b*) for practice. A system or constitution, in its notion, implies variety; and so complicated an one as this world, very great variety. So that were revelation universal, yet, from men's different capacities of understanding, from the different lengths of their lives, their different educations and other external circumstances, and from their difference of temper and bodily constitution; their religious situations would be widely different, and the disadvantage of some in comparison of others, perhaps, altogether as much as at present. And (*c*) the true account, whatever it be, why mankind, or such a part of mankind, are placed in this condition of ignorance, must be supposed also the true account of our further ignorance, in not knowing the reasons why, or whence it is, that they are placed in this condition. But the following practical reflections may deserve the serious consideration of those persons, who think the circumstances of mankind or their own, in the forementioned respects, a ground of complaint.

Practical reflections: (1) The imperfection of evidence may form part of our trial, in our moral and religious capacity.

[8.] First, The evidence of religion not appearing obvious, may constitute one particular part of some men's trial in the religious sense:[6] as it gives scope, for a virtuous exercise, or vicious neglect of their understanding, in examining or not examining into that evidence. There seems no possible reason to be given, why we may not be in a state of moral probation, with regard to the exercise of our understanding upon the subject of religion, as we are with regard to our behaviour in common affairs. The former is as much a thing within our power and choice as the latter. And I suppose it is to be laid down for certain, that the same character, the same inward principle, which, after a man is convinced of the truth of religion,

[6] [The germ of this valuable discussion may be traced in Serm. xv. § 9, "Difficulties in speculation as much come into the notion of a state of discipline, as difficulties in practice; and so the same reason or account is to be given of both."]

renders him obedient to the precepts of it, would, were he not thus convinced, set him about an examination of it, upon its system and evidence being offered to his thoughts: and that in the latter state his examination would be with an impartiality, seriousness, and solicitude, proportionable to what his obedience is in the former. And as inattention, negligence, want of all serious concern, about a matter of such a nature and such importance, when offered to men's consideration, is, before a distinct conviction of its truth, as real immoral depravity and dissoluteness; as neglect of religious practice after such conviction:[7] so active solicitude about it, and fair impartial consideration of its evidence before such conviction is as really an exercise of a morally right temper; as is religious practice after. Thus, that religion is not intuitively true, but a matter of deduction and inference; that a conviction of its truth is not forced upon every one, but left to be, by some, collected with heedful attention to premises; this as much constitutes religious probation, as much affords sphere, scope, opportunity, for right and wrong behaviour, as anything whatever does. And their manner of treating this subject, when laid before them, shews what is in their heart, and is an exertion of it.

(2) Even if the evidence be highly doubtful, the obligation of duty remains,

[9.] Secondly, It appears to be a thing as evident, though it is not so much attended to, that if, upon consideration of religion, the evidence of it should seem to any persons doubtful, in the highest supposable degree; even this doubtful evidence will, however, put them into a general state of probation in the moral and religious sense. For, suppose a man to be really in doubt, whether such a person had not done him the greatest favour; or, whether his whole temporal interest did not depend upon that person: no one, who had any sense of gratitude and of prudence, could possibly consider himself in the same situation, with regard to such person, as if he had no such doubt. In truth, it is as just to say, that certainty and doubt are the same; as to say, the situations now mentioned would leave a man as entirely at liberty in point of gratitude or prudence, as he would be, were he certain he had received no favour from such person, or that he no way depended upon him. And thus, though the evidence

as in the *moral*,

[7] [Cp. page 42 above.]

so in the *religious* sphere.

of religion which is afforded to some men should be little more than that they are given to see the system of Christianity, or religion in general, to be supposable and credible; this ought in all reason to beget a serious practical apprehension, that it may be true. And even this will afford matter of exercise for religious suspense and deliberation, for moral resolution and self-government; because the apprehension that religion may be true does as really lay men under obli-
α gations, as a full conviction that it is true. It gives occasion and motives to consider further the important subject; to
β preserve attentively upon their minds a general implicit sense that they may be under Divine moral government, an awful solicitude about religion, whether natural or revealed. Such
γ apprehension ought to turn men's eyes to every degree of new light which may be had, from whatever side it comes;
δ and induce them to refrain, in the mean time, from all immoralities, and live in the conscientious practice of every common virtue. Especially are they bound to keep at the
ε greatest distance from all dissolute profaneness;[8] for this the very nature of the case forbids; and to treat with highest reverence a matter, upon which their own whole interest and being, and the fate of Nature, depends. This behaviour, and an active endeavour to maintain within themselves this temper, is the business, the duty, and the wisdom of those persons, who complain of the doubtfulness of religion: is what they are under the most proper obligations to. And such behaviour is an exertion of, and has a tendency to improve in them, that character, which the practice of all the several duties of religion, from a full conviction of its truth, is an exertion of, and has a tendency to improve in others: others, I say, to whom God has afforded such conviction. Nay, considering the infinite importance of religion, revealed as well as natural, I think it may be said in general, that whoever will weigh the matter thoroughly may see, there is not near so much difference, as is commonly imagined, between what ought in reason to be the rule of life, to those persons who are fully convinced of its truth, and to those who have only a serious doubting apprehension, that it may be true. Their hopes, and fears, and obligations, will be in various degrees: but,

To behave in such a manner promotes the religious character.

[8] [Cp. the language of the Advertisement to the *Analogy*, and the editor's note there.]

as the subject-matter of their hopes and fears is the same; so the subject-matter of their obligations what they are bound to do and to refrain from, is not so very unlike.

Men of high intellect or position are especially under such obligation.

[10.] It is to be observed further, that, from a character of understanding, or a situation of influence in the world, some persons have it in their power to do infinitely more harm or good, by setting an example of profaneness and avowed disregard to all religion, or, on the contrary, of a serious, though perhaps doubting, apprehension of its truth, and of a reverend regard to it under this doubtfulness; than they can do, by acting well or ill in all the common intercourses amongst mankind. And consequently they are most highly accountable for a behaviour, which, they may easily foresee, is of such importance, and in which there is most plainly a right and a wrong; even admitting the evidence of religion to be as doubtful as is pretended.

Doubt implies *some* positive evidence.

[11.] The ground of these observations, and that which renders them just and true, is, that doubting necessarily implies some degree of evidence for that, of which we doubt. For no person would be in doubt concerning the truth of a number of facts so and so circumstanced, which should accidentally come into his thoughts, and of which he had no evidence at all. And though in the case of an even chance, and where consequently we were in doubt, we should in common language say, that we had no evidence at all for either side; yet that situation of things, which renders it an even chance and no more, that such an event will happen, renders this case equivalent to all others, where there is such evidence on both sides of a question,[9] as leaves the mind in doubt concerning the truth. Indeed in all these cases, there is no more evidence on one side than on the other; but there is (what is equivalent to) much more for either, than for the truth of a number of facts, which come into one's thoughts at random. And thus, in all these cases, doubt as much presupposes evidence, lower degrees of evidence, as belief presupposes higher, and certainty higher still. Any one, who will a little attend to the nature of evidence, will easily carry this observation on, and see, that between no evidence at all, and that degree of it which affords ground

As there are degrees of evidence, so of assent;

[9] Introduction [§ 4. Cp. Part II. vii. 31.]

of doubt, there are as many intermediate degrees, as there are, between that degree which is the ground of doubt, and demonstration. And though we have not faculties to distinguish these degrees of evidence with any sort of exactness; yet, in proportion as they are discerned, they ought to influence our practice.[10] For it is as real an imperfection in the moral character, not to be influenced in practice by a lower degree of evidence when discerned, as it is in the understanding, not to discern it. And as, in all subjects which men consider, they discern the lower as well as higher degrees of evidence, proportionably to their capacity of understanding; so, in practical subjects, they are influenced in practice, by the lower as well as higher degrees of it, proportionably to their fairness and honesty. And as, in proportion to defects in the understanding, men are unapt to see lower degrees of evidence, are in danger of overlooking evidence when it is not glaring, and are easily imposed upon in such cases; so, in proportion to the corruption of the heart, they seem capable of satisfying themselves with having no regard in practice to evidence acknowledged real, if it be not overbearing. From these things it must follow, that doubting concerning religion implies such a degree of evidence for it, as, joined with the consideration of its importance,

but, low or high,

in speculation,

and in morals,

evidence imposes an obligation.

[10] [Compare Introd. § 1. This is the doctrine of assent which Butler had inherited from the sober English thinkers who had preceded him. Thus Hooker writes: "When it cometh to the point of trial, such as the evidence is which the truth hath either in itself or through proof, such is the heart's assent thereunto; neither can it be stronger, being grounded as it should be" (*Eccl. Pol.* II. vii. 5). And Locke, in his chapter on Enthusiasm (*Essay* IV. xix. 1), notes as the "one unerring mark" of sincerity, "the not entertaining any proposition with greater assurance than the proofs it is built upon will warrant." So again, at a later date, Hume, in his *Essay on Miracles*, urges that when probabilities are balanced against each other, "there is a mutual destruction of arguments, and the superior only gives us an assurance suitable to that degree of force which remains, after deducting the inferior." This view has been combated by Newman in his *Grammar of Assent*, and it must be confessed that it does not allow sufficiently for the fact that in practical matters, when once the mind is made up after due consideration of all the evidence, the adverse probabilities must be ignored. If we did not do this in ordinary life, action would be rendered impossible. We may think that in political controversies both sides have a good deal to say for themselves, but nevertheless, when it comes to a contested election, we vote for that side which seems, on the whole, to have the stronger position. That is, we must (if we wish to act at all) cast away from us all the adverse criticisms that we have heard, and act as if they did not exist. *Evidence* admits of degrees, but practical assent to a proposition does not. Our vote must be "Aye" or "No." But it is *conduct*, not *conviction*, which Butler has in his mind throughout.]

unquestionably lays men under the obligations before mentioned, to have a dutiful regard to it in all their behaviour.

(3) Theoretical analogous to practical difficulties;

[12.] Thirdly, The difficulties in which the evidence of religion is involved, which some complain of, is no more a just ground of complaint, than the external circumstances of temptation, which others are placed in; or than difficulties in the practice of it, after a full conviction of its truth. Temptations render our state a more improving state of discipline,[11] than it would be otherwise: as they give occasion for a more attentive exercise of the virtuous principle, which confirms and strengthens it more, than an easier or less attentive exercise of it could. Now speculative difficulties are, in this respect, of the very same nature with these external temptations. For the evidence of religion not appearing obvious, is to some persons a temptation to reject it, without any consideration at all; and therefore requires such an attentive exercise of the virtuous principle, seriously to consider that evidence, as there would be no occasion for, but for such temptation. And the supposed doubtfulness of its evidence, after it has been in some sort considered, affords opportunity to an unfair mind of explaining away, and deceitfully hiding from itself, that evidence which it might see; and also for men's encouraging themselves in vice, from hopes of impunity, though they do clearly see thus much at least, that these hopes are uncertain: in like manner as the common temptation to many instances of folly, which end in temporal infamy and ruin, is the ground for hope of not being detected, and of escaping with impunity; *i.e.* the doubtfulness of the proof beforehand, that such foolish behaviour will thus end in infamy and ruin. On the contrary, supposed doubtfulness in the evidence of religion calls for a more careful and attentive exercise of the virtuous principle, in fairly yielding themselves up to the proper influence of any real evidence, though doubtful; and in practising conscientiously all virtue, though under some uncertainty, whether the government in the universe may not possibly be such, as that vice may escape with impunity. And in general, temptation, meaning by this word the lesser allurements to wrong and difficulties in the discharge of our

as temptations make the present state one of improving discipline, so do speculative difficulties.

[11] Part I. v. [§ 13 ff.]

duty, as well as the greater ones; temptation, I say, as such and of every kind and degree, as it calls forth some virtuous efforts, additional to what would otherwise have been wanting, cannot but be an additional discipline and improvement of virtue, as well as probation of it in the other senses of that word.[12] So that the very same account is to be given, why the evidence of religion should be left in such a manner, as to require, in some, an attentive, solicitous, perhaps painful exercise of their understanding about it; as why others should be placed in such circumstances, as that the practice of its common duties, after a full conviction of the truth of it, should require attention, solicitude, and pains: or, why appearing doubtfulness should be permitted to afford matter of temptation to some; as why external difficulties and allurements should be permitted to afford matter of temptation to others. The same account also is to be given, why some should be exercised with temptations of both these kinds; as why others should be exercised with the latter in such very high degrees, as some have been, particularly as the primitive Christians were.

Thus the same reason may be assigned for both.

[13.] Nor does there appear any absurdity in supposing, that the speculative difficulties, in which the evidence of religion is involved, may make even the principal part of some persons' trial. For as the chief temptations of the generality of the world are the ordinary motives to injustice or unrestrained pleasure; or to live in the neglect of religion from that frame of mind, which renders many persons almost without feeling as to anything distant, or which is not the object of their senses: so there are other persons without this shallowness of temper, persons of a deeper sense as to what is invisible and future; who not only see, but have a general practical feeling, that what is to come will be present, and that things are not less real for their not being the objects of sense; and who, from their natural constitution of body and of temper, and from their external condition, may have small temptations to behave ill, small difficulty in behaving well, in the common course of life. Now when these latter persons have a distinct full conviction of the truth of religion, without any possible doubts or difficulties, the practice of it is to them unavoidable,

Speculative difficulties the chief part of some men's trial,

especially of those whose practical temptations are small:

[12] Part I. chap. iv. and pp. 98, 99.

unless they will do a constant violence to their own minds; and religion is scarce any more a discipline to them, than it is to creatures in a state of perfection. Yet these persons may possibly stand in need of moral discipline and exercise in a higher degree, than they would have by such an easy practice of religion. Or it may be requisite, for reasons unknown to us, that they should give some further manifestation[13] what is their moral character, to the creation of God, than such a practice of it would be. Thus in the great variety of religious situations in which men are placed, what constitutes, what chiefly and peculiarly constitutes, the probation, in all senses, of some persons, may be the difficulties in which the evidence of religion is involved: and their principal and distinguished trial may be, how they will behave under and with respect to these difficulties. Circumstances in men's situation in their temporal capacity, analogous in good measure to this respecting religion, are to be observed. We find some persons are placed in such a situation in the world, as that their chief difficulty with regard to conduct, is not the doing what is prudent when it is known; for this, in numberless cases, is as easy as the contrary: but to some the principal exercise is, recollection and being upon their guard against deceits, the deceits suppose of those about them; against false appearances of reason and prudence. To persons in some situations, the principal exercise with respect to conduct is, attention in order to inform themselves what is proper, what is really the reasonable and prudent part to act.[14]

(α) these need discipline;

(β) requisite that their character be exhibited to the world.

Analogy in the natural order.

[14.] But as I have hitherto gone upon supposition, that men's dissatisfaction with the evidence of religion is not owing to their neglects or prejudices; it must be added, on the other hand, in all common reason, and as what the truth of the case plainly requires should be added, that such dissatisfaction possibly may be owing to those, possibly may be men's own fault. For,

Dissatisfaction with evidence may be men's own fault;

[15.] If there are any persons, who never set themselves heartily and in earnest to be informed in religion; if there are any, who secretly wish it may not prove true; and are less attentive to evidence than to difficulties, and more to objections than to what is said in answer to them: these persons will

for the indolent, careless, and superstitious may miss plain evidence.

[13] Pp. 98, 99.

[14] [See Part I. iv. 7.]

scarce be thought in a likely way of seeing the evidence of religion, though it were most certainly true, and capable of being ever so fully proved. If any accustom themselves to consider this subject usually in the way of mirth and sport: if they attend to forms and representations, and inadequate manners of expression, instead of the real things intended by them: (for signs often can be no more than inadequately expressive of the things signified:) or if they substitute human errors in the room of Divine truth; why may not all, or any of these things, hinder some men from seeing that evidence, which really is seen by others; as a like turn of mind, with respect to matters of common speculation and practice, does, we find by experience, hinder them from attaining that knowledge and right understanding, in matters of common speculation and practice, which more fair and attentive minds attain to? And the effect will be the same, whether their neglect of seriously considering the evidence of religion, and their indirect behaviour with regard to it, proceed from mere carelessness, or from the grosser vices; or whether it be owing to this, that forms and figurative manners of expression, as well as errors, administer occasions of ridicule, when the things intended, and the truth itself, would not. Men may indulge a ludicrous turn so far as to lose all sense of conduct and prudence in worldly affairs, and even, as it seems, to impair their faculty of reason. And in general, levity, carelessness, passion, and prejudice, *do* hinder us from being rightly informed, with respect to common things: and they *may*, in like manner, and perhaps in some further providential manner, with respect to moral and religious subjects: may hinder evidence from being laid before us, and from being seen when it is. The Scripture[15] does declare, that every one "shall not

Analogy in worldly affairs.

[15] *Dan.* xii. 10. See also *Isa.* xxix. 13, 14; *St. Matt.* vi. 23 and xi. 25 and xiii. 11, 12; *St. John* iii. 19 and v. 44; *1 Cor.* ii. 14, and *2 Cor.* iv. 4; *2 Tim.* iii. 13; and that affectionate as well as authoritative admonition, so very many times inculcated, "He that hath ears to hear, let him hear." Grotius saw so strongly the thing intended in these and other passages of Scripture of the like sense, as to say, that the proof given us of Christianity was less than it might have been, for this very purpose: *Ut ita sermo Evangelii tanquam lapis esset Lydius ad quem ingenia sanabilia explorarentur.* De Ver. *R. C.* lib. ii. towards the end. [I have no doubt that Butler found this quotation from Grotius in Bishop Wilkins' *Natural Religion.* This book he had undoubtedly read; in particular, the arguments of this chapter are in many points identical with those of Wilkins (Bk. i. c. 3.) The words of Wilkins which are here in view are: "And therefore God is pleased to

understand." And it makes no difference, by what providential conduct this comes to pass: whether the evidence of Christianity was, originally and with design, put and left so, as that those who are desirous of evading moral obligations should not see it; and that honest-minded persons should: or, whether it comes to pass by any other means.

The general proofs of religion, natural and revealed, lie level to ordinary men.

[16.] Further: The general proof of natural religion and of Christianity does, I think, lie level to common men; even those, the greatest part of whose time, from childhood to old age, is taken up with providing for themselves and their families the common conveniences, perhaps necessaries, of life: those, I mean, of this rank, who ever think at all of asking after proof, or attending to it. Common men, were they as much in earnest about religion, as about their temporal affairs, are capable of being convinced upon real evidence, that there is a God Who governs the world: and they feel themselves to be of a moral nature, and accountable creatures. And as Christianity entirely falls in with this their natural sense of things, so they are capable, not only of being persuaded, but of being made to see, that there is evidence of miracles wrought in attestation of it, and many appearing completions of prophecy. But though this proof is real and conclusive, yet it is liable to objections, and may be run up into difficulties; which, however, persons who are capable, not only of talking of, but of really seeing, are capable also of seeing through: *i.e.* not of clearing up and answering them, so as to satisfy their curiosity, for of such knowledge we are not capable with respect to any one thing in Nature; but capable of seeing that the proof is not lost in these difficulties, or destroyed by these objections. But then a thorough examination into religion, with regard to these objections, which cannot be the business of every man, is a matter of pretty large compass, and, from the nature of it, requires some knowledge, as well as time and attention; to see, how the evidence comes out, upon balancing one thing with another, and what, upon the whole, is the amount of it. Now if persons who

Those who see the difficulties can see the answers,

propose these matters of belief to us in such a way as that we might give some testimony of our teachable dispositions, and of our obedience by our assent to them. *Ut sermo Evangelii tanquam lapis esset Lydius, ad quem ingenia sanabilia explorarentur,* as the learned Grotius speaks concerning the doctrine of the Gospel, whereby God was pleased as with a touchstone to prove and try men," etc. (p. 32, ed. 1675).]

doubtful what will be the consequence, are often naturally, *i.e.* providentially, altogether as fatal, as misconduct occasioned by heedless inattention to what we certainly know, or disregarding it from overbearing passion.

To serious persons this will be quite intelligible.

[19.] Several of the observations here made may well seem strange, perhaps unintelligible, to many good men. But if the persons for whose sake they are made think so; persons who object as above, and throw off all regard to religion under pretence of want of evidence; I desire them to consider again, whether their thinking so be owing to anything unintelligible in these observations, or to their own not having such a sense of religion and serious solicitude about it, as even their state of scepticism does in all reason require? It ought to be forced upon the reflection of these persons, that our nature and condition necessarily require us, in the daily course of life, to act upon evidence much lower than what is commonly called probable; to guard, not only against what we fully believe will, but also against what we think it supposable may, happen; and to engage in pursuits when the probability is greatly against success, if it be credible, that possibly we may succeed in them.

CHAPTER VII.

Of the particular Evidence for Christianity.

[1.] THE presumptions against revelation, and objections against the general scheme of Christianity, and particular things relating to it, being removed; there remains to be considered, what positive evidence we have for the truth of it: chiefly in order to see, what the analogy of Nature suggests with regard to that evidence, and the objections against it: or to see what is, and is allowed to be, the plain natural rule of judgment and of action, in our temporal concerns, in cases where we have the same kind of evidence, and the same kind of objections against it, that we have in the case before us.

Positive evidence for Christianity

[2.] Now in the evidence of Christianity there seem to be several things of great weight, not reducible to the head, either of miracles, or the completion of prophecy, in the common acceptation of the words. But these two are its direct and fundamental proofs: and those other things, however considerable they are, yet ought never to be urged apart from its direct proofs, but always to be joined with them. Thus the evidence of Christianity will be a long series of things, reaching, as it seems, from the beginning of the world to the present time, of great variety and compass, taking in both the direct, and also the collateral, proofs; and making up, all of them together, one argument: the conviction arising from which kind of proof may be compared to what they call *the effect* in architecture or other works of art; a result from a great number of things so and so disposed, and taken into one view.[1] I shall therefore, first, make some observations relating to miracles, and the appearing completions of prophecy; and

is **(A)** *direct*, viz. I Miracles, II. Prophecy;

and **(B)** *cumulative*, from the direct and collateral proofs taken together.

A

[1] [This *cumulative* force of the evidences of Christianity is admirably described by Davison, *On Prophecy*, p. 21. Cp. § 43 below.]

sufficient to invalidate it. But no man will deny the consequence to be, that it cannot be rejected, or thrown by as of no authority, till it can be proved to be of none; even though the evidence now mentioned for its authority were doubtful.

α This evidence may be confronted by historical evidence on
β the other side, if there be any: or general incredibility in the
γ things related, or inconsistence in the general turn of the history, would prove it to be of no authority. But since, upon the face of the matter, upon a first and general view, the appearance is, that it is an authentic history; it cannot be determined to be fictitious without some proof that it is so. And the following observations in support of these, and coincident with them, will greatly confirm the historical evidence for the truth of Christianity.

(2) The Pauline Epistles confirm the Gospel miracles.

(*a*) They are genuine letters of St. Paul.

[7.] 2. The Epistles of St. Paul, from the nature of epistolary writing, and moreover from several of them being written, not to particular persons, but to churches, carry in them evidences of their being genuine, beyond what can be in a mere historical narrative, left to the world at large.[4] This evidence, joined with that which they have in common with the rest of the New Testament, seems not to leave so much as any particular pretence for denying their genuineness, considered as an ordinary matter of fact, or of criticism: I say *particular* pretence, for *denying* it; because any single fact, of such a kind and such antiquity, may have *general doubts* raised concerning it, from the very nature of human affairs and human testimony. There is also to be mentioned a distinct and particular evidence of the genuineness of the Epistle chiefly referred to here, the first to the Corinthians; from the manner in which it is quoted by Clemens Romanus, in an epistle of his own to that church.[5] Now these epistles afford a proof of Christianity, detached from all others, which is, I think, a thing of weight; and also a proof of a nature and kind peculiar to itself. For,

4 [This was developed with great ingenuity by Paley in his *Horae Paulinae*.]

5 Clem. Rom. Ep. 1, c. 47. ["Take up the epistle of the blessed Paul the Apostle. What wrote he first unto you in the beginning of the Gospel? of a truth he charged you in the Spirit concerning himself and Cephas and Apollos, because that even then ye had made parties," where the reference is evidently to *1 Cor*. i. 12, etc. The date of this letter, written by Clement to the Corinthians in the name of the Roman Church, is about 95 A.D.]

[8.] In them the author declares, that he received the Gospel in general, and the institution of the Communion in particular, not from the rest of the Apostles, or jointly together with them, but alone, from Christ Himself; Whom he declares likewise, conformably to the history in the Acts, that he saw after His ascension.[6] So that the testimony of St. Paul is to be considered, as detached from that of the rest of the Apostles.

(*b*) His testimony distinct from that of the Twelve.

[9.] And he declares further, that he was endued with a power of working miracles, as what was publicly known to those very people, speaks of frequent and great variety of miraculous gifts as then subsisting in those very churches, to which he was writing; which he was reproving for several irregularities; and where he had personal opposers:[7] he mentions these gifts incidentally, in the most easy manner, and without effort; by way of reproof to those who had them, for their indecent use of them; and by way of depreciating them, in comparison of moral virtues: in short he speaks to these churches, of these miraculous powers, in the manner, any one would speak to another of a thing, which was as familiar and as much known in common to them both, as anything in the world.[8] And this, as hath been observed by several persons, is surely a very considerable thing.

(*c*) He claims the power of working miracles in his own person.

[10.] 3. It is an acknowledged historical fact, that Christianity offered itself to the world, and demanded to be received, upon the allegation, *i.e.* as unbelievers would speak, upon the pretence, of miracles, publicly wrought to attest the truth of it, in such an age: and that it was actually received by great numbers in that very age, and upon the professed belief of the reality of these miracles. And Christianity, including the dispensation of the Old Testament, seems distinguished by this from all other religions. I mean, that this does not appear to be the case with regard to any other: for surely it will not be supposed to lie upon any person, to prove by

(3) Christianity was accepted on the ground of its miracles;

(*a*) herein differing from other religions.

[6] *Gal.* i. 1; *1 Cor.* xi. 23, etc.; *1 Cor.* xv. 8.

[7] [This is an important point. If it had not been an acknowledged fact that some such exhibitions of power had followed St. Paul's ministry, it would have been incredible folly that he should have made such a claim in letters to be read by unfavourable critics as well as by personal friends.]

[8] *Rom.* xv. 19; *1 Cor.* xii. 8, 9, 10-28, etc., and xiii. 1, 2, 8, and the whole xivth chapter; *2 Cor.* xii. 12, 13; *Gal.* iii. 2, 5.

(α) Mahomet's claim not supported by visible miracle.

positive historical evidence, that it was not. It does in no sort appear that Mahometanism was first received in the world upon the foot of supposed miracles,[9] *i.e.* public ones: for, as revelation is itself miraculous, all pretence to it must necessarily imply some pretence of miracles. And it is a known fact, that it was immediately, at the very first, propagated by other means.[10] And as particular institutions, whether in Paganism or Popery, said to be confirmed by miracles after those institutions had obtained, are not to the purpose: so, were there what might be called historical proof, that any of them were introduced by a supposed Divine command believed to be attested by miracles; these would not be in any wise parallel. For single things of this sort are easy to be accounted for, after parties are formed, and have power in their hands; and the leaders of them are in veneration with the multitude; and political interests are blended with religious claims, and religious distinctions. But before anything of this kind, for a few persons, and those of the lowest rank, all at once, to bring over such great numbers to a new religion, and get it to be received upon the particular evidence of miracles; this is quite another thing. And I think it will be allowed by any fair adversary, that the fact now mentioned, taking in all the circumstances of it, is peculiar to the Christian religion. However, the fact itself is allowed, that Christianity obtained, *i.e.* was professed to be received in the world, upon the belief of miracles, immediately in the age in which it is said those miracles were wrought: or that this is what its first converts would have alleged, as the reason for their embracing it. Now certainly it is not to be supposed, that such numbers of men, in the most distant parts of the world, should forsake the religion of

(β) Heathen and Roman miracles *followed* the establishment of the tenets they supported.

But the miracles of Christianity were prior to its establishment.

(*b*) Thus its first adherents must *themselves* have been convinced of the truth of these miracles.

[9] See the *Koran*, c. xiii. and c. xvii. [See pp. 201, 203, 232, 235 of Sale's Translation, ed. 1850. In the passages alluded to, the Koreish are represented as demanding miracles of Mohammed, as the certificate of his Divine mission, which the prophet uniformly refused. "Am I other than a man, an apostle? And nothing hindereth men from believing when a direction is come unto them, except that they say, Hath God sent a man for His apostle?"]

[10] [The same thing had been urged by Clarke in his *Evidences* (p. 320), "The Mahometan religion was . . . propagated merely by violence and force of arms, was confirmed by no public and uncontestable miracles, etc." For a defence of the missionary methods of Mohammedanism, see T. W. Arnold's *Preaching of Islam*, where it is contended that they are less violent than Western writers have usually represented them to be.]

their country, in which they had been educated;[11] separate themselves from their friends, particularly in their festival shows and solemnities, to which the common people are so greatly addicted, and which were of a nature to engage them much more, than anything of that sort amongst us; and embrace a religion, which could not but expose them to many inconveniences, and indeed must have been a giving up the world in a great degree, even from the very first, and before the empire engaged in form against them: it cannot be supposed, that such numbers should make so great, and, to say the least, so inconvenient a change in their whole institution of life, unless they were really convinced of the truth of those miracles, upon the knowledge or belief of which they professed to make it. And it will, I suppose, readily be acknowledged, that the generality of the first converts to Christianity must have believed them: that as by becoming Christians they declared to the world, they were satisfied of the truth of those miracles; so this declaration was to be credited. And this their testimony is the same kind of evidence for those miracles, as if they had put it in writing, and these writings had come down to us. And it is real evidence, because it is of facts, which they had capacity and full opportunity to inform themselves of. It is also distinct from the direct or express historical evidence, though it is of the same kind: and it would be allowed to be distinct in all cases. For were a fact expressly related by one or more ancient historians, and disputed in after-ages; that this fact is acknowledged to have been believed by great numbers of the age in which the historian says it was done, would be allowed an additional proof of such fact, quite distinct from the express testimony of the historian. The credulity of mankind is acknowledged: and the suspicions of mankind ought to be acknowledged too; and their backwardness even to believe, and greater still to practise, what makes against their interest. And it must particularly be remembered, that education, and prejudice, and authority, were against Christianity, in the age I am speaking of. So that the immediate conversion of such numbers is a real presumption of somewhat more than human in this matter: I say presumption, for it is not

Their testimony considerable.

[11] [All this, and more, is worked out by Paley in the opening chapters of his *Evidences*.]

alleged as a proof alone and by itself. Nor need any one of the things mentioned in this chapter be considered as a proof by itself: and yet all of them together may be one of the strongest.[12]

Objections to the credibility of this evidence for the Christian miracles:

[11.] Upon the whole: as there is large historical evidence, both direct and circumstantial, of miracles wrought in attestation of Christianity, collected by those who have writ upon the subject; it lies upon unbelievers to shew, why this evidence is not to be credited. This way of speaking is, I think, just; and what persons who write in defence of religion naturally fall into. Yet, in a matter of such unspeakable importance, the proper question is, not whom it lies upon, according to the rules of argument, to maintain or confute objections: but whether there really are any, against this evidence, sufficient, in reason, to destroy the credit of it. However, unbelievers seem to take upon them the part of shewing that there are.

(i) Enthusiasm for ill-founded opinions may beget self-sacrifice.

[12.] They allege, that numberless enthusiastic people, in different ages and countries, expose themselves to the same difficulties which the primitive Christians did; and are ready to give up their lives for the most idle follies imaginable. But it is not very clear, to what purpose this objection is brought. For every one, surely, in every case, must distinguish between opinions and facts.[13] And though testimony is no proof of enthusiastic opinions, or of any opinions at all; yet it is allowed, in all other cases, to be a proof of facts. And a person's laying down his life in attestation of facts or of opinions, is the strongest proof of his believing them. And if the Apostles and their contemporaries did believe the facts, in attestation of which they exposed themselves to sufferings and death; this their belief, or rather knowledge, must be a proof of those facts: for they were such as came under the observation of their senses. And though it is not of equal weight, yet it is of weight, that the martyrs of the next age, notwithstanding they were not eyewitnesses of those facts, as were the Apostles and their contemporaries, had, however, full oppor-

Answer: Self-sacrifice proves the belief of the witness as to facts.

[12] § 43 below.

[13] [Butler seems to have derived this way of putting his answer from Clarke: "'Tis very remarkable, the Apostles did not lay down their lives for their *opinions* (which enthusiasts may possibly be supposed to do), but in attestation to *facts* of their own knowledge" (*Evidences*, p. 441).]

tunity to inform themselves, whether they were true or not, and gave equal proof of their believing them to be true.

(ii) Enthusiasm weakens testimony to facts.

[13.] But enthusiasm, it is said, greatly weakens the evidence of testimony even for facts, in matters relating to religion: some seem to think it totally and absolutely destroys the evidence of testimony upon this subject. And indeed the powers of enthusiasm, and of diseases too, which operate in a like manner, are very wonderful, in particular instances. But if great numbers of men, not appearing in any peculiar degree weak, nor under any peculiar suspicion of negligence, affirm that they saw and heard such things plainly with their eyes and their ears, and are admitted to be in earnest; such testimony is evidence of the strongest kind we can have, for any matter of fact. Yet possibly it may be overcome, strong as it is, by incredibility in the things thus attested, or by contrary testimony. And in an instance where one thought it was so overcome, it might be just to consider, how far such evidence could be accounted for, by enthusiasm; for it seems as if no other imaginable account were to be given of it. But till such incredibility be shewn, or contrary testimony produced, it cannot surely be expected, that so far-fetched, so indirect and wonderful an account of such testimony, as that of enthusiasm must be; an account so strange, that the generality of mankind can scarce be made to understand what is meant by it: it cannot, I say, be expected, that such account will be admitted of such evidence; when there is this direct, easy, and obvious account of it, that people really saw and heard a thing not incredible, which they affirm sincerely and with full assurance, they did see and hear. Granting then that enthusiasm is not (strictly speaking) an absurd, but a possible account of such testimony; it is manifest, that the very mention of it goes upon the previous supposition that the things so attested are incredible: and therefore need not be considered, till they are shewn to be so. Much less need it be considered, after the contrary has been proved. And I think it has been proved, to full satisfaction, that there is no incredibility in a revelation, in general; or in such an one as the Christian in particular. However; as religion is supposed peculiarly liable to enthusiasm, it may just be observed, that prejudices almost without number, and with-

Answer: (a) The testimony of large numbers is only to be overcome (α) by general incredibility of the statements made, or (β) by contrary testimony.

(b) In the absence of these, enthusiasm not a sufficient account;

and the Christian revelation has been proved credible.

(*c*) Such an objection applies to *all* testimony.

out name, romance, affectation, humour, a desire to engage attention, or to surprise, the party-spirit, custom, little competitions, unaccountable likings and dislikings; these influence men strongly in common matters. And as these prejudices are often scarce known or reflected upon by the persons themselves who are influenced by them, they are to be considered as influences of a like kind to enthusiasm. Yet human testimony in common matters is naturally and justly believed notwithstanding.

(iii) The Apostles were partly deceivers and partly deceived.

[14.] It is intimated further, in a more refined way of observation, that though it should be proved, that the Apostles and first Christians could not, in some respects, be deceived themselves, and, in other respects, cannot be thought to have intended to impose upon the world; yet it will not follow, that their general testimony is to be believed, though truly handed down to us: because they might still in part, *i.e.* in other respects, be deceived themselves, and in part also designedly impose upon others; which, it is added, is a thing very credible, from that mixture of real enthusiasm, and real knavery, to be met with in the same characters. And, I must confess, I think the matter of fact contained in this observation upon mankind is not to be denied; and that somewhat very much akin to it is often supposed in Scripture as a very common case,[14] and most severely reproved. But it were to have been expected, that persons capable of applying this observation as applied in the objection, might also frequently have met with the like mixed character, in instances where religion was quite out of the case. The thing plainly is, that mankind are naturally endued with reason, or a capacity of distinguishing between truth and falsehood; and as naturally they are endued with veracity, or a regard to truth in what they say: but from many occasions they are liable to be prejudiced and biassed and deceived themselves, and capable of intending to deceive others, in every different degree: insomuch that, as we are all liable to be deceived by prejudice, so likewise it seems to be not an uncommon thing, for persons, who, from their regard to truth, would not invent a lie

Answer: Psychologically possible;

but the objection would apply to *all* testimony.

[14] [Probably Butler had in his mind such a case as that of Balaam. See *Sermons* vii. and x. and *Public Sermons*, iii. 2 note, for many references.]

entirely without any foundation at all, to propagate it with heightening circumstances, after it is once invented and set agoing. And others, though they would not *propagate* a lie, yet, which is a lower degree of falsehood, will let it pass without contradiction. But, notwithstanding all this, human testimony remains still a natural ground of assent; and this assent a natural principle of action.

(iv) Men deluded often by false miracles. Answer: No more than in other ways.

[15.] It is objected further, that however it has happened, the *fact* is, that mankind have, in different ages, been strangely deluded with pretences to miracles and wonders. But it is by no means to be admitted, that they have been oftener, or are at all more liable to be deceived by these pretences, than by others.

(v) Considerable evidence for false miracles.

Answer: (*a*) Not so good as for the Gospel miracles;

(*b*) each case should be judged on its own merits.

[16.] It is added that there is a very considerable degree of historical evidence for miracles, which are, on all hands, acknowledged to be fabulous.[15] But suppose there were even *the like* historical evidence for these, to what there is for those alleged in proof of Christianity, which yet is no wise allowed, but suppose this; the consequence would not be, that the evidence of the latter is not to be admitted. Nor is there a man in the world, who, in common cases, would conclude thus. For what would such a conclusion really amount to but this, that evidence, confuted by contrary evidence, or any way overbalanced, destroys the credibility of other evidence, neither confuted, nor overbalanced? To argue, that because there is, if there were, like evidence from testimony, for miracles acknowledged false, as for those in attestation of Christianity, therefore the evidence in the latter case is not to be credited; this is the same as to argue, that if two men of equally good reputation had given evidence in different cases no way connected, and one of them had been convicted of perjury, this confuted the testimony of the other.

Deceit and self-deceit weaken, but do not destroy, testimony.

[17.] Upon the whole then, the general observation, that human creatures are so liable to be deceived, from enthusiasm in religion, and principles equivalent to enthusiasm in common matters, and in both from negligence; and that they are so capable of dishonestly endeavouring to deceive others; this does indeed weaken the evidence of testimony in all cases, but does not destroy it in any. And these things will appear,

15 [This objection was powerfully urged a little later by Hume, and Paley devoted a large part of his *Evidences* to the consideration of it.]

to different men, to weaken the evidence of testimony, in different degrees: in degrees proportionable to the observations they have made, or the notions they have any way taken up, concerning the weakness and negligence and dishonesty of mankind; or concerning the powers of enthusiasm, and prejudices equivalent to it. But it seems to me, that people do not know what they say, who affirm these things to destroy the evidence from testimony, which we have of the truth of Christianity. Nothing can destroy the evidence of testimony in any case, but a proof or probability, that persons are not competent judges of the facts to which they give testimony; or that they are actually under some indirect influence in giving it, in such particular case. Till this be made out, the *natural* laws of human actions require, that testimony be admitted. It can never be sufficient to overthrow direct historical evidence, indolently to say, that there are so many principles, from whence men are liable to be deceived themselves, and disposed to deceive others, especially in matters of religion, that one knows not what to believe. And it is surprising persons can help reflecting, that this very manner of speaking supposes they are not satisfied that there is nothing in the evidence, of which they speak thus; or that they can avoid observing, if they do make this reflection, that it is, on such a subject, a very material one.[16]

Its force remains unless the witness is (α) incompetent or (β) under undue influence.

[18.] And over against all these objections is to be set the importance of Christianity, as what must have engaged the attention of its first converts, so as to have rendered them less liable to be deceived from carelessness, than they would in common matters; and likewise the strong obligations to veracity, which their religion laid them under: so that the first and most obvious presumption is, that they could not be deceived themselves, nor would deceive others. And this presumption, in this degree, is peculiar to the testimony we have been considering.

The force of such objections here lessened, because of (*a*) the importance of Christianity; (*b*) its obligations to veracity.

[19.] In argument, assertions are nothing in themselves, and have an air of positiveness, which sometimes is not very easy: yet they are necessary, and necessary to be repeated; in order to connect a discourse, and distinctly to lay before the view of the reader, what is proposed to be

Thus, the direct proof by miracle is very considerable.

[16] See the foregoing chapter [especially § 11].

proved, and what is left as proved. Now the conclusion from the foregoing observations is, I think, beyond all doubt, this: that unbelievers must be forced to admit the external evidence for Christianity, *i.e.* the proof of miracles wrought to attest it, to be of real weight and very considerable; though they cannot allow it to be sufficient, to convince them of the reality of those miracles. And as they must, in all reason, admit this; so it seems to me, that upon consideration they would, in fact, admit it; those of them, I mean, who know anything at all of the matter: in like manner as persons, in many cases, own they see strong evidence from testimony, for the truth of things, which yet they cannot be convinced are true: cases, suppose, where there is contrary testimony; or things which they think, whether with or without reason, to be incredible. But there is no testimony contrary to that which we have been considering: and it has been fully proved, that there is no incredibility in Christianity in general, or in any part of it.

[20.] II. As to the evidence for Christianity from prophecy, I shall only make some few general observations, which are suggested by the Analogy of Nature; *i.e.* by the acknowledged natural rules of judging in common matters, concerning evidence of a like kind to this from prophecy. **II. Prophecy.**

[21.] 1. The obscurity or unintelligibleness of one part of a prophecy does not, in any degree, invalidate the proof of foresight, arising from the appearing completion of those other parts which are understood. For the case is evidently the same, as if those parts, which are not understood, were lost, or not written at all, or written in an unknown tongue. Whether this observation be commonly attended to or not, it is so evident, that one can scarce bring oneself to set down an instance in common matters, to exemplify it. However, suppose a writing, partly in cypher, and partly in plain words at length; and that in the part one understood, there appeared mention of several known facts; it would never come into any man's thoughts to imagine, that if he understood the whole, perhaps he might find, that those facts were not in reality known by the writer. Indeed, both in this example, and the thing intended to be exemplified by it, our not understanding the whole (the whole, suppose, of a sentence or a paragraph) might sometimes occasion a doubt, whether

(1) Obscurity of part of a prophecy does not invalidate the proof from the rest.

Illustration.

satisfied to such degree, that one knew the whole meaning of that book: for the meaning of a book is nothing but the meaning of the author. But if one knew a person to have compiled a book out of memoirs, which he received from another, of vastly superior knowledge in the subject of it, especially if it were a book full of great intricacies and difficulties; it would in no wise follow, that one knew the whole meaning of the book, from knowing the whole meaning of the compiler: for the original memoirs, *i.e.* the author of them, might have, and there would be no degree of presumption, in many cases, against supposing him to have, some further meaning than the compiler saw. To say then, that the Scriptures, and the things contained in them, can have no other or further meaning than those persons thought or had, who first recited or wrote them; is evidently saying, that those persons were the original, proper, and sole authors of those books, *i.e.* that they are not inspired: which is absurd, whilst the authority of these books is under examination; *i.e.* till you have determined they are of no Divine authority at all. Till this be determined, it must in all reason be supposed, not indeed that they have, for this is taking for granted that they are inspired; but that they may have, some further meaning than what the compilers saw or understood. And, upon this supposition, it is supposable also, that this further meaning may be fulfilled. Now events corresponding to prophecies, interpreted in a different meaning from that, in which the prophets are supposed to have understood them; this affords, in a manner, the same proof, that this different sense was originally intended, as it would have afforded, if the prophets had not understood their predictions in the sense it is supposed they did: because there is no presumption of their sense of them being the whole sense of them. And it has been already shewn, that the apparent completions of prophecy must be allowed to be explanatory of its meaning. So that the question is, whether a series of prophecy has been fulfilled, in a natural or proper, *i.e.* in any real, sense of the words of it. For such completion is equally a proof of foresight more than human, whether the prophets are, or are not, supposed to have understood it in a different sense. I say, supposed: for, though I think it clear, that the prophets did not understand the full meaning of their

A meaning other than the prophet knew perhaps intended.

Double sense of prophecy.

predictions;[18] it is another question, how far they thought they did, and in what sense they understood them.

Applicability of the prophecy to the present or past might cause a difficulty at the time.

[26.] Hence may be seen, to how little purpose those persons busy themselves, who endeavour to prove, that the prophetic history is applicable to events of the age in which it was written, or of ages before it. Indeed to have proved this, before there was any appearance of a further completion of it, might have answered some purpose; for it might have prevented the expectation of any such further completion. Thus could Porphyry have shewn, that some principal parts of the book of Daniel, for instance, the seventh verse of the seventh chapter, which the Christians interpreted of the latter ages, was applicable to events, which happened before or about the age of Antiochus Epiphanes; this might have prevented them from expecting any further completion of it. And, unless there was then, as I think there must have been, external evidence concerning that book, more than is come down to us; such a discovery might have been a stumbling-block in the way of Christianity itself: considering the authority which our Saviour has given to the book of Daniel,[19] and how much the general scheme of Christianity presupposes the truth of it. But even this discovery, had there been any such,[20] would be of very little weight with reasonable men

E.g. the Book of Daniel.

But it does not affect the proof from the

[18] [The same might be said of every work of genius. The poet to whom it is given to use words vastly greater than the fragment of the truth which he sees is only one instance. Perhaps it is also true of the great painter that he is unconscious of the manifold suggestiveness of his work. Certainly it is not surprising that the prophets who were moved by a spirit other than their own should use language transcending their thought. See Keble, *Christian Year*, 13 S. aft. Trinity.

It would be impossible within the compass of a note adequately to discuss the doctrine of the "double sense" of prophecy which Butler has in view in § 25. It is fully expounded in many books, *e.g.* Davison, *On Prophecy*, p. 144. It is enough to observe here that the utterances of genius have eternal vitality, and are interpreted afresh by each age in relation to its own needs. And so every "true word of prophecy" may have many different "senses." Thus a principle of God's dealings with men which a prophet and his hearers referred to their own times might have repeated fulfilments in after days, under different circumstances and changed conditions. And it is therefore not unreasonable to believe that prophecies originally directed to the national policy of the Jewish people have found a wider fulfilment in the Advent and the Kingdom of Christ, and that this wider fulfilment was part of the Divine purpose behind the prophetic inspiration.]

[19] [See *St. Matt.* xxiv. 15 = *St. Mark* xiii. 14.]

[20] It appears, that Porphyry did nothing worth mentioning in this way. For Jerome on the place says, *Duas posteriores bestias—in uno Macedonum regno ponit*. And as to the ten kings; *Decem reges enumerat, qui fuerunt sævissimi: ipsosque reges*

hinders the weight of them from being seen, as from having its due influence upon practice.

Thesis.

Christianity is a revelation

(*a*) of natural religion,

[29.] The thing asserted, and the truth of which is to be inquired into, is this: That over and above our reason and affections, which God has given us for the information of our judgment and the conduct of our lives, He has also, by external revelation, given us an account of Himself and His moral government over the world, implying a future state of rewards and punishments; *i.e.* hath revealed the system of natural religion: for natural religion may be externally[22] revealed by God, as the ignorant may be taught it by mankind their fellow-creatures—that God, I say, has given us the evidence of revelation, as well as the evidence of reason, to ascertain this moral system; together with an account of a particular dispensation of Providence, which reason could no way have discovered, and a particular institution of religion founded on it, for the recovery of mankind out of their present wretched condition, and raising them to the perfection and final happiness of their nature.

(*b*) of new truths.

It is a historical revelation,

[30.] This revelation, whether real or supposed, may be considered as wholly historical. For prophecy is nothing but the history of events before they come to pass;[23] doctrines also are matters of fact; and precepts come under the same notion. And the general design of Scripture, which contains in it this revelation, thus considered as historical, may be said to be, to give us an account of the world, in this one single view as God's world: by which it appears essentially distinguished from all other books, so far as I have found, except such as are copied from it. It begins with an account

Scripture giving an account (*a*) of the world as God's world,

[22] Part II. i. 4.

[23] [This is far too narrow a definition. Prediction is by no means the only function of the prophet; even more than they were *seers*, the Hebrew prophets were moral teachers, preachers of righteousness. They not only foresaw the future; they gave counsel for the present. And, again, it was counted part of their province to record the past. The schools of the prophets supplied the civil *historians* of Judæa: and the Jews still classify under "the prophets," such books as Joshua, Judges, 1 and 2 Samuel, and 1 and 2 Kings. But their most conspicuous office was that of *preacher*. And, in fact, the larger sense of the word *prophecy* in English, as including more than prediction, has not been quite lost. Bacon describes the exposition of Scripture as "an exercise commonly called prophesying"; and the titles of Jeremy Taylor's treatise "On the Liberty of Prophesying" and of Newman's "On the Prophetical Office of the Church" are familiar. The word prophecy connotes not only prediction, but exposition and moral instruction. Cp. Milton, *Par. Reg.* iv. 353 ff.]

of God's creation of the world, in order to ascertain, and distinguish from all others, Who is the object of our worship, by what He has done: in order to ascertain, Who He is, concerning Whose providence, commands, promises, and threatenings, this sacred book, all along, treats; the Maker and Proprietor of the world, He Whose creatures we are, the God of nature: in order likewise to distinguish Him from the idols of the nations, which are either imaginary beings, *i.e.* no beings at all; or else part of that creation, the historical relation of which is here given. And St. John, not improbably, with an eye to this Mosaic account of the creation, begins his Gospel with an account of our Saviour's pre-existence, and that "all things were made by Him; and without Him was not anything made that was made":[24] agreeably to the doctrine of St. Paul, that "God created all things by Jesus Christ."[25] This being premised, the Scripture, taken together, seems to profess to contain a kind of an abridgment of the history of the world, in the view just now mentioned: that is, a general account of the condition of religion and its professors, during the continuance of that apostasy from God, and state of wickedness, which it every where supposes the world to lie in. And this account of the state of religion carries with it some brief account of the political state of things, as religion is affected by it. Revelation indeed considers the common affairs of this world, and what is going on in it, as a mere scene of distraction; and cannot be supposed to concern itself with foretelling at what time Rome, or Babylon, or Greece, or any particular place, should be the most conspicuous seat of that tyranny and dissoluteness, which all places equally aspire to be; cannot, I say, be supposed to give any account of this wild scene for its own sake. But it seems to contain some very general account of the chief governments of the world, as the general state of religion has been, is, or shall be, affected by them, from the first transgression, and during the whole interval of the world's continuing in its present state, to a certain future period, spoken of both in the Old and New Testament, very distinctly, and in great variety of expression: "The times

and (*b*) of its chief governments,

so far as they affect religion.

[24] *St. John* i. 3.
[25] *Eph.* iii. 9. [However, in the best MS. authorities, followed by the R.V., the words *by Jesus Christ* are not found; and so the text is not apposite here.]

of the restitution of all things":[26] when "the mystery of God shall be finished, as He hath declared to His servants the prophets":[27] when "the God of heaven shall set up a kingdom, which shall never be destroyed: and the kingdom shall not be left to other people,"[28] as it is represented to be during this apostasy, but "judgment shall be given to the saints,"[29] and "they shall reign":[30] "and the kingdom and dominion, and the greatness of the kingdom under the whole heaven, shall be given to the people of the saints of the Most High."[31]

This covers a long period.

[31.] Upon this general view of the Scripture, I would remark, how great a length of time the whole relation takes up, near six thousand years of which are past;[32] and how great a variety of things it treats of; the natural and moral system or history of the world, including the time when it was formed, all contained in the very first book, and evidently written in a rude and unlearned age; and in subsequent books, the various common and prophetic history, and the particular dispensation of Christianity. Now all this together gives the largest scope for criticism; and for confutation of what is capable of being confuted, either from reason, or from common history, or from any inconsistence in its several parts. And it is a thing which deserves, I think, to be mentioned, that whereas some imagine the supposed doubtfulness of the evidence for revelation implies a positive argument that it is not true; it appears, on the contrary, to imply a positive argument that it is true. For, could any common relation, of such antiquity, extent and variety, (for in these things the stress of what I am now observing lies,) be proposed to the examination of the world: that it could not, in an age of knowledge and liberty, be confuted, or shewn to have nothing in it, to the satisfaction of reasonable men; this would be thought a strong presumptive proof of its truth. And indeed it must be a proof of it, just in proportion to the probability, that if it were false, it might be shewn

If untrue, would have been confuted, either α or β or γ

Thus the *doubtfulness* of the evidence is a positive argument.

26 *Acts* iii. 21.
27 *Rev.* x. 7.
28 *Dan.* ii. 44.
29 *Dan.* vii. 22.
30 *Rev.* xxii. 5.
31 *Dan.* vii. 27.
32 [Butler adopts the old system of chronology, introduced into our Authorised Version through the influence of Archbishop Ussher. But we could not expect him to be in advance of his age in such a matter. Lord Kelvin's calculation in 1897 was that probably between 20 and 30 million years have elapsed since the consolidation of the earth (*The Age of the Earth*, p. 10).]

to be so: and this I think, is scarcely pretended to be shewn, but upon principles and in ways of arguing, which have been clearly obviated.[33] Nor does it at all appear, that any set of men, who believe natural religion, are of the opinion, that Christianity has been thus confuted. But to proceed.

[32.] Together with the moral system of the world, the Old Testament contains a chronological account of the beginning of it, and from thence, an unbroken genealogy of mankind for many ages before common history begins; and carried on as much further as to make up a continued thread of history of the length of between three and four thousand years. It contains an account of God's making a covenant with a particular nation, that they should be His people, and He would be their God, in a peculiar sense; of His often interposing miraculously in their affairs; giving them the promise, and, long after, the possession, of a particular country; assuring them of the greatest national prosperity in it, if they would worship Him, in opposition to the idols which the rest of the world worshipped, and obey His commands; and threatening them with unexampled punishments, if they disobeyed Him, and fell into the general idolatry: insomuch that this one nation should continue to be the observation and the wonder of all the world. It declares particularly, that "God would scatter them among all people, from one end of the earth unto the other": but that "when they should return unto the Lord their God, He would have compassion upon them, and gather them from all the nations, whither He had scattered them": that "Israel should be saved in the Lord, with an everlasting salvation; and not be ashamed or confounded world without end." And as some of these promises are conditional, others are as absolute, as anything can be expressed: that the time should come, when "the people should be all righteous, and inherit the land for ever": that "though God would make a full end of all nations whither He had scattered them, yet would He not make a full end of them:" that "He would bring again the captivity of His people Israel, and plant them upon their land, and they should be no more pulled up out of their land": that "the seed of Israel should

(*c*) Scripture is also a history of the Chosen People;

[33] Chaps. ii., iii., etc.

foretells Messiah as (α) their desired Prince,

not cease from being a nation for ever."[34] It foretells, that God would raise them up a particular person, in Whom all His promises should finally be fulfilled; the Messiah, Who should be, in an high and eminent sense, their anointed Prince and Saviour. This was foretold in such a manner, as raised a general expectation of such a person in the nation, as appears from the New Testament, and is an acknowledged fact; an expectation of His coming at such a particular time before any one appeared claiming to be that person, and when there was no ground for such an expectation, but from the prophecies: which expectation, therefore, must in all reason be presumed to be explanatory of those prophecies, if there were any doubt about their meaning. It seems moreover to foretell, that this person should be rejected by that nation, to whom He had been so long promised, and though He was so much desired by them.[35] And it expressly foretells, that He should be the Saviour of the Gentiles; and even that the completion of the scheme, contained in this book, and then begun, and in its progress, should be somewhat so great, that, in comparison with it, the restoration of the Jews alone would be but of small account. "It is a light thing that Thou shouldest be My servant to raise up the tribes of Jacob, and to restore the preserved of Israel: I will also give Thee for a light to the Gentiles, that Thou mayest be for salvation unto the end of the earth." And, "In the last days, the mountain of the Lord's house shall be established in the top of the mountains, and shall be exalted above the hills; and all nations shall flow into it—for out of Zion shall go forth the law, and the word of the Lord from Jerusalem. And He shall judge among the nations—and the Lord alone shall be exalted in that day, and the idols He shall utterly abolish."[36] The Scripture further contains an account, that at the time the Messiah was expected, a person rose up, in this nation, claiming to be that Messiah, to be the person, Whom all the prophecies referred to, and in Whom they should centre: that

(β) to be rejected when He came,

(γ) the Saviour of the Gentiles;

and records that in time He came and established His Kingdom.

[34] *Deut.* xxviii. 64, xxx. 2, 3; *Is.* xlv. 17, lx. 21; Jer. xxx. 11, xlvi. 28; *Amos* ix. 14, 15; *Jer.* xxxi. 36.

[35] *Is.* viii. 14, 15, xlix. 5, ch. liii.; *Mal.* i. 10, 11, and ch. iii.

[36] *Is.* xlix. 6, ch. ii., ch. xi., ch. lvi. 7; *Mal.* i. 11. To which must be added, the other prophecies of the like kind, several in the New Testament, and very many in the Old; which describe what shall be the completion of the revealed plan of Providence.

He spent some years in a continued course of miraculous works; and endued His immediate disciples and followers with a power of doing the same, as a proof of the truth of that religion, which He commissioned them to publish: that, invested with this authority and power, they made numerous converts in the remotest countries, and settled and established His religion in the world; to the end of which the Scripture professes to give a prophetic account of the state of this religion amongst mankind.

[33.] Let us now suppose a person utterly ignorant of history, to have all this related to him out of the Scripture. Or suppose such an one, having the Scripture put into his hands, to remark these things in it, not knowing but that the whole, even its civil history, as well as the other parts of it, might be, from beginning to end, an entire invention; and to ask, What truth was in it, and whether the revelation here related was real, or a fiction? And, instead of a direct answer, suppose him, all at once, to be told the following confessed facts; and then to unite them into one view.

If an ignorant reader were to ask, was this true? he should be reminded that

[34.] Let him first be told, in how great a degree the profession and establishment of natural religion, the belief that there is one God to be worshipped, that virtue is His law, and that mankind shall be rewarded and punished hereafter, as they obey and disobey it here; in how very great a degree, I say, the profession and establishment of this moral system in the world is owing to the revelation, whether real or supposed, contained in this book: the establishment of this moral system, even in those countries which do not acknowledge the proper authority of the Scripture.[37] Let him be told also, what number of nations do acknowledge its proper authority. Let him then take in the consideration, of what importance religion is to mankind. And upon these things he might, I think, truly observe, that this supposed revelation's α
obtaining and being received in the world, with all the circumstances and effects of it, considered together as one event, is the most conspicuous and important event in the history of mankind: that a book of this nature, and thus promulged and β
recommended to our consideration, demands, as if by a voice from heaven, to have its claims most seriously examined into:

(1) The world's religion and morality are largely due to acceptance of the Bible revelation.

[37] Part II. vi. 4.

γ and that, before such examination, to treat it with any kind of scoffing and ridicule, is an offence against natural piety.

This does not destroy the proofs of religion from reason.

But it is to be remembered, that how much soever the establishment of natural religion in the world is owing to the Scripture-revelation, this does not destroy the proof of religion from reason, any more than the proof of Euclid's Elements is destroyed, by a man's knowing or thinking, that he should never have seen the truth of the several propositions contained in it, nor had those propositions come into his thoughts, but for that mathematician.

(2) This history is ancient

[35.] Let such a person as we are speaking of be, in the next place, informed of the acknowledged antiquity of the first parts of this book; and that its chronology, its account of the time when the earth, and the several parts of it, were first peopled with human creatures, is no way contradicted, but is really confirmed, by the natural and civil history of the world,[38] collected from common historians, from the state of the earth, and from the late invention of arts and sciences. And as the Scripture contains an unbroken thread of common and civil history, from the Creation to the Captivity, for between three and four thousand years; let the person we are speaking of be told, in the next place, that this general history, as it is not contradicted, but is confirmed by profane history as much as there would be reason to expect, upon supposition

and credible in itself

of its truth; so there is nothing in the whole history *itself*, to give any reasonable ground of suspicion of its not being, in the general, a faithful and literally true genealogy of men, and

(here excluding miracle);

series of things. I speak here only of the common Scripture-history, or of the course of ordinary events related in it, as distinguished from miracles, and from the prophetic history. In all the Scripture-narrations of this kind, following events

(α) no anachronisms,

arise out of foregoing ones, as in all other histories. There appears nothing related as done in any age, not conformable to the manners of that age: nothing in the account of a succeeding age, which, one would say, could not be true, or was improbable, from the account of things in the preceding

(β) characters real,

one. There is nothing in the characters, which would raise a thought of their being feigned; but all the internal marks imaginable of their being real. It is to be added also, that

[38] [Cp. § 31 note, above.]

mere genealogies, bare narratives of the number of years, which persons called by such and such names lived, do not carry the face of fiction; perhaps do carry some presumption of veracity: and all unadorned narratives, which have nothing to surprise, may be thought to carry somewhat of the like presumption too. And the domestic and the political history is plainly credible. There may be incidents in Scripture, which, taken alone in the naked way they are told, may appear strange; especially to persons of other manners, temper, education: but there are also incidents of undoubted truth, in many or most persons' lives, which, in the same circumstances, would appear to the full as strange.[39] There may be mistakes of transcribers, there may be other real or seeming mistakes,[40] not easy to be particularly accounted for: but there are certainly no more things of this kind in the Scripture, than what were to have been expected in books of such antiquity; and nothing, in any wise, sufficient to discredit the general narrative. Now, that a history, claiming to commence from the creation, and extending in one continued series, through so great a length of time, and variety of events, should have such appearances of reality and truth in its whole contexture, is surely a very remarkable circumstance in its favour. And as all this is applicable to the common history of the New Testament, so there is a further credibility, and a very high one, given to it by profane authors: many of these writing of the same times, and confirming the truth of customs and events which are incidentally as well as more purposely mentioned in it. And this credibility of the common Scripture-history, gives some credibility to its miraculous history: especially as this is interwoven with the common,[41] so as that they imply each other, and both together make up one relation.

(γ) narratives unadorned.

As to (*a*) strange incidents,

or (*b*) mistakes,

they might be expected in any ancient book.

[36.] Let it then be more particularly observed to this person, that it is an acknowledged matter of fact, which is indeed implied in the foregoing observation, that there was such a nation as the Jews, of the greatest antiquity, whose

(3) The existence of the Jews as a nation

[39] [FitzGerald refers, for illustration of this, to Whately's *Historic Doubts concerning Napoleon Buonaparte*, a once famous pamphlet, in in which Butler's point here is well brought out.]

[40] [Observe the caution with which Butler expresses himself. He is very careful not to assume that inspiration guarantees *inerrancy*, and distinctly implies that in Scripture there *may* be mistakes in unimportant details, other than those due to the blunders of scribes.]

[41] [Cp. § 5 above.]

government and general polity was founded on the law, here related to be given them by Moses as from heaven: that natural religion, though with rites additional yet no way contrary to it, was their established religion, which cannot be said of the Gentile world: and that their very being as a nation, depended upon their acknowledgment of one God, the God of the universe. For, suppose in their captivity in Babylon, they had gone over to the religion of their conquerors, there would have remained no bond of union, to keep them a distinct people. And whilst they were under their own kings, in their own country, a total apostasy from God would have been the dissolution of their whole government. They in such a sense nationally acknowledged and worshipped the Maker of heaven and earth, when the rest of the world were sunk in idolatry, as rendered them, in fact, the peculiar people of God. And this so remarkable an establishment and preservation of natural religion amongst them, seems to add some peculiar credibility to the historical evidence for the miracles of Moses and the Prophets: because these miracles are a full satisfactory account of this event, which plainly wants to be accounted for, and cannot otherwise.

depended on their religion,

the preservation of which confirms the evidence for its miracles.

(4) As a matter of fact, One claiming to be Messiah came and was rejected by Jews,

[37.] Let this person, supposed wholly ignorant of history, be acquainted further, that one claiming to be the Messiah, of Jewish extraction, rose up at the time when this nation, from the prophecies above mentioned, expected the Messiah: that He was rejected, as it seemed to have been foretold He should, by the body of the people, under the direction of their rulers: that in the course of a very few years, He was believed on and acknowledged as the promised Messiah, by great numbers among the Gentiles, agreeably to the prophecies of Scripture, yet not upon the evidence of prophecy, but of miracles,[42] of which miracles we also have strong historical evidence; (by which I mean here no more than must be acknowledged by unbelievers; for let pious frauds and follies be admitted to weaken, it is absurd to say they destroy, our evidence of miracles wrought in proof of Christianity:[43]) that this religion approving itself to the reason of mankind, and carrying its own evidence with it, so far as reason is a judge of its system, and being no way contrary to reason in those parts

but accepted by Gentiles because of His miracles.

His religion is rational,

[42] § 10 above.

[43] § 17 above.

of it which require to be believed upon the mere authority of its Author; that this religion, I say, gradually spread and supported itself for some hundred years, not only without any assistance from temporal power, but under constant discouragements, and often the bitterest persecutions from it; and then became the religion of the world: that in the meantime, the Jewish nation and government were destroyed in a very remarkable manner, and the people carried away captive and dispersed through the most distant countries; in which state of dispersion they have remained fifteen hundred years: and that they remain a numerous people, united amongst themselves, and distinguished from the rest of the world, as they were in the days of Moses, by the profession of his law; and everywhere looked upon in a manner, which one scarce knows how distinctly to express, but in the words of the prophetic account of it, given so many ages before it came to pass; "Thou shalt become an astonishment, a proverb, a byword, among all nations whither the Lord shall lead thee."[44]

and has spread despite opposition,

while the Jewish nation was dispersed,

though remaining distinct.

[38.] The appearance of a standing miracle, in the Jews remaining a distinct people in their dispersion,[45] and the confirmation which this event appears to give to the truth of revelation, may be thought to be answered, by their religion's forbidding them intermarriages with those of any other, and prescribing them a great many peculiarities in their food, by which they are debarred from the means of incorporating with the people in whose countries they live. This is not, I think, a satisfactory account of that which it pretends to account for. But what does it pretend to account for? The correspondence between this event and the prophecies; or the coincidence of both, with a long dispensation of Providence, of a peculiar nature, towards that people formerly? No. It is only the event itself, which is offered to be thus accounted for; which single event, taken alone, abstracted from all such correspondence and coincidence, perhaps would not have appeared miraculous: but that correspondence and coincidence may be so, though the event itself be supposed not. Thus the concurrence of our Saviour's

This standing miracle not explicable by Jewish exclusiveness,

for it is their separate existence *as prophesied* which is the problem.

[44] *Deut.* xxviii. 37.

[45] [This familiar argument had been urged in much the same way by Clarke (*Evidences*, p. 391) and by Wilkins (*Natural Religion*, p. 89).]

of very great weight to a considerate reasonable person: of much greater indeed, upon having them first laid before him, than is easy for us, who are so familiarized to them, to conceive, without some particular attention for that purpose.

All this direct and circumstantial evidence very weighty,

[42.] All these things, and the several particulars contained under them, require to be distinctly and most thoroughly examined into; that the weight of each may be judged of, upon such examination, and such conclusion drawn as results from their united force. But this has not been attempted here. I have gone no further than to shew, that the general imperfect view of them now given, the confessed historical evidence for miracles, and the many obvious appearing completions of prophecy, together with the collateral things[47] here mentioned, and there are several others of the like sort; that all this together, which, being fact, must be acknowledged by unbelievers, amounts to real evidence of somewhat more than human in this matter: evidence much more important, than careless men, who have been accustomed only to transient and partial views of it, can imagine; and indeed abundantly sufficient to act upon. And these things, I apprehend, must be acknowledged by unbelievers. For though they may say, that the historical evidence of miracles wrought in attestation of Christianity, is not sufficient to convince them, that such miracles were really wrought; they cannot deny, that there is such historical evidence, it being a known matter of fact that there is. They may say, the conformity between the prophecies and events is by accident: but there are many instances in which such conformity itself cannot be denied. They may say, with regard to such kind of collateral things as those above mentioned, that any odd accidental events, without meaning, will have a meaning found in them by fanciful people: and that such as are fanciful in any one certain way, will make out a thousand coincidences, which seem to favour their peculiar follies. Men, I say, may talk thus: but no one who is serious, can possibly think these things to be nothing, if he considers the importance of collateral things, and even of lesser circumstances, in the evidence of proba-

and not to be set aside because of objections to any one point.

[47] All the particular things mentioned in this chapter, not reducible to the head of certain miracles, or determinate completions of prophecy. See § 2 above.

bility, as distinguished, in Nature, from the evidence of demonstration. In many cases indeed it seems to require the truest judgment, to determine with exactness the weight of circumstantial evidence: but it is very often altogether as convincing, as that which is the most express and direct.

Important to omit no line of proof,

[43.] This general view of the evidence for Christianity, considered as making one argument, may also serve to recommend to serious persons, to set down everything which they think may be of any real weight at all in proof of it, and particularly the many seeming completions of prophecy: and they will find, that, judging by the natural rules, by which we judge of probable evidence in common matters, they amount to a much higher degree of proof, upon such a joint review, than could be supposed upon considering them separately, at different times; how strong soever the proof might before appear to them, upon such separate views of it. For probable proofs, by being added, not only increase the evidence, but multiply it.[48] Nor should I dissuade any one from setting down, what he thought made for the contrary side. But then it is to be remembered, not in order to influence his judgment, but his practice, that a mistake on one side may be, in its consequences, much more dangerous, than a mistake on the other.[49] And what course

for the sum of probabilities *multiplies* the evidence.

A mistake on the negative side more dangerous than on the positive.

[48] [This is mathematically demonstrable. Thus if there are three *independent* probabilities for an event, each represented by the fraction $\frac{4}{5}$, the *total* probability in its favour will be $\frac{124}{125}$.]

[49] [The famous passage, sometimes called the 'Wager,' in which Pascal expounds the same idea, may perhaps be quoted once more. "Car il ne sert de rien de dire qu'il est incertain si on gagnera, et qu'il est certain qu'on hasarde; et que l'infinie distance qui est entre la *certitude* de ce qu'on s'expose et *l'incertitude* de ce qu'on gagnera égale le bien fini qu'on expose certainement, à l'infini qui est incertain. Cela n'est pas ainsi: tout joueur hasarde avec certitude pour gagner avec incertitude; et néanmoins il hasarde certainement le fini pour gagner incertainement le fini, sans pécher contre la raison. Il n'y a pas infinité de distance entre cette certitude de ce qu'on s'expose et l'incertitude du gain; cela est faux. Il y a, à la vérité, infinité entre la certitude de gagner et la certitude de perdre. Mais l'incertitude de gagner est proportionnée à la certitude de ce qu'on hasarde, selon la proportion des hasards de gain et de perte; et de là vient que s'il y a autant de hasards d'un côté que de l'autre, le parti est à jouer égal contre égal; et alors la certitude de ce qu'on s'expose est égale à l'incertitude du gain; tant s'en faut qu'elle en soit infiniment distante. Et ainsi notre proposition est dans une force infinie, quand il y a le fini à hasarder à un jeu où il y a pareils hasards de gain que de perte, et l'infini à gagner" (*Pensées*, ed. Faugère, ii. 167). See above, Introd. § 4, and Note A at the end of the Introduction.]

CHAPTER VIII.

Of the Objections which may be made against arguing from the Analogy of Nature, to Religion.

Objections against arguing from the Analogy of Nature to Religion,

[1.] If every one would consider, with such attention as they are bound, even in point of morality, to consider, what they judge and give characters of; the occasion of this chapter would be, in some good measure at least, superseded. But since this is not to be expected; for some we find do not concern themselves to understand even what they write against: since this treatise, in common with most others, lies open to objections, which may appear very material to thoughtful men at first sight; and, besides that, seems peculiarly liable to the objections of such as can judge without thinking, and of such as can censure without judging; it may not be amiss to set down the chief of these objections which occur to me, and consider them to their hands. And they are such as these:

e.g. (i) §§ 4, 5. (ii) §§ 6, 7. (iii) § 8.

[2.] "That it is a poor thing to solve difficulties in revelation, by saying, that there are the same in natural religion; when what is wanting is to clear both of them of these their common, as well other their respective, difficulties: but that it is a strange way indeed of convincing men of the obligations of religion, to shew them, that they have as little reason for their worldly pursuits: and a strange way of vindicating the justice and goodness of the Author of Nature, and of removing the objections against both, to which the system of religion lies open, to shew, that the like objections lie against natural providence; a way of answering objections against religion, without so much as pretending to make out, that the system of it, or the particular things in it objected against, are reasonable——especially, perhaps some may be inattentive enough to add, must this be thought strange, when it is confessed that analogy is no answer to such objections: that when this sort of reasoning is carried to the utmost length (iv) § 9. it can be imagined capable of, it will yet leave the mind in a very unsatisfied state: and that it must be unaccountable (v) § 10. ignorance of mankind, to imagine they will be prevailed with to forego their present interests and pleasures, from regard to religion, upon doubtful evidence."

Such objections due to (*a*) half-views;

[3.] Now, as plausible as this way of talking may appear, that appearance will be found in a great measure owing to half-views, which shew but part of an object, yet shew that indistinctly, and to undeterminate language. By these means weak men are often deceived by others, and ludicrous men, by themselves. And even those, who are serious and considerate, cannot always readily disentangle, and at once clearly see through the perplexities, in which subjects themselves are involved; and which are heightened by the deficiencies and the abuse of words. To this latter sort of persons, the following reply to each part of this objection severally, may be of some assistance; as it may also tend a little to stop and silence others.

(*b*) abuse of words.

(i) (*a*) Impossible to remove *all* difficulties:

[4.] First, The thing wanted, *i.e.* what men require, is to have all difficulties cleared. And this is, or, at least for anything we know to the contrary, it may be, the same, as requiring to comprehend the Divine nature, and the whole plan of Providence from everlasting to everlasting. But it hath always been allowed to argue, from what is acknowledged, to what is disputed. And it is in no other sense a poor thing, to argue from natural religion to revealed, in the manner found fault with, than it is to argue in numberless other ways of probable deduction and inference, in matters of conduct, which we are continually reduced to the necessity of doing. Indeed the epithet *poor* may be applied, I fear, as properly to great part or the whole of human life, as it is to the things mentioned in the objection. Is it not a poor thing, for a physician to have so little knowledge in the cure of diseases, as even the most eminent have? to act upon conjecture and guess, where the life of man is concerned? Undoubtedly it is: but not in comparison of having no skill at all in that useful art, and being obliged to act wholly in the dark.

these are present everywhere;

(*b*) useful to shew that

[5.] Further: since it is as unreasonable, as it is common,

objections to Christianity lie against natural religion,

to urge objections against revelation, which are of equal weight against natural religion; and those who do this, if they are not confused themselves, deal unfairly with others, in making it seem, that they are arguing only against revelation, or particular doctrines of it, when in reality they are arguing against moral providence; it is a thing of consequence to shew, that such objections are as much levelled against natural religion as against revealed. And objections, which are equally applicable to both, are properly speaking answered, by its being shewn that they are so, provided the former be admitted to be true. And, without taking in the consideration how distinctly this is admitted, it is plainly very material to observe, that as the things objected against in natural religion are of the same kind with what is certain matter of experience in the course of providence, and in the information which God affords us concerning our temporal interest under His government; so the objections against the system of Christianity, and the evidence of it, are of the very same kind with those which are made against the system and evidence of natural religion. However, the reader upon review may see, that most of the analogies insisted upon, even in the latter part of this treatise, do not necessarily require to have more taken for granted than is in the former; that there is an Author of Nature, or natural Governor of the world: and Christianity is vindicated, not from its analogy to natural religion, but chiefly from its analogy to the experienced constitution of Nature.[1]

which is admitted by objectors.

(*c*) Most of our analogies are between *religion* and *nature*.

(ii) Religion a practical thing,

[6.] Secondly, Religion is a practical thing, and consists in such a determinate course of life, as being what, there is reason to think, is commanded by the Author of Nature, and will, upon the whole, be our happiness under His government.[2] Now if men can be convinced, that they have the like reason to believe this, as to believe, that taking care of their temporal affairs will be to their advantage; such conviction cannot but be an argument to them for the practice of religion. And

hence it is (*a*) useful to justify it by the analogy of nature,

[1] [This is, in fact, set forth in the *title* of the Treatise, "The Analogy of Religion, natural and revealed, to the constitution and course of Nature."]

[2] [This amounts to a definition of the religious life in Butler's view; the stress laid upon its *prudence* is characteristic both of the man and of his age. It is this aspect, called by Coleridge "other-worldliness," which is specially prominent in Paley's ethical and theological system.]

if there be really any reason for believing one of these, and endeavouring to preserve life, and secure ourselves the necessaries and conveniences of it; then there is reason also for believing the other, and endeavouring to secure the interest it proposes to us. And if the interest, which religion proposes to us, be infinitely greater than our whole temporal interest; then there must be proportionably greater reason for endeavouring to secure one, than the other; since, by the supposition, the probability of our securing one is equal to the probability of our securing the other. This seems plainly unanswerable; and has a tendency to influence fair minds, who consider what our condition really is, or upon what evidence we are naturally appointed to act; and who are disposed to acquiesce in the terms upon which we live, and attend to and follow that practical instruction, whatever it be, which is afforded us.

(*b*) especially as it is so vastly important;

[7.] But the chief and proper force of the argument referred to in the objection, lies in another place. For, it is said that the proof of religion is involved in such inextricable difficulties, as to render it doubtful; and that it cannot be supposed, that, if it were true, it would be left upon doubtful evidence. Here then, over and above the force of each particular difficulty or objection, these difficulties and objections taken together are turned into a positive argument against the truth of religion; which argument would stand thus. If religion were true, it would not be left doubtful, and open to objections to the degree in which it is: therefore that it is thus left, not only renders the evidence of it weak, and lessens its force, in proportion to the weight of such objections; but also shews it to be false, or is a general presumption of its being so. Now the observation, that, from the natural constitution and course of things, we must in our temporal concerns, almost continually, and in matters of great consequence, act upon evidence of a like kind and degree to the evidence of religion, is an answer to this argument; because it shews, that it is according to the conduct and character of the Author of Nature to appoint we should act upon evidence like to that, which this argument presumes He cannot be supposed to appoint we should act upon; it is an instance, a general one made up of numerous particular ones, of somewhat in His dealing with us, similar to what is said to be incredible.

(*c*) that its evidence is only doubtful, not fatal, for so it is with our worldly concerns.

And as the force of this answer lies merely in the parallel, which there is between the evidence for religion and for our temporal conduct; the answer is equally just and conclusive, whether the parallel be made out, by shewing the evidence of the former to be higher, or the evidence of the latter to be lower.

(iii) Our purpose not to justify God, but to exhibit duty, by shewing that the things objected to

[8.] Thirdly, The design of this treatise is not to vindicate the character of God, but to shew the obligations of men: it is not to justify His providence, but to shew what belongs to us to do.[3] These are two subjects, and ought not to be confounded. And though they may at length run up into each other, yet observations may immediately tend to make out the latter, which do not appear, by any immediate connexion, to the purpose of the former; which is less our concern, than many seem to think.

(*a*) *may* be consistent with goodness;

For, first, it is not necessary we should justify the dispensations of Providence against objections, any further than to shew, that the things objected against may, for ought we know, be consistent with justice and goodness. Suppose then, that there are things in the system of this world, and plan of Providence relating to it, which taken alone would be unjust: yet it has been shewn unanswerably, that if we could take in the reference, which these things may have to other things present, past, and to come; to the whole scheme, which the things objected against are parts of; these very things might, for ought we know, be found to be, not only consistent with justice, but instances of it.[4] Indeed it has been shewn, by the analogy of what we see, not only possible that this may be the case, but credible that it is. And thus objections, drawn from such things, are answered, and Providence is vindicated, as far as religion makes its vindication necessary.

(*b*) are found also in the constitution of Nature and are there inconclusive;

Hence it appears, secondly, that objections against the Divine justice and goodness are not endeavoured to be removed, by shewing that the like objections, allowed to be really conclusive, lie against natural providence: but those objections being supposed and shewn not to be conclusive, the things objected

[3] ["Revelation was not given to satisfy doubts, but to make us better men, and it is as we become better men that it becomes light and peace to our souls, even though to the end of life we shall find difficulties in it and in the world around us" (Newman, *Parochial Sermons*, i. Serm. 18). Cp. also Part II. v. 23 above and *Sermons* xv. § 10.].

[4] [Cp. Part I. vii. 3.]

against, considered as matters of fact, are further shewn to be credible, from their conformity to the constitution of Nature; for instance, that God will reward and punish men for their actions hereafter, from the observation, that He does reward and punish them for their actions here. And this, I apprehend, is of weight. And I add, thirdly, it would be of weight, even though those objections were not answered. For, there being the proof of religion above set down; and religion implying several facts; for instance again, the fact last mentioned, that God will reward and punish men for their actions hereafter; the observation, that His present method of government is by rewards and punishments, shews that future fact not to be incredible: whatever objections men may think they have against it, as unjust or unmerciful, according to their notions of justice and mercy; or as improbable from their belief of necessity. I say, *as improbable*: for it is evident no objection against it, *as unjust*, can be urged from necessity; since this notion as much destroys injustice, as it does justice.[5] Then, fourthly, Though objections against the reasonableness of the system of religion cannot indeed be answered without entering into consideration of its reasonableness; yet objections against the credibility or truth of it may. Because the system of it is reducible into what is properly matter of fact: and the truth, the probable truth, of facts, may be shewn without consideration of their reasonableness. Nor is it necessary, though, in some cases and respects, it is highly useful and proper, yet it is not necessary, to give a proof of the reasonableness of every precept enjoined us, and of every particular dispensation of Providence, which comes into the system of religion. Indeed the more thoroughly a person of a right disposition is convinced of the perfection of the Divine nature and conduct, the further he will advance towards that perfection of religion, which St. John speaks of.[6] But the general obligations of religion are fully made out, by proving the

(*c*) future retribution is credible,

despite theories of necessity;

(*d*) whether theoretically reasonable or not, religion is

(α) credible

and

(β) practically reasonable.

[5] [See Part I. vi. 8.]

[6] *I John* iv. 18. ["There is no fear in love; but perfect love casteth out fear: because fear hath torment. He that feareth is not made perfect in love." Butler's point is that the ideal is to serve God for love's sake, without the motives of hope or fear. But nevertheless the latter motive will lead to the practice of religion, though it may not supply a rational theory of it. Cp. Part I. v. 19 and Note D at the end of that chapter.]

reasonableness of the practice of it. And that the practice of religion *is* reasonable, may be shewn, though no more could be proved, than that the system of it *may be* so, for ought we know to the contrary: and even without entering into the distinct consideration of this. And from hence, fifthly, it is easy to see, that though the analogy of Nature is not an immediate answer to objections against the wisdom, the justice, or goodness, of any doctrine or precept of religion: yet it may be, as it is, an immediate and direct answer to what is really intended by such objections; which is, to shew that the things objected against are incredible.

(*e*) Thus analogy proves the *credibility* if not the *morality*, of the scheme.

(iv) No theory of life is satisfactory.

[9.] Fourthly, It is most readily acknowledged, that the foregoing treatise is by no means satisfactory; very far indeed from it: but so would any natural institution of life appear, if reduced into a system, together with its evidence. Leaving religion out of the case, men are divided in their opinions, whether our pleasures overbalance our pains:[7] and whether it be, or be not, eligible to live in this world. And were all such controversies settled, which perhaps, in speculation, would be found involved in great difficulties; and were it determined upon the evidence of reason, as Nature has determined it to our hands, that life is to be preserved: yet still, the rules which God has been pleased to afford us, for escaping the miseries of it, and obtaining its satisfactions, the rules, for instance, of preserving health, and recovering it when lost, are not only fallible and precarious, but very far from being exact. Nor are we informed by Nature, in future contingencies and accidents, so as to render it at all certain, what is the best method of managing our affairs. What will be the success of our temporal pursuits, in the common sense of the word Success, is highly doubtful. And what will be the success of them in the proper sense of the word; *i.e.* what happiness or enjoyment we shall obtain by them, is doubtful in a much higher degree. Indeed the unsatisfactory nature of the evidence, with which we are obliged to take up, in the daily course of life, is scarce to be expressed. Yet men do not throw away life, or disregard the interests of it, upon account of this doubtfulness. The evidence of religion then being admitted real, those who object against it, as not

Hard to prove

(*a*) life worth living,

or

(*b*) the rules for extracting the best from it,

or

(*c*) how to reach success.

Yet we act on the evidence, though unsatisfactory.

To refuse to do so is to forget

[7] [Cp. Part I. iii. 5 and iv. 7.]

Value of Visible Church p 142, 3

Objections to Christianity met p 144

Importance of Christianity

Proved by fact that

1. It is a republication of Natural Religion

e.g. a It represents God as infinitely Perfect & governing the world & to be Judge of mankind. (reason reveals this)

b It is supported by Miracles & Prophecy

c It brings Life & Immortality to Light

d It has an instituted form of External religion i.e. the visible Church

e. It is essentially practical

∴ it is important

---

2. It is a Revelation of New Truth

a. It reveals our relations to the Son & Spirit not only to the Father. (Christianity reveals these)

b. These relations being revealed our regard to the Son & Spirit is a moral duty

∴ A moral precept is one, the reason for which we see

∴ A positive precept is one, the reason for wh. we do not see

Christ wd. have men obey because of a clear reason not a blind obedience Matt 9.13

satisfactory, *i.e.* as not being what they wish it,[8] plainly forget the very condition of our being: for satisfaction, in this sense, does not belong to such a creature as man. And, which is more material, they forget also the very nature of religion. For, religion presupposes, in all those who will embrace it, a certain degree of integrity and honesty; which it was intended to try whether men have or not, and to exercise in such as have it, in order to its improvement. Religion presupposes this as much, and in the same sense, as speaking to a man presupposes he understands the language in which you speak; or as warning a man of any danger presupposes that he hath such a regard to himself, as that he will endeavour to avoid it. And therefore the question is not at all, Whether the evidence of religion be satisfactory; but, Whether it be, in reason, sufficient to prove and discipline that virtue, which it presupposes. Now the evidence of it is fully sufficient for all those purposes of probation; how far soever it is from being satisfactory, as to the purposes of curiosity, or any other: and indeed it answers the purposes of the former in several respects, which it would not do, if it were as overbearing as is required. One might add further; that whether the motives or the evidence for any course of action be satisfactory, meaning here, by that word what satisfies a man, that such a course of action will in event be for his good; this need never be, and I think, strictly speaking, never is, the practical question in common matters. But the practical question in all cases is, Whether the evidence for a course of action be such, as, taking in all circumstances, makes the faculty within us, which is the guide and judge of conduct,[9] determine that course of action to be prudent. Indeed, satisfaction that it will be for our interest or happiness, abundantly determines an action to be prudent: but evidence almost infinitely lower than this, determines actions to be so too; even in the conduct of every day.

(α) the condition of our being

and (β) the nature of religion.

The real question is: Is the evidence sufficient for probation of virtue?

We do not ask in daily life, Is the evidence satisfactory? but, Is it prudent to act on it?

[10.] Fifthly, As to the objection concerning the influence which this argument, or any part of it, may, or may not, be expected to have upon men; I observe, as above, that religion

To say that such evidence will not influence men

[8] [Note the sense in which he uses the word *satisfactory*, as equivalent to "satisfying our *wishes*." The evidence, he would say, is sufficient for our *needs*, though not for our *desires*.]

[9] See *Dissert.* II. [§ 6; and cp. Note A at end of the Introduction above].

much is irrelevant.

being intended for a trial and exercise of the morality of every person's character, who is a subject of it; and there being, as I have shewn, such evidence for it, as is sufficient, in reason, to influence men to embrace it: to object, that it is not to be imagined mankind will be influenced by such evidence, is nothing to the purpose of the foregoing treatise. For the purpose of it is not to inquire, what sort of creatures mankind are; but what the light and knowledge, which is afforded them, requires they should be: to shew how, in reason, they ought to behave; not how, in fact, they will behave. This depends upon themselves, and is their own concern; the personal concern of each man in particular. And how little regard the generality have to it, experience indeed does too fully shew. But religion, considered as a probation, has had its end upon all persons, to whom it has been proposed with evidence sufficient in reason to influence their practice: for by this means they have been put into a state of probation; let them behave as they will in it. And thus, not only revelation, but reason also, teaches us, that by the evidence of religion being laid before men, the designs of Providence are carrying on, not only with regard to those who will, but likewise with regard to those who will not, be influenced by it. However, lastly, the objection here referred to, allows the things insisted upon in this treatise to be of some weight: and if so, it may be hoped it will have some influence. And if there be a probability that it will have any at all, there is the same reason in kind, though not in degree, to lay it before men, as there would be, if it were likely to have a greater influence.

(*a*) The question is, *Ought* it to influence them?

(*b*) The objection concedes that the evidence has *some* force.

Butler's whole argument is *ad hominem*.

[11.] And further, I desire it may be considered, with respect to the whole of the foregoing objections, that in this treatise I have argued upon the principles of others,[10] not my own: and have omitted what I think true, and of the utmost importance, because by others thought unintelligible, or not true. Thus I have argued upon the principles of the Fatalists, which I do not believe: and have omitted a thing of the utmost importance which I do believe, the moral fitness and unfitness of actions, prior to all will whatever; which I apprehend as

He does not assume (*a*) freedom or (*b*) immutable morality,

[10] By *arguing upon the principles of others*, the reader will observe is meant; not proving anything *from* those principles, but *notwithstanding* them. Thus religion is proved, not *from* the opinion of necessity; which is absurd: but, *notwithstanding* or *even though* that opinion were admitted to be true. [Cp. Part II. Concl. § 3 below.]

certainly to determine the Divine conduct, as speculative truth and falsehood necessarily determine the Divine judgment.[11] Indeed the principle of liberty, and that of moral fitness, so force themselves upon the mind, that moralists, the ancients as well as moderns, have formed their language upon it. And probably it may appear in mine:[12] though I have endeavoured to avoid it; and, in order to avoid it, have sometimes been obliged to express myself in a manner, which will appear strange to such as do not observe the reason for it: but the general argument here pursued does not at all suppose or proceed upon these principles. Now, these two abstract principles of liberty and moral fitness being omitted, religion can be considered in no other view, than merely as a question of fact: and in this view it is here considered. It is obvious, that Christianity, and the proof of it, are both historical. And even natural religion is, properly, a matter of fact. For, that there is a righteous Governor of the world, is so: and this proposition contains the general system of natural religion. But then, several abstract truths, and in particular those two principles, are usually taken into consideration in the proof of it: whereas it is here treated of only as a matter of fact. To explain this: that the three angles of a triangle are equal to two right ones, is an abstract truth: but that they appear so to our mind, is only a matter of fact. And this last must have been admitted, if anything was, by those ancient sceptics, who would not have admitted the former: but pretended to doubt, Whether there were any such thing as truth, or, Whether we could certainly depend upon our faculties of understanding for the knowledge of it in any case. So likewise, that there is, in the nature of things, an original standard of right and wrong in actions, independent upon all will, but which unalterably determines the will of God, to exercise that moral government over the world, which religion teaches, *i.e.* finally and upon the whole to reward and punish men respectively as they act right or wrong; this assertion contains an abstract truth, as well as matter of fact. But suppose, in the present state, every man, without exception, was rewarded and punished,

although his language shews his belief.

Thus he treats religion, revealed and natural, as a concrete fact, not as an abstract truth.

Illustration.

So, immutable morality an abstract truth.

but moral government a concrete fact,

[11] [Cp. Part I. vi. 12 note.]

[12] [Cp., for example, his definition of *government* as "the annexing pleasure to some actions and pain to others, *in our power to do or forbear*," etc. (Part I. ii. 6), and the dictum that "all wickedness is voluntary" (Part I. v. 1), both of which presuppose a belief in human freedom.]

CONCLUSION.

Evidence for Natural Religion plain.

[1.] WHATEVER account may be given of the strange inattention and disregard, in some ages and countries, to a matter of such importance as Religion; it would, before experience, be incredible, that there should be the like disregard in those, who have had the moral system of the world laid before them, as it is by Christianity, and often inculcated upon them: because this moral system carries in it a good degree of evidence for its truth, upon its being barely proposed to our thoughts. There is no need of abstruse reasonings and distinctions, to convince an unprejudiced understanding, that there is a God Who made and governs the world, and will judge it in righteousness; though they may be necessary to answer abstruse difficulties, when once such are raised: when the very meaning of those words, which express most intelligibly the general doctrine of religion, is pretended to be uncertain; and the clear truth of the thing itself is obscured by the intricacies of speculation. But to an unprejudiced mind ten thousand thousand instances of design cannot but prove a designer. And it is intuitively manifest, that creatures ought to live under a dutiful sense of their Maker; and that justice and charity must be His laws, to creatures whom He has made social, and placed in society.

Revealed Religion needs external proof; but neglect of it is immoral.

Indeed the truth of revealed religion, peculiarly so called, is not self-evident, but requires external proof, in order to its being received. Yet inattention, among us, to revealed religion, will be found to imply the same dissolute immoral temper of mind, as inattention to natural religion: because, when both are laid before us, in the manner they are in Christian countries of liberty, our obligations to inquire into both, and to embrace both upon supposition of their truth, are obligations of the same nature. For, revelation claims to be the voice of God: and our obligation to attend to His voice is surely moral in all cases.[1] And as it is insisted, that its evidence is conclusive, upon thorough consideration of it; so it offers itself to us with manifest obvious appearances of having something more than human in it, and therefore in all reason requires to have its claims most seriously examined into. It is to be added, that though light and knowledge, in what manner soever afforded us, is equally from God; yet a miraculous revelation has a peculiar tendency, from the first principles of our nature, to awaken mankind, and inspire them with reverence and awe: and this is a peculiar obligation, to attend to what claims to be so with such appearances of truth. It is therefore most certain, that our obligations to inquire seriously into the evidence of Christianity, and, upon supposition of its truth, to embrace it, are of the utmost importance, and moral in the highest and most proper sense. Let us then suppose, that the evidence of religion in general, and of Christianity, has been seriously inquired into, by all reasonable men among us. Yet we find many professedly to reject both, upon speculative principles of infidelity. And all of them do not content themselves with a bare neglect of religion, and enjoying their imaginary freedom from its restraints. Some go much beyond this. They deride God's moral government over the world. They renounce His protection, and defy His justice. They ridicule and vilify Christianity, and blaspheme the Author of it: and take all occasions to manifest a scorn and contempt of revelation. This amounts to an active setting themselves against religion; to what may be considered as a positive principle of irreligion; which they cultivate within themselves, and, whether they intend this effect or not, render habitual, as a good man does the contrary principle. And others, who are not chargeable with all this profligateness, yet are in avowed opposition to religion, as if discovered to be groundless. Now admitting, which is the supposition we go upon, that these persons act upon what they think principles of reason, and otherwise they are not to be argued with; it is really inconceivable, that they should imagine they clearly see the whole evidence of it, considered in itself, to be nothing at all: nor do

Its peculiar claims to attention.

Some reject evidence for all religion, and deride

(α) its restraints, (β) its doctrines.

[1] [Cp. Part II. i. 14.]

things; one dispensation preparatory to another, this to a further one, and so on through an indefinite number of ages, before the end of the scheme proposed can be completely accomplished; a scheme conducted by infinite wisdom, and executed by almighty power. But now, on the contrary, our finding that everything in the constitution and course of Nature is thus carried on, shews such expectations concerning revelation to be highly unreasonable; and is a satisfactory answer to them, when urged as objections against the credibility, that the great scheme of Providence in the redemption of the world may be of this kind, and to be accomplished
Ch. v. in this manner. As to the particular method of our redemption, the appointment of a Mediator between God and man:
§ 2. this has been shewn to be most obviously analogous to the general conduct of Nature, *i.e.* the God of Nature, in appointing others to be the instruments of His mercy, as we experi-
§ 10. ence in the daily course of Providence. The condition of this world, which the doctrine of our redemption by Christ presupposes, so much falls in with natural appearances, that
§ 11. heathen moralists inferred it from those appearances: inferred, that human nature was fallen from its original rectitude, and, in consequence of this, degraded from its primitive happiness.[4] Or, however this opinion came into the world, these appearances must have kept up the tradition, and confirmed the belief of it. And as it was the general opinion under
§ 8. the light of Nature, that repentance and reformation, alone and by itself, was not sufficient to do away sin, and procure a full remission of the penalties annexed to it; and as the reason of the thing does not at all lead to any such con-
§ 7. clusion; so every day's experience shews us, that reformation is not, in any sort, sufficient to prevent the present disadvantages and miseries, which, in the natural course of things, God has annexed to folly and extravagance. Yet

[4] [Cp. Part II. v. 11 above. I suppose Butler to have taken this from Clarke, who writes (*Evidences*, Prop. xiii. 6) of "the general opinion that the ancient learnedest heathens entertained, upon very obscure and uncertain tradition, that the original state of man was innocent and simple, and the earth whereon they dwelt, fruitful of itself, and abundant with all plenty; but that God, for the sin of man, changed this happy constitution of things, and made labour necessary for the support of our lives." Clarke's marginal reference for this is a passage from 'Calanus Indus, *apud Strabon.* lib. 15.' Calanus was a philosopher who accompanied Alexander the Great in his Indian expedition.]

there may be ground to think, that the punishments, which, § 6.
by the general laws of Divine government, are annexed to vice, may be prevented: that provision may have been, even originally, made, that they should be prevented by some means or other, though they could not by reformation alone. For we have daily instances of such mercy, in the general conduct of Nature: compassion provided for misery,[5] medi- § 5.
cines for diseases, friends against enemies. There is provision made, in the original constitution of the world, that much of the natural bad consequences of our follies, which persons themselves alone cannot prevent, may be prevented by the assistance of others; assistance, which Nature enables, and disposes, and appoints them to afford. By a method of goodness analogous to this, when the world lay in wickedness, and consequently in ruin, "God so loved the world, § 10.
that He gave His only begotten Son" to save it: and "He being made perfect by suffering, became the Author of eternal salvation to all them that obey Him."[6] Indeed neither reason nor analogy would lead us to think, in particular, that the interposition of Christ, in the manner in which He did interpose, would be of that efficacy for § 20.
recovery of the world, which the Scripture teaches us it was: but neither would reason nor analogy lead us to think, that other particular means would be of the efficacy, which experience shews they are, in numberless instances. And therefore, as the case before us does not admit of experience; so, that neither reason nor analogy can shew how, or in what particular § 19.
way, the interposition of Christ, as revealed in Scripture, is of that efficacy, which it is there represented to be; this is no kind nor degree of presumption against its being really of that efficacy. Further: the objections against Christianity, Ch. vi.
from the light of it not being universal, nor its evidence so strong as might possibly be given us, have been answered by the general analogy of Nature. That God has made such variety of creatures, is indeed an answer to the former: but that He dispenses His gifts in such variety, both of degrees § 3.
and kinds, amongst creatures of the same species, and even to the same individuals at different times; is a more obvious and full answer to it. And it is so far from being the

[5] Serm. vi. § 5. [See also Part II. v. 5.]

[6] *St. John* iii. 16; *Heb.* v. 9.

method of Providence in other cases, to afford us such overbearing evidence, as some require in proof of Chris-
§ 18. tianity; that, on the contrary, the evidence upon which we are naturally appointed to act in common matters, throughout a very great part of life, is doubtful in a high degree. And
§ 12. admitting the fact, that God has afforded to some no more than doubtful evidence of religion; the same account may be given of it, as of difficulties and temptations with regard to practice. But as it is not impossible,[7] surely, that this
§ 14. alleged doubtfulness may be men's own fault; it deserves their most serious consideration, whether it be not so. How-
§ 11. ever, it is certain that doubting implies a degree of evidence
§ 9. for that of which we doubt: and that this degree of evidence as really lays us under obligations, as demonstrative evidence.

[3.] The whole then of religion is throughout credible: nor is there, I think, anything relating to the revealed dispensation of things, more different from the experienced constitution and course of Nature, than some parts of the constitution of
Ch. vii. Nature are from other parts of it. And if so, the only question which remains is, what positive evidence can be alleged for the truth of Christianity. This too in general has been considered, and the objections against it estimated. Deduct, therefore, what is to be deducted from that evidence, upon account of any weight which may be thought to remain in these objections, after what the analogy of Nature has suggested in answer to them: and then consider, what are the practical consequences from all this, upon the most sceptical principles one can argue upon: (for I am writing to persons who entertain these principles:)[8] and upon such consideration it will be obvious, that immorality, as little excuse as it admits of in itself, is greatly aggravated, in persons who have been made acquainted with Christianity, whether they believe it or not: because the moral system of Nature, or natural religion, which Christianity lays before us, approves itself, almost intuitively, to a reasonable mind, upon seeing it proposed. In the next place, with regard to Christianity, it will be observed; that there is a middle between a full satisfaction of the truth of it, and a satisfaction of the contrary. The middle state of mind

Allowing for all such objections,

(a) the mere acquaintance with Christianity carries moral obligation with it;

(b) the sceptic cannot go beyond doubt *of its truth,*

[7] Part II. vi. 14, etc.

[8] [Cp. Part II. viii. 11 above.]

between these two consists in a serious apprehension, that it may be true, joined with doubt whether it be so. And this, upon the best judgment I am able to make, is as far towards speculative infidelity, as any sceptic can at all be supposed to go, who has had true Christianity, with the proper evidence of it, laid before him, and has in any tolerable measure considered them. For I would not be mistaken to comprehend all who have ever heard of it: because it seems evident, that in many countries called Christian, neither Christianity, nor its evidence, are fairly laid before men. And in places where both are, there appear to be some, who have very little attended to either, and who reject Christianity with a scorn proportionate to their inattention; and yet are by no means without understanding in other matters. Now it has been shewn, that a serious apprehension that Christianity may be true, lays persons under the strictest obligations of a serious regard to it, throughout the whole of their life: a regard not the same exactly, but in many respects nearly the same, with what a full conviction of its truth would lay them under. Lastly, it will appear, that blasphemy and profaneness, I mean with regard to Christianity, are absolutely without excuse. For there is no temptation to it, but from the wantonness of vanity or mirth: and these, considering the infinite importance of the subject, are no such temptations as to afford any excuse for it. If this be a just account of things, and yet men can go on to vilify or disregard Christianity, which is to talk and act as if they had a demonstration of its falsehood; there is no reason to think they would alter their behaviour to any purpose, though there were a demonstration of its truth.

if Christianity and its evidence are fairly laid before him;

(*c*) blasphemy and profanity are inexcusable.

TWO BRIEF

DISSERTATIONS

I. OF PERSONAL IDENTITY.

II. OF THE NATURE OF VIRTUE.

ADVERTISEMENT.

In the first copy of these papers, I had inserted the two following Dissertations into the chapters, *Of a Future Life*, and, *Of the Moral Government of God*; with which they are closely connected. But as they do not directly fall under the title of the foregoing treatise, and would have kept the subject of it too long out of sight; it seemed more proper to place them by themselves.

DISSERTATION I.

Of Personal Identity.[1]

[1.] WHETHER we are to live in a future state, as it is the most important question which can possibly be asked, so it is the most intelligible one which can be expressed in language. Yet strange perplexities have been raised about the meaning of that identity or sameness of person, which is implied in the notion of our living now and hereafter, or in any two successive moments. And the solution of these difficulties hath been stranger than the difficulties themselves. For, personal identity has been explained so by some, as to render the inquiry concerning a future life of no consequence at all to us the persons who are making it. And though few men can be misled by such subtleties; yet it may be proper a little to consider them.

The question important.

[2.] Now when it is asked, wherein personal identity consists, the answer should be the same, as if it were asked, wherein consists similitude, or equality; that all attempts to define would but perplex it. Yet there is no difficulty at all in ascertaining the idea. For as, upon two triangles being compared or viewed together, there arises to the mind the idea of similitude; or upon twice two and four, the idea of equality: so likewise, upon comparing the consciousnesses of one's self, or one's own existence, in any two moments, there as immediately arises to the mind the idea of personal identity. And as the two former comparisons not only give us the ideas of similitude and equality; but also shew us, that two triangles are alike, and twice two and four are equal: so the latter comparison not only gives us the idea of personal

Personal identity revealed by consciousness.

[[1] See above, Part I. i. 1, 9, for the relevance of this Dissertation to the argument of the *Analogy*.]

identity, but also shews us the identity of ourselves in those two moments; the present, suppose, and that immediately past; or the present, and that a month, a year, or twenty years past. Or in other words, by reflecting upon that, which is myself now, and that, which was myself twenty years ago, I discern they are not two, but one and the same self.

Consciousness presupposes it, but is not essential to it.

[3.] But though consciousness of what is past does thus ascertain our personal identity to ourselves, yet to say, that it makes personal identity, or is necessary to our being the same persons, is to say, that a person has not existed a single moment, nor done one action, but what he can remember; indeed none but what he reflects upon. And one should really think it self-evident, that consciousness of personal identity presupposes, and therefore cannot constitute, personal identity; any more than knowledge, in any other case, can constitute truth, which it presupposes.

Confusion between consciousness and personality.

[4.] This wonderful mistake may possibly have arisen from hence; that to be endued with consciousness is inseparable from the idea of a person, or intelligent being. For, this might be expressed inaccurately thus, that consciousness makes personality: and from hence it might be concluded to make personal identity. But though present consciousness of what we at present do and feel is necessary to our being the persons we now are; yet present consciousness of past actions or feelings is not necessary to our being the same persons who performed those actions, or had those feelings.

Identity of vegetables

[5.] The inquiry, what makes vegetables the same in the common acceptation of the word does not appear to have any relation to this of personal identity: because, the word *same*, when applied to them and to person, is not only applied to different subjects, but it is also used in different senses. For when a man swears to the same tree, as having stood fifty years in the same place, he means only the same as to all the purposes of property and uses of common life, and not that the tree has been all that time the same in the strict philosophical sense of the word. For he does not know, whether any one particle of the present tree be the same with any one particle of the tree which stood in the same place fifty years ago. And if they have not one common particle of matter, they cannot be the same tree in the proper philosophical sense of the word *same*: it being evidently a con-

not the sameness of material substance,

tradiction in terms, to say they are, when no part of their substance, and no one of their properties is the same: no part of their substance, by the supposition; no one of their properties, because it is allowed, that the same property cannot be transferred from one substance to another. And therefore when we say the identity or sameness of a plant consists in a continuation of the same life, communicated under the same organization, to a number of particles of matter, whether the same or not; the word *same*, when applied to life and to organization, cannot possibly be understood to signify, what it signifies in this very sentence, when applied to matter. In a loose and popular sense then, the life and the organization and the plant are justly said to be the same, notwithstanding the perpetual change of the parts. But in a strict and philosophical manner of speech, no man, no being, no mode of being, no anything, can be the same with that, with which it hath indeed nothing the same. Now sameness is used in this latter sense, when applied to persons. The identity of these, therefore, cannot subsist with diversity of substance.

but continuity of life.

Identity of persons the sameness of mental substance.

[6.] The thing here considered, and demonstratively, as I think, determined, is proposed by Mr. Locke in these words, *Whether it*, i.e. the same self or person, *be the same identical substance?* And he has suggested what is a much better answer to the question, than that which he gives it in form. For he defines Person, *a thinking intelligent being*, etc., and personal identity, *the sameness of a rational being*.[2] The question then is, whether the same rational being is the same substance: which needs no answer, because Being and Substance, in this place, stand for the same idea. The ground of the doubt, whether the same person be the same substance, is said to be this; that the consciousness of our own existence, in youth and in old age, or in any two joint successive moments, is not the *same individual action*,[3] i.e. not the same consciousness, but different successive consciousnesses. Now it is strange that this should have occasioned such perplexities. For it is surely conceivable, that a person may have a capacity of knowing some object or other to be the same now, which it was when he contemplated it formerly: yet in this case,

Locke's view leads up to this.

[2] Locke's *Works*, vol. i. p. 146. [*Essay concerning Human Understanding*, II. xxvii. 10.]

[3] Locke, pp. 146, 147.

but must be owing to an inward unfairness, and secret corruption of heart.

(ii) Identity of beings, not of ideas, is here in question.

[9.] Secondly, It is not an idea, or abstract notion, or quality, but a being only, which is capable of life and action, of happiness and misery. Now all beings confessedly continue the same, during the whole time of their existence. Consider then a living being now existing, and which has existed for any time alive: this living being must have done and suffered and enjoyed, what it has done and suffered and enjoyed formerly, (this living being, I say, and not another,) as really as it does and suffers and enjoys, what it does and suffers and enjoys this instant. All these successive actions, enjoyments, and sufferings, are actions, enjoyments, and sufferings, of the same living being. And they are so, prior to all consideration of its remembering or forgetting: since remembering or forgetting can make no alteration in the truth of past matter of fact. And suppose this being endued with limited powers of knowledge and memory, there is no more difficulty in conceiving it to have a power of knowing itself to be the same living being which it was some time ago, of remembering some of its actions, sufferings, and enjoyments, and forgetting others, than in conceiving it to know or remember or forget anything else.

(iii) Consciousness implies and reveals identity of mental substance.

[10.] Thirdly, Every person is conscious, that he is now the same person or self he was as far back as his remembrance reaches: since when any one reflects upon a past action of his own, he is just as certain of the person who did that action, namely, himself, the person who now reflects upon it, as he is certain that the action was at all done. Nay, very often a person's assurance of an action having been done, of which he is absolutely assured, arises wholly from the consciousness that he himself did it. And this he, person, or self, must either be a substance, or the property of some substance. If he, if person, be a substance; then consciousness that he is the same person is consciousness that he is the same substance. If the person, or he, be the property of a substance, still consciousness that he is the same property is as certain a proof that his substance remains the same, as consciousness that he remains the same substance would be: since the same property cannot be transferred from one substance to another.

[11.] But though we are thus certain, that we are the same agents, living beings, or substances, now, which we were as far back as our remembrance reaches; yet it is asked, whether we may not possibly be deceived in it? And this question may be asked at the end of any demonstration whatever: because it is a question concerning the truth of perception by memory. And he who can doubt, whether perception by memory can in this case be depended upon, may doubt also, whether perception by deduction and reasoning, which also include memory, or indeed whether intuitive perception can. Here then we can go no further. For it is ridiculous to attempt to prove the truth of those perceptions, whose truth we can no otherwise prove, than by other perceptions of exactly the same kind with them, and which there is just the same ground to suspect; or to attempt to prove the truth of our faculties, which can no otherwise be proved, than by the use or means of those very suspected faculties themselves.

We must trust consciousness,

for we have no more trustworthy guide.

including active principles.

or practical principles: those principles from which men would act, if occasions and circumstances gave them power; and which, when fixed and habitual in any person, we call his character.[7] It does not appear, that brutes have the least reflex sense of actions, as distinguished from events: or that will and design, which constitute the very nature of actions as such, are at all an object to their perception. But to ours they are: and they are the object, and the only one, of the approving and disapproving faculty. Acting, conduct, behaviour, abstracted from all regard to what is, in fact and event, the consequence of it, is itself the natural object of the moral discernment; as speculative truth and falsehood is of speculative reason. Intention of such and such consequences, indeed, is always included; for it is part of the action itself: but though the intended good or bad consequences do not follow, we have exactly the same sense of the action as if they did.[8] In like manner we think well or ill of characters, abstracted from all consideration of the good or the evil, which persons of such characters have it actually in their power to do. We never, in the moral way, applaud or blame either ourselves or others, for what we enjoy or what we suffer, or for having impressions made upon us which we consider as altogether out of our power: but only for what we do, or would have done, had it been in our power; or for what we leave undone, which we might have done, or would have left undone, though we could have done it.

(Brutes do not distinguish actions from events.)

Thus it looks

(*a*) to intention, not consequence;

(*b*) to character, not power.

(*c*) to voluntary, not involuntary action or inaction.

(ii) Our sense of moral good and evil implies good and ill desert.

[3.] Secondly, Our sense or discernment of actions as morally good or evil, implies in it a sense or discernment of them as of good or ill desert.[9] It may be difficult to explain this perception, so as to answer all the questions which may be asked concerning it: but every one speaks of such and such actions as deserving punishment; and it is not, I suppose, pretended, that they have absolutely no meaning at all to the expression. Now the meaning plainly is not, that we conceive it for the good of society, that the doer of such actions should

Idea of ill desert not that of pain

consistit." Cic. *Off.* lib. i. cap. 6. [It is possible that Butler laid special stress on this point, because it had been little attended to in the ethical philosophy of Shaftesbury and Hutcheson. See Stewart, *Works*, vi. pp. 304-6.]

[7] [Cp. Part I. vi. 8 note.]

[8] [The necessary qualifications of this statement are given in Serm. viii. § 7, *sub fin.*]

[9] [Cp. Part I. vi. 11.]

be made to suffer. For if unhappily it were resolved, that a man, who, by some innocent action, was infected with the plague,[10] should be left to perish, lest, by other people's coming near him, the infection should spread; no one would say he deserved this treatment. Innocence and ill-desert are inconsistent ideas. Ill-desert always supposes guilt: and if one be no part of the other, yet they are evidently and naturally connected in our mind. The sight of a man in misery raises our compassion towards him; and, if this misery be inflicted on him by another, our indignation against the author of it. But when we are informed, that the sufferer is a villain, and is punished only for his treachery or cruelty; our compassion exceedingly lessens, and in many instances our indignation wholly subsides. Now what produces this effect is the conception of that in the sufferer, which we call ill-desert. Upon considering then, or viewing together, our notion of vice and that of misery, there results a third, that of ill-desert. And thus there is in human creatures an association of the two ideas, natural and moral evil, wickedness and punishment. If this association were merely artificial or accidental, it were nothing: but being most unquestionably natural, it greatly concerns us to attend to it, instead of endeavouring to explain it away.

inflicted for the common good.

It supposes guilt,

e.g.

and results from association of guilt and misery.

[4.] It may be observed further, concerning our perception of good and of ill-desert, that the former is very weak with respect to common instances of virtue. One reason of which may be, that it does not appear to a spectator, how far such instances of virtue proceed from a virtuous principle, or in what degree this principle is prevalent: since a very weak regard to virtue may be sufficient to make men act well in many common instances. And on the other hand, our perception of ill-desert in vicious actions lessens, in proportion to the temptations men are thought to have had to such vices. For, vice in human creatures consisting chiefly in the absence or want of the virtuous principle; though a man be overcome, suppose, by tortures, it does not from thence appear to what degree the virtuous principle was wanting. All that appears is, that he had it not in such a degree, as to prevail

Our perception of good desert weak in ordinary cases, for the motive is doubtful;

and of ill desert, lessened in proportion to the temptation.

[10] [The illustration seems to have been borrowed from Shaftesbury: "We do not however say of anyone that he is an ill man, because he has the plague-spots upon him" (*Inquiry*, p. 21; cp. further, p. 120).]

over the temptation: but possibly he had it in a degree, which would have rendered him proof against common temptations.

(iii) Perception of ill desert has regard to the agent's capacity;

[5.] Thirdly, Our perception of vice and ill-desert arises from, and is the result of, a comparison of actions with the nature and capacities of the agent.[11] For the mere neglect of doing what we ought to do would, in many cases, be determined by all men to be in the highest degree vicious. And this determination must arise from such comparison, and be the result of it; because such neglect would not be vicious in creatures of other natures and capacities, as brutes. And it is the same also with respect to positive vices, or such as consist in doing what we ought not. For, every one has a different sense of harm done by an idiot, madman, or child, and by one of mature and common understanding; though the action of both, including the intention, which is part of the action, be the same: as it may be, since idiots and madmen, as well as children, are capable not only of doing mischief, but also of intending it. Now this difference must arise from somewhat discerned in the nature or capacities of one, which renders the action vicious; and the want of which, in the other, renders the same action innocent or less vicious: and this plainly supposes a comparison, whether reflected upon or not, between the action and capacities of the agent, previous to our determining an action to be vicious. And hence arises a proper application of the epithets, *incongruous*, *unsuitable*, *disproportionate*, *unfit*, to actions which our moral faculty determines to be vicious.[12]

e.g. (*a*) negligence in brutes not vicious;

(*b*) harm done by children or madmen leniently judged.

Thus what is vicious is *unfit*.

(iv) Prudence is a virtue,

(definition)

[6.] Fourthly, It deserves to be considered, whether men are more at liberty, in point of morals, to make themselves miserable without reason, than to make other people so: or dissolutely to neglect their own greater good, for the sake of a present lesser gratification, than they are to neglect the good of others, whom Nature has committed to their care. It should seem, that a due concern about our own interest or happiness, and a reasonable endeavour to secure and promote it,[13] which is, I think, very much the meaning of the word *prudence*, in

[11] [Cp. Serm. ii. § 10 and iii. § 9.]

[12] [Cp. Part I. vi. 12 note; see also Note E at end of ch. vi.]

[13] [Cp. Part I. iv. 4 and the note there. This paragraph was probably written in view of the doctrines of Francis Hutcheson (1694-1747), who had pushed his doctrine that benevolence is the sum of virtue so far as to deny that prudent actions can be morally approved.]

our language; it should seem, that this is virtue, and the contrary behaviour faulty and blamable; since, in the calmest way of reflection, we approve of the first, and condemn the other conduct, both in ourselves and others. This approbation and disapprobation are altogether different from mere desire of our own, or of their happiness, and from sorrow upon missing it. For the object or occasion of this last kind of perception is satisfaction or uneasiness: whereas the object of the first is active behaviour. In one case, what our thoughts fix upon is our condition: in the other, our conduct. It is true indeed, that Nature has not given us so sensible a disapprobation of imprudence and folly, either in *ourselves* or *others*, as of falsehood, injustice, and cruelty: I suppose, because that constant habitual sense of private interest and good, which we always carry about with us, renders such sensible disapprobation less necessary, less wanting, to keep us from imprudently neglecting our own happiness, and foolishly injuring ourselves, than it is necessary and wanting to keep us from injuring others, to whose good we cannot have so strong and constant a regard: and also because imprudence and folly, appearing to bring its own punishment more immediately and constantly than injurious behaviour, it less needs the additional punishment, which would be inflicted upon it by others, had they the same sensible indignation against it, as against injustice, and fraud, and cruelty. Besides, unhappiness being in itself the natural object of compassion; the unhappiness which people bring upon themselves, though it be wilfully, excites in us some pity for them: and this of course lessens our displeasure against them. But still it is matter of experience, that we are formed so as to reflect very severely upon the greater instances of imprudent neglects and foolish rashness, both in ourselves and others. In instances of this kind, men often say of themselves with remorse, and of others with some indignation, that they deserved to suffer such calamities, because they brought them upon themselves, and would not take warning. Particularly when persons come to poverty and distress by a long course of extravagance, and after frequent admonitions, though without falsehood or injustice; we plainly do not regard such people as alike objects of compassion with those, who are brought into the same condition by unavoidable accidents. From these things it

for conscience approves it.

This approbation not a mere desire of happiness.

Disapprobation of imprudence not so strong as of falsehood, for

(*a*) it is less necessary;

(*b*) imprudence brings its own punishment,

(*c*) which breeds compassion.

Yet disapprobation of it is sometimes strongly expressed.

appears, that prudence is a species of virtue, and folly of vice: meaning by *folly*, somewhat quite different from mere incapacity; a thoughtless want of that regard and attention to our own happiness, which we had capacity for. And this the word properly includes; and, as it seems, in its usual acceptation: for we scarce apply it to brute creatures.

Def. of *folly*.

Whether it be called *virtue* or not, still prudence as such is approved by conscience.

[7.] However, if any person be disposed to dispute the matter, I shall very willingly give him up the words Virtue and Vice, as not applicable to prudence and folly: but must beg leave to insist, that the faculty within us, which is the judge of actions, approves of prudent actions, and disapproves imprudent ones; I say prudent and imprudent *actions* as such, and considered distinctly from the happiness or misery which they occasion. And, by the way, this observation may help to determine what justness there is in that objection against religion, that it teaches us to be interested and selfish.[14]

(v) Benevolence is not the whole of virtue;

[8.] Fifthly, Without inquiring how far, and in what sense, virtue is resolvable into benevolence, and vice into the want of it; it may be proper to observe, that benevolence, and the want of it, singly considered, are in no sort the whole of virtue and vice.[15] For if this were the case, in the review of one's own character, or that of others, our moral understanding and moral sense would be indifferent to everything, but the degrees in which benevolence prevailed, and the degrees in which it was wanting. That is, we should neither approve of benevolence to some persons rather than to others, nor disapprove injustice and falsehood upon any other account, than merely as an overbalance of happiness was foreseen likely to be produced by the first, and of misery by the second. But now, on the contrary, suppose two men competitors for anything whatever, which would be of equal advantage to each of them; though nothing indeed would be more impertinent, than for a stranger to busy himself to get one of them preferred to the other; yet such endeavour would be virtue, in behalf of a friend or benefactor, abstracted from all consideration of distant consequences:[16] as that examples of gratitude, and the cultivation of friendship, would be of general

for conscience considers other things,

e.g. (*a*) gratitude

[14] [Compare the objection raised and answered in Part I. v. 19; see also Note D at end of ch. V.]

[15] [This question had been already discussed in Serm. xii. §§ 25-32; see especially the note on § 31, and cp. Part I. iii. 3 above.]

[16] [This case was cited in the Sermons (I. § 6 note) in a slightly different reference.]

good to the world. Again, suppose one man should, by fraud or violence, take from another the fruit of his labour, with intent to give it to a third, who he thought would have as much pleasure from it as would balance the pleasure which the first possessor would have had in the enjoyment, and his vexation in the loss of it; suppose also that no bad consequences would follow: yet such an action would surely be vicious. Nay further, were treachery, violence and injustice, no otherwise vicious, than as foreseen likely to produce an overbalance of misery to society; then, if in any case a man could procure to himself[17] as great advantage by an act of injustice, as the whole foreseen inconvenience, likely to be brought upon others by it, would amount to; such a piece of injustice would not be faulty or vicious at all: because it would be no more than, in any other case, for a man to prefer his own satisfaction to another's in equal degrees. The fact then appears to be, that we are constituted so as to condemn falsehood, unprovoked violence, injustice, and to approve of benevolence to some preferably to others, abstracted from all consideration, which conduct is likeliest to produce an overbalance of happiness or misery. And therefore, were the Author of Nature to propose nothing to Himself as an end but the production of happiness, were His moral character merely that of benevolence; yet ours is not so. Upon that supposition indeed the only reason of His giving us the above-mentioned approbation of benevolence to some persons rather than others, and disapprobation of falsehood, unprovoked violence, and injustice, must be, that He foresaw this constitution of our nature would produce more happiness, than forming us with a temper of mere general benevolence. But still, since this is our constitution; falsehood, violence, injustice, must be vice in us, and benevolence to some, preferably to others, virtue; abstracted from all consideration of the overbalance of evil or good, which they may appear likely to produce.

(*b*) justice between other men;

(*c*) justice between ourselves and others.

Even if benevolence were the whole of virtue in God, it is not so in man, as the dictates of conscience shew.

[9.] Now if human creatures are endued with such a moral nature as we have been explaining, or with a moral faculty, the natural object of which is actions; moral government must consist in rendering them happy and unhappy, in re-

Hence moral government consists in requiting men according as they

[17] [It appears from this illustration that in Butler's use of the word, *benevolence* may have *self* for its object, as well as *others*.]

follow conscience.

warding and punishing them, as they follow, neglect, or depart from, the moral rule of action interwoven in their nature, or suggested and enforced by this moral faculty;[18] in rewarding and punishing them upon account of their so doing.

Some writers have said that the promotion of happiness is the sum of virtue.

[10.] I am not sensible that I have, in this fifth observation, contradicted what any author designed to assert. But some of great and distinguished merit[19] have, I think, expressed themselves in a manner, which may occasion some danger, to careless readers, of imagining the whole of virtue to consist in singly aiming, according to the best of their judgment, at promoting the happiness of mankind in the present state; and the whole of vice, in doing what they foresee, or might foresee, is likely to produce an overbalance of unhappiness in it; than which mistakes, none can be conceived more terrible. For it is certain, that some of the most shocking instances of injustice, adultery, murder, perjury, and even of persecution, may, in many supposable cases, not have the appearance of being likely to produce an overbalance of misery in the present state; perhaps sometimes may have the contrary appearance. For this reflection might easily be carried on, but I forbear—. The happiness of the world is the concern of Him, Who is the Lord and the Proprietor of it: nor do we know what we are about, when we endeavour to promote the good of mankind in any ways, but those which He has directed; that is indeed in all ways not contrary to veracity and justice. I speak thus upon supposition of persons really endeavouring, in some sort, to do good without regard to these. But the truth seems to be, that such supposed endeavours proceed, almost always, from ambition, the spirit of party, or some indirect principle, concealed perhaps in great measure from persons themselves. And though it is our business and our duty to endeavour, within the bounds of veracity and justice, to contribute to the ease, convenience, and even cheerfulness and diversion of our fellow-creatures: yet, from our short views, it is greatly uncertain, whether this endeavour will in particular instances, produce an overbalance of happiness upon the whole; since so many and distant things must come

This would lead to bad consequences.

The world's happiness is the concern of God.

In promoting it, *we* must have regard to veracity and justice, which will probably have the best results.

[18] Part I. vi. 14.

[19] [Butler probably had in his mind Ralph Cudworth, Henry More, and John Smith, the Cambridge Platonists, and especially Francis Hutcheson, whose books had recently appeared.]

into the account. And that which makes it our duty is, that there is some appearance that it will, and no positive appearance sufficient to balance this, on the contrary side; and also, that such benevolent endeavour is a cultivation of that most excellent of all virtuous principles, the active principle of benevolence.

α β

Veracity not violated where there is no intent to deceive.

[11.] However, though veracity, as well as justice, is to be our rule of life; it must be added, otherwise a snare will be laid in the way of some plain men, that the use of common forms of speech, generally understood, cannot be falsehood; and, in general, that there can be no designed falsehood without designing to deceive. It must likewise be observed, that in numberless cases, a man may be under the strictest obligations to what he foresees will deceive, without his intending it. For it is impossible not to foresee, that the words and actions of men, in different ranks and employments, and of different educations, will perpetually be mistaken by each other; and it cannot but be so, whilst they will judge with the utmost carelessness, as they daily do, of what they are not, perhaps, enough informed to be competent judges of, even though they considered it with great attention.

INDEX[1]

[1] [The editor's notes are not indexed, as they form no proper part of the work. See Preface, p. xii.]

7 And conformable.—*Butler.*

[8] The expectation that His goodness would have induced Him to make us perfect creatures all at once, contradicted by the analogy of what we experience.—*Butler.*

[14] Conformable to the whole constitution and course of nature.—*Butler*.

[15] Like historical evidence of fabulous ones, to that there is for those which are alleged in proof of Christianity, would not destroy the evidence of the latter.—*Butler*.

16 Query.—*Butler.*

17 Parallel.—*Butler.*

S.

GLASGOW: PRINTED AT THE UNIVERSITY PRESS BY ROBERT MACLEHOSE AND CO.